Like the readers below, you may be asking yourself, "How Do I…"

… know and avoid all the pitfalls I hear about… budget overruns, delays, bad work?

… keep the reins on my budget and prevent extra costs—ahead of time?

… choose the contractor that will make my dream come true… not be my worst nightmare?

… pay an architect for only the services I need?

… get a building contract together?

… sail through the intimidating process of getting a permit?

… be a knowledgeable, confident participant in my own project—building from smart to finish?

If so, then this is the book for you!

★★★★★ A Terrific Book

First of all, I couldn't put the book down. I'm planning to build a house and frankly, hadn't a clue how to begin. Not now. I have a blueprint in the form of a book which explains in a step-by-step manner how to go about getting the right people, information and materials to do the job. I continue to reread the book and bought a second copy for my wife (mine is dog-eared and full of notes). If you're planning to build or do a renovation of an existing home, the first step is to get this book.

★★★★★ Good money-saving advice on your most expensive purchase

Every chapter is focused on another phase of the project, and her clear writing opens up the mysteries along the way. She describes who is doing what (or should be doing it), what choices need to be made, and what the alternatives are. Better yet, she is fair. She makes sure that neither you nor anyone is getting cheated. I refer to the book constantly and appreciate the wide margins that allow for notes to be made.

★★★★ Useful detailed practical information for building a home

I am looking to build my own home, and have purchased half a dozen books in hopes of learning how to start. This is by far the most informative, useful book of the lot. It is written for someone like myself, an ordinary Joe who has zero experience in design, building or construction.

★★★★★ Chock full of sound advice!

Ms. Johnston's book does not provide head-spinning technical information, rather it is a project management guide for the general public. We are first-time home builders, and the understanding of the construction process gained from this book has served us well. Our confidence to complete our project on-time and on-budget is sound. This book is a true bargain when measured against the costs and anxiety of home building and renovation!

★★★★★ Without question, the most important investment in your project

I bought all the construction books... $1,000 worth to prepare for building our house. This book is far and away the most valuable resource available. I have read it cover to cover three times now, and referred back to it at the appropriate stages to be sure I follow the author's very sage advice. It is so well written, I think I would find it quite entertaining even if I weren't building a house. The book provides neophytes like myself with excellent insight into the building industry. Things are not necessarily as they seem on the surface!

★★★★★ Avoid building contract problems

This is one 'How To' guide that delivers as promised. A few dollars invested here could literally save you thousands and give you results you desire while maintaining a good working relationship and understanding with your contractor.

★★★★★ A requirement for anyone even thinking of renovating!

This is a great book! It's easy to understand, the organization's easy to follow and I cannot even count how many pitfalls we avoided by following her advice. Thanks so much!!!

★★★★★ Your build/renovation must start with this book

After reading just about every construction book available, I stumbled across this one. It is the most important investment that you will make in your home. Amy Johnston details the steps in your construction project from an insider's perspective. She provides invaluable advice in selecting and working with contractors in a down-to-earth manner. The book includes anecdotes and personal experiences, and reads like a novel while providing you with fundamental information for your project. Make sure to have a pen handy while you read, because you're likely to want to take notes!

★★★★★ The Most Imformative Book on the Market!

Thank you Amy! You are a true innovator! This book is the pirate ship in the yacht club. The issues are well written and strategically laid out. After reading this, I now have the education I need.

★★★★★ A Consumer's Guide without Bashing Contractors or Tradesmen

The author presents valuable notes and cautions highlighted for clients as 'Insider Tips' or 'Pitfalls.' The strategies and educational pointers are worth many times the cost of the book. It's very informative without being preachy, boring, or bashing.

★★★★★ Everything you NEED to know about the construction process

This book is an indispendable resource. Read it and you will be able to converse professionally with architects, engineers, builders and sub-contractors. Johnston's check lists and recommendations for various parts of the process are spot-on. Follow her guidance and you will save thousands in time and money.

What Your Contractor Can't Tell You

The Essential Guide to Building and Renovating

by Amy Johnston

SHUBE PUBLISHING

This book was formerly published under the title *What the "Experts" May Not Tell You About... Building or Renovating Your Home* (Warner Books, 2004, ISBN 0-446-69083-X).

Design by Sylvie Vidrine

Illustrations for *Pitfalls* and *Insider Tips* by Jeff Danziger

Printed in the United States of America

10 9 8 7 6 5 4 3

ISBN 978-0-9799838-0-1

To Louise Johnston,
who provided the unwavering vision;
to Fred Johnston,
who taught that the impossible just takes a little longer;
and to Tom O'Brien,
for his boundless generosity of knowledge.

Acknowledgments

My thanks to Tom O'Brien, Steve Pitkin, Ken Lerner, John Racys, Annie Bessette, Mark Landry, William Fead, Kate Stephenson, Jean Poulin, Duane Webster, and some indispensable anonymous sources for their invaluable technical advice.

To Sylvie Vidrine, Tanya Herbick, Cathy Purdy, Julie Stillman, John Pitts, Vicky Brucia, Bill Harvey, Steve Wetherby, Kris Kimball, Jim Gish, Jennifer Arbuckle, Karen Johnson, and Sam Press, my thanks for their reviews of the written word and guidance in the publishing world.

Most especially, I thank all the friends, colleagues, clients, and family members who supported and encouraged me to wrestle this information to the page.

Contents

Introduction: Building from Smart to Finish xiii

Chapter 1: **Ready, Set, Think:**
How the Savvy Owner Starts a Project 1

The Mind-Set: How to Approach a Project 1

The Players List: The People Who Will Be on
Your Team 4

A Gleam in Your Eye: Can You Build? 8

Don't Bank On It: Is Your Loan Officer Your Ally? 9

The Scary Money: Down Payments. 13

Chapter 2: **The Plan Is the Thing:**
Making a Successful Project 14

Task-Oriented: Your To-Do List 14

Getting What You Need: How to Approach
Your Design 15

Sneaking Up On Your Design: Do's and Don'ts to
Get You Started 18

What's It Worth to You? Money and Design 20

Beyond Eenie, Meenie, Miney, Mo: A Formula for
Balanced Choices 21

A House United: Working Together as a Couple 22

Chapter 3: **Design as a Noun:**
Refining and Conveying Your Vision 24

Decisions, Decisions: Your Design 24

Conveying Your Decisions: Construction
Documents 24

Building In Flexibility: Allowances, Unit Pricing
and Alternate Pricing 28

Chapter 4: **Help with Your Vision:**
When and How to Employ an Architect 30

Do You Need a Professional? Considering an Architect . . 30

The Yin to Your Yang: The Right Architect for You 36

Everyone Pick Up Your #2 Pencils:
Working with an Architect 42

Chapter 5: **Bang for the Buck and the Sixteen Divisions:**
What Can You Have and What Should You Worry About? 45

Divide and Conquer: The Sweet Sixteen Divisions 45

The Devil's in the Details: Where to Focus
Your Attention and Money 46

And Another Thing: Considerations When
Determining Materials and Scope of Work 68

Chapter 6: **And the Grand Total Is . . . :**
Cost Estimating and the Budget 72

Follow the Money: How It Works on a
Construction Project 72

Where'd You Get That Number? Four Methods of
Cost Estimating 73

Crunching Their Numbers: Assessing a Cost Estimate . . 76

It's Alive! Your Budget as a Living Document 78

Chapter 7: **Setting Up Your Deal:**
Contract Structures 83

Who Knew You Had a Choice? Options for
Contract Structures 83

Chapter 8: **The Second Oldest Profession:**
Selecting and Working with a Contractor 90

He Was Such a Nice Guy: Choosing More Wisely 90

Welcome to His World: Working with a Contractor 96

To Protect and Serve: Protecting Your Project
and Serving Your Contractor 98

Chapter 9: **How Low Can They Go?**
Bidding the Project 104

You Talkin' to Me? Should You Bid Your Project? 104

Package Deal: Getting Your Bid Package
Together—the Four Elements 105

Going Out: What You and They Need to Do—
the Four Stages 108

Chapter 10: **Cover Your Assets:**
Contracts, Insurance, Liens, and Other Commitments . 116

If You Only Knew: Where Laypeople Go Wrong 116

Whose to Use? Construction Contracts 117

Don't Build Home Without It: Must-Haves 120

It Couldn't Hurt: Optional Additional Protection 129

Chapter 11: **Believe It! Time Really Is Money:**
Schedules 132

Tick Tock: How Time = Money on a
Construction Project 132

More Than One Way to Tell Time: Types of Schedules . 134

What Was That Other Thing? Additional Things to Track 138

Chapter 12: **Mother, May I?**
Getting Through the Permit Process 139

Nothing to Fear: Knowing the Process and Its Players . . 139

People Pleasing: The Steps for Permit Approval 142

Good to Go: Once You've Got the Permit 147

Step Lightly: Making Changes to the Neighborhood. . . 148

Chapter 13: **Ready to Build? . . . Not So Fast:**
Pulling It All Together 150

Just Like Santa: Make a List and Check It Twice 150

Long Time No See: The Preconstruction Meeting 151

Ensurance: Make Sure These Things Are Done 153

When Are They Leaving?! Renovation Tips 154

Chapter 14: **Let the Games Begin:**
Managing the Construction-Phase 158

Who's on First: Establishing the Roles and Rules for All 158

Watching the Store: Monitoring the Project 164

For Richer or Poorer: Budget Management 170

The Homestretch: Project Closeout 181

Conclusion   185

Talk the Talk: A Glossary of Terms 187

Inspirations: Other Resources 197

Index   200

Building from Smart to Finish

A Wing and a Prayer

Every day, unsuspecting people wander into construction projects like babes in the woods, and they come out wondering what the heck happened in there. They suffer cost overruns, disputes, missed deadlines, and poor workmanship. Remarkably, no one thinks it can happen to him, but according to the Better Business Bureau, it happens to many. Contractors are the most complained-about group in America. Why is getting something built such a high risk endeavor? For starters, owners enter a culture that's much less straightforward than it appears from the outside, and everyone in it knows more than they do. They can expect to make fifteen hundred decisions when building a new home. Add to that a dozen new relationships, deadlines, taste, quality standards, and more money than they'll ever spend on anything else, and you have a formula for potential disaster. Most people don't know how to get themselves prepared for this undertaking, and to date, few in the industry have wanted to tell them.

Not for Dummies

It might surprise you to know that when people in the construction industry get together socially, the conversation often turns to ethical and philosophical debate regarding all the fascinating scenarios that grow out of construction projects. There are no easy answers for problem projects, only lost opportunities for prevention, because all successful projects start with a great plan. The biggest difference between a professional and a layperson managing a construction project is that a professional spends about 80 percent of his time in the setup, the work done before a shovel hits the turf. An informed homeowner needs to be likewise proactive, not reactive.

This book reveals the real deal about how to be a proactive owner. It explains the work you'll have to do and the strategies you'll have to employ to maximize your chances of a successful project. The laypeople I've met who want to undergo such projects are ambitious and bright. They surprise me with their ability to handle the sometimes heady information that I now convey in this book, and they go on to have sensational projects. This book is written for them . . . and I hope you.

About This Book

This book wasn't my idea. I was told to write it.

When I meet people for the first time, they tend to gush forth with their building horror stories once they find out I manage construction projects for people. After ten years of this, I thought, "There's got to be a better way." I began offering seminars on construction management to homeowners. At the end of each seminar, at least one overachiever would come up to me and say, "I've read fifteen books on this. None of them has this stuff, and this is what I needed. You have to write a book." I investigated and found that they were right. Most of the books on this subject are written by contractors and focus on technical aspects of the construction trades. While this information may be interesting and certainly can help you in monitoring your project, it's not what keeps a project from derailing. Plus, a little knowledge can be dangerous and just make you an annoyance on the construction site. This book is written from the perspective of someone who has been in your shoes. I have designed and built or renovated more than two hundred buildings as a function of my work, and restored six of my own homes as well. This book reveals lessons hard-learned, and it focuses on an owner's strategies for setting up a project that preempts problems, just like the pros do it.

This book is not about how to swing a hammer, or even how to be your own general contractor. It is about how to be a savvy consumer of design and construction services and a competent participant in your own project. It lays out how a professional owner's representative goes about mitigating risk to bring a construction project to completion. However, no one can prove a negative. I can't tell you if you don't drive defensively, you will be hit by another car. But your odds are greatly increased. I can't say if you don't have a construction contract for your project, it will be an unbearable hassle and you'll lose a lot of money. But your odds are greatly increased. This book hits all the low points where risks lie. Nonetheless, no two projects are alike, and so, few people, whether professionals or laypeople, would carry out every task described in these pages. Based on your standards, your budget, your time, and all the other factors of your project, it's up to you to weigh your options and choose the tasks you want to execute to avoid risk.

Like the people in my seminars, you may feel overwhelmed as you take in this information. It's a lot. But also like them, as you learn the principles behind the owner's tasks, you'll see they're undeniable, and you'll likely find yourself understanding how projects can go so wrong for the uninitiated. As you come to accept all you have to do, try to think of it this way: Wouldn't you rather learn all this the easy way, before you're in the middle of a project, than the hard way like those tellers of horror stories? Sure, you won't follow every step in this book, but your project will benefit just from your heightened knowledge. If you hear a plumber complain to a general contractor about late payment, you'll take notice because you'll learn how that might affect your bank loan. If you're quoted a price that you worry you can't afford, maybe you'll flip back to the section on how to build in options now for what you might be able to afford later. So while there's great benefit in doing all the tasks spelled out in this book, the greater benefit is simply understanding them.

You may come away more knowledgeable than some of the professionals on your project. Licensed architects and large contractors will be familiar with all this information, but some designers and small contractors may not. Plus, everyone has his own slight variations on how to do things. Be prepared to do a little training of your own, and accommodate where needed, even as you insist on protecting your project. The tone of this book is very hands-on for you, the owner. However, there are plenty of professionals out there able to help you with whatever tasks you don't want to take on yourself.

This book includes samples of some of the paperwork associated with a project: a budget, a construction schedule, a draw schedule, a site plan, a floor plan, a set of job meeting minutes, a change order, a lien waiver, and a requisition. These all work in concert and are based on the following project:

The Dorseys are building a 1,250-square-foot, two-story addition to their home. It will have a full basement, clapboard siding, and an asphalt shingled roof. The first floor will be a family room with hardwood floors, a brick fireplace, six windows, stairs leading to the second floor, and French doors leading out to the location of a future deck. It will also have a half bathroom with ceramic tile floors. The second floor will be the new master bedroom with carpeted floors, seven windows, and a full bath with ceramic tile floors and walls. Both floors will be heated and wired to code.

There were three challenges unique to writing on this topic. The biggest challenge was the sequencing of information. If you were to lay out everything related to a building project in its proper sequence, it wouldn't be a bit linear, but rather look more like a family tree, with things interconnecting and doubling back. For instance, dealing with your budget happens from the first day of your project to the last. Town officials will hop in and out of your project at various intervals. So the information in this book has been laid out roughly chronologically, but also by theme. You will see page numbers in parentheses indicating where you can jump forward or back in the book to see how else and when else this topic pertains to your project. I recommend you read through the whole book and then use it as a reference on a chapter-by-chapter basis. Words you may not know are defined in the glossary. Speaking of words, although the role of women is ever expanding in this field, I'm sorry, but *The Chicago Manual of Style* dictates that "he" is the pronoun of choice.

The second challenge was accurately presenting the weird workings of an industry wherein you guard against those you employ. You address in planning and contracts against the worst eventualities and then work hard to make sure the contracts just gather dust. Maybe the closest parallel would be the design and negotiation of a prenuptial agreement followed by a great marriage. At any rate, I would like to state for the record that a good share of people undergoing construction projects have a pleasant and successful time of it. That's a nice thing to know, but it doesn't help you much. No, in order to prepare you well I had to write this book to the highest common denominator for risk, spelling out every potential problem, what generates it, how you spot it, and what your options are for avoiding it. I would be remiss to do otherwise. This means I'm making reference to some level of malevolence or incompetence at almost every turn. In its totality, does this book represent life in the design and building world fairly? No, not at all! I would give up this line of work today if it did. But each individual problem explained in these pages is common. I've done my best to be fair to all parties, but this book has a slanted perspective because it's you and your risk I'm addressing foremost.

The third challenge was writing this book for all projects when no two are alike in terms of scale or the nature of the work. Some of you are planning a little bathroom remodel. Some of you will be building the retirement home you've dreamed of your whole life. So the only solution was to write it to the highest common denominator again, the full blown, custom designed and constructed home, which requires everything covered herein. In other words, this is how a professional would do the tasks associated with a very large project if he never cut one corner.

Whether you're renovating your beloved older home, putting on an addition, building a barn, or just updating your home office, I hope you'll still find much that pertains to you and your project. Take what you need from it.

CHAPTER 1

Ready, Set, Think
How the Savvy Owner
Starts a Project

This chapter takes the broad view of the project and answers a lot of important questions. What's your job as an owner? Is your project feasible? Is the money in place? Whom will you encounter? How do you keep control of this project?

- The Mind-Set: How to Approach a Project
- The Players List: The People Who Will Be on Your Team
- A Gleam in Your Eye: Can You Build?
- Don't Bank On It: Is Your Loan Officer Your Ally?
- The Scary Money: Down Payments

The Mind-Set:
How to Approach a Project

I see construction projects as being made up of five elements: the existing building or site where the construction will take place, the owner, the designs, the contractor, and the budget. I have come to expect that, on average, two of these things will pose big challenges. More than that and I'm in trouble. Fewer than that and I'm in heaven, but I have been on only one perfect project in my life. No one could believe it. We all just kept basking in our own glow and saying how much we loved each other. There must have been something in the water.

You, the owner, are the axis around which your project revolves. You have the money and the dream. You are the final arbiter of the form and function of the design. You will monitor the execution of that design and live with the results. You will also rely on others along the way. You will provide the money, but it will likely flow through a loan officer and appraiser. You have the dream, but an architect or designer might shape it and then convey it to a contractor. You will watch the construction, but it will be done by a team under the contractor you hire.

You're about to enter into several new relationships, and there's a lot of your hard-earned money at stake. You will make hundreds of decisions and maybe a few mistakes. You will learn more than you can imagine right now. You must navigate through risk and guard against those who are incompetent or may seek to take advantage of you. It's a big undertaking and a lot of responsibility. Try to embrace it and be proactive. Educate yourself about

> *If you find a path with no obstacles, it probably doesn't lead anywhere.*
>
> —FRANK CLARK

the tasks ahead and how you'll lead this group to achieve your goals. Do this and you will not only get the end result you hope for, you will also be that rarest of creatures—the savvy owner who's an indispensable asset to the project.

If they had one, the professionals' mantra to make this all work would be "foresight good, hindsight bad" as they approach each task that will make their projects secure. They manage the owner's risk by defining as many things as possible up front. They do their best to make sure that each project will be financially, aesthetically, structurally, and emotionally sound for all parties involved. And you can do that too.

So in the story above, what exactly did this couple do right?

There Are No Coincidences

I have yet to hear about either a great project or a terrible project that happened by dumb luck. When people regale me with horror stories of their home construction projects, I bite my tongue and offer sympathy, but where they went wrong is evident in under a minute. What a nice surprise, then, when I met a woman whose building project was a job well done. It was no coincidence either—just less common an outcome.

I was introduced to her at a party. The host told me she and her husband had built a great house. He explained to her that I was writing a book on that very topic. To that she said kind of sheepishly, "Well, I'm sure we did it all wrong."

I asked, "Are you happy with the house?"

"We love it," she said. "We've been in it for a year and wouldn't change a thing."

I said, "Well, then, you must have done something right."

"We had a great contractor," she said.

"And how'd you find him?"

"We'd been thinking and dreaming about building a house for almost ten years. We live in a small town with only three contractors who are really appropriate for that kind of work. So every time one of them finished a project similar to what we were planning, we contacted the owners and talked to them about it. We ended up dropping one of them from consideration. When it came time to build, we interviewed the other two and chose the one that seemed more in sync with us."

"Sounds perfect so far. And what about your designs?" I asked.

She said, sounding more confident now, "We drove around a lot, took lots of pictures, and jotted down things we liked about a bunch of houses. Then we started looking at those house plan magazines. We ended up buying a set of plans for about $500, took them to a local architect, and he made some minor changes. He offered to come supervise the work every other week and answer questions by phone. He was a great bargain, really. We couldn't have done it without him, or our lawyer either. She drew up our contracts with the architect and builder, but kept the cost down by starting with stock contracts. It was crazy once the work started, but we liked the guys on the crew. We had some problems with the plumber, but the contractor straightened him out. We all met with the architect every other week, but my husband and I were there almost every day."

"Did your budget hold up?" I asked.

"We did pretty well. The plans were complete, so there were no surprises with that, but once the framing was up, we made a couple changes. We widened a hallway and moved a closet in my daughter's bedroom because it was blocking the light."

"And you love it?" I said.

"Yup, we just love it." She beamed.

"And was the contractor at the housewarming party?"

"He was the belle of the ball!" she said. "He was so proud of the place, and he's gotten other work from it since."

I told her she and her husband had managed the perfect project.

- They educated themselves before each step in the process.
- They gave great thought to what they wanted and needed.
- They researched other homes and used periodicals to find the design elements that suited those needs and wants.
- They got very detailed plans at a bargain price.
- They weighed their risks and benefits and chose only the most valuable services they needed from an architect.
- They called contractor references.
- They interviewed contractors.
- They had a contract with the builder and didn't reinvent the wheel doing it.
- They were a constant presence on their own project.
- They monitored what was built and made the necessary changes to get it just right.
- They were social with the crew members but let the contractor supervise his people and solve problems.

I'm sure if I'd pumped her for more information, I would have found they had a sound budget, insurance, and meeting notes too!

The Players List:
The People Who Will Be on Your Team

You will be amazed by the number of people you come in contact with over the course of a construction project. Some you will employ, some you will answer to, some you will befriend, and some you might rather live without. As you read through this list of players and their roles, keep in mind how your current definition of your own role may change and expand. Like they say, where you sit is where you stand.

Owner

The owner is you, the one who requests, monitors, pays for, and lives with the work done. From the point of view of others on this list, the owner also includes your budget, your family and friends, your kids and pets, your competency, your availability, and your attitude.

Bankers

Loan officer: processes your construction loan and mortgage.

Appraiser: determines the value of construction work planned and later completed.

Townspeople

Staff members: people at the Town Clerk's Office, the Planning and Zoning Department, and the Public Works Department who assist you in getting through the permit process.

Board members: often volunteer citizens, residents of the town who review your project for appropriateness and compliance with town ordinances (Design Review, and Planning and Zoning).

Architect

The architect is a designer of buildings who is licensed to practice in your state and provide stamped drawings. Members of an architectural firm may include:

Principals: partners in the firm.

Associates: employee architects.

Draftspeople: those who turn ideas into blueprints for your project.

Office personnel: administrative workers who will call you for appointments or send you things.

Engineers

These are designers licensed in your state to provide stamped drawings on specific aspects of the project.

Civil engineer: addresses the site.

Structural engineer: addresses the structure of a building.

Electrical engineer: addresses electrical systems.

Mechanical engineer: addresses plumbing, heating, ventilating, and air-conditioning systems.

Landscape architect

This is the designer of terrain and exterior architecture.

Cost estimator

Whether working for you, an architect, or a contractor, this person reviews your plans and prices the work.

Designer

This is a very broad term meaning anyone who designs. Find out what meaning this service provider is giving that title, and consider what it means to you. While an architect is a designer, a "designer" is likely not an architect. This person may or may not have any credentials and is not a licensed architect. Of course, it's fine to use a designer's services, but keep in mind that a designer is to an architect what a bookkeeper is to a CPA.

Interior decorator

This is a designer who creates the finished look of the space, including colors, furnishings, and window treatments. The decorator is often brought in early in a project to specify materials that will be installed by the contractor, like cabinetry, plumbing and electrical fixtures, flooring materials, and paint colors.

Surveyor

This person measures land to determine its location, volume, form, and boundaries. He also locates structures on land and utilities under it.

Testing services

There are several outfits that specialize in testing different things related to buildings. You may be required to perform a perk test for drainage, or a soil test for contamination. You can have the concrete for your foundation tested to ensure it meets density standards. You may be renovating an older home and want the old furnace and pipes tested for asbestos or the paint tested for lead.

Clerk of the works

This person is the eyes and ears of someone who wants the project monitored from a technical perspective. The "clerk" can be hired by you, an architect, the bank, even the contractor—anyone with a vested interest in ensuring that things are built according to the plans and a record be kept. Clerks are rare on residential jobs, but they don't charge a lot for the service they give, so just know they are an option for you.

Construction manager

This title can be confusing, since people in several jobs use it. (1) A construction manager (CM) is like a clerk in that he can monitor the project, but he usually has much more authority and responsibility. A CM representing owners could guide them through all facets of a project from design review and cost estimating to construction completion. (2) More commonly called a project manager, a CM employed by a general contractor provides the same services on the general contractor's behalf. (3) Architects may employ a CM to provide monitoring services during the construction phase. (4) CM is the title of a contractor working under the contract structure called construction management (page 86).

General contractor

A builder who works under contract is a contractor. A general contractor is a builder who coordinates other workers, subcontractors, and suppliers involved in a construction project. He is the ringleader responsible for the labor and materials for his crew and all those it takes to get the job done. Depending on the size of his company, the people who work directly for him are:

Superintendent (super) or foreman: on-site person coordinating the project, managing the crews, interpreting the plans, ordering materials, setting the pace. He is the owner's on-site link to the contractor.

Carpenters: the folks swinging the hammers. "Framers" do rough carpentry, and "finish carpenters" do things like building a mantel for your fireplace.

Laborers: the foot soldiers of the site. Their work is unglamorous but essential. They are the gofers, the cleanup crew, the heavy lifters, and the extra set of hands. They are often hired on a job-by-job basis and are not long-term employees of the general contractor.

Office personnel: administrative workers, bookkeepers, receptionists. It is imperative to know that in many small companies, there is only one administrative person: the spouse of the contractor who is carrying out your project.

Subcontractors (subs)

These are non-general contractors who specialize in specific trades. They are called subcontractors because their work is often part of a larger contract, in which case they work "under" a general contractor.

Excavators: operate heavy equipment like backhoes and bulldozers to dig foundations, install septic systems, and shape the land.

Masons: lay brick, block, stone, and tile to create structural work like block walls and chimneys, as well as finish work like fireplace hearths and walkways. If it involves mortar, chances are it's a mason doing it.

Roofers: apply the four layers to the top of the house that make a roof: sheathing, felt paper, metal flashing, and shingles, or tile, membrane, standing-seam metal, etc.

Framers: do the rough carpentry using dimensional lumber such as 2" x 6"s to create the studs and rafters that are the skeleton of your building project.

Electricians: install everything that uses electricity, including electrical panels, electrical wire, light fixtures, thermostats, alarm systems, even phone lines, cable and fiber-optic wire.

Plumbers: install everything that uses water, including sinks, tubs, showers, toilets, water meters, and water-flow restrictors, along with incoming water pipes and outgoing drain pipes.

Mechanical subcontractors: install heating, ventilation, and air-conditioning (HVAC) systems. Many companies provide both plumbing and mechanical services.

Sheetrockers: install or "hang" Sheetrock (drywall, gypsum board). They apply tape over the edges that butt together, using three coats of compound, which is sanded smooth to appear invisible once painted.

Painters: prepare and paint surfaces. In renovation work, their preparation "prep" work can be the bulk of their job and includes sanding, burning off old paint, lead-paint abatement, and/or priming. Due to the popularity of faux finishes, many painters have become expert in techniques such as rag rolling, glazing, stippling, combing and Venetian plaster.

Landscapers: shape the land surface, define exterior spaces, prepare the soil, and install the plantings: trees, shrubs, ground cover, and flowers.

Paving subcontractors: apply and finish asphalt paving. More than anyone, these subcontractors are limited by the temperature if you live in the North. The hot mix plants that supply asphalt close down in cold weather.

Suppliers

These are the purveyors of all tangible materials that will go into your project. Some also provide design and even subcontracting services related to the following materials:

- Gravel, fill, soils

- Lumber: dimensional and finish

- General supplies: nails, screws, felt paper, hardware

- Windows and doors

- Electrical supplies

- Plumbing and mechanical supplies

- Paint

- Flooring: carpet, vinyl, ceramic tile, synthetic wood

- Cabinets

- Appliances

Lawyer

With luck, this is a person who may help you prevent problems by reviewing your contracts before signing. Other than that, hiring one is not a good sign.

Arbiter

A much better choice than a lawyer, an arbiter is hired to hear the complaints of two grieved parties in conflict. The arbiter then decides the fair solution and compensation for both parties. Arbitration is often built into contracts as a means of dispute resolution that is binding.

Mediator

A mediator also hears the complaints of two aggrieved parties, but usually negotiates a midrange solution that each party can live with. The mediator's input is not usually binding, but rather based on bringing the grieved parties to consensus.

A Gleam in Your Eye: Can You Build?

Before you start in earnest on planning your project, make sure you can have one. If you are hoping to construct a custom home on a building lot:

- Make sure it's a buildable lot. In other words, make sure it's not in a flood zone, wetlands, a restrictive slope, easement, or natural habitat, over toxic waste, in a lava flow, whatever. You'd·be amazed by the number of people who buy a piece of land only to find they cannot build on it. Many of these limitations can be found in the deed, but they don't necessarily throw up any red flags in a title search, because the land can be sold just fine. It just can't be built on. Read the deed yourself before you start spending money on designs or builders.

- Make sure you can get water in and out. Be sure you have access to the town water line or that you're likely to drill for a well successfully. If you need a well, do that first so you know how much money is left for the project. To get wastewater out, you need to tie into the town sewer system or put in a septic system. For the latter, you will need to know how the land tests for drainage and design your system accordingly.

- Make sure you can get power, gas, phone, cable, and any other desired and required services and utilities to your home. Really be sure of this. Just because you see a pole doesn't mean you can access it.

- Make sure you're building the right kind of thing in the right place at the right size. Stop by your town offices and check the zoning and the setback requirements for your lot, especially if you've owned it a long time. The town may have made some zoning changes to your lot or those within sight (page 139).

- If you're building an addition, first check the deed to make sure there are no covenants restricting you from adding on. Then make sure you can comply with any requirements regarding lot coverage, height, physical and visual encroachment on the neighbors, and continuity in design with your existing building.

Don't Bank On It:
Is Your Loan Officer Your Ally?

If you need a construction loan, any loan officer will guide you through the process. You'll get a list of tasks you must complete and things you must provide. Your contractor may get one too. The items will likely include:

- Plans and specifications for the construction project (page 25)

- A budget broken down by divisions (page 78)

- A certificate of insurance from the contractor (page 123)

- A draw schedule laying out a plan for payment to the contractor as work is completed (page 135)

- A building permit (page 144)

- A contractor's signature on a contract the bank provides. This could be in addition to your more detailed contract. Its primary purpose is to protect the bank's interest in this investment of theirs.

- A building inspection schedule for the bank's appraiser (pages 138)

- Lien waivers (page 129)

The loan officer gathers information and materials from you and gives them to an appraiser, who determines the value of the proposed finished project. If the loan sought is for no more than that value, you are in good shape to get the loan, assuming you're otherwise qualified.

During the construction phase, the appraiser will inspect the work progress to see that work has been completed as planned before each disbursement of loan funds is made to the contractor. He will use a form like that shown on page 11. It's important to note that appraisers are assessing the value, not the quality, of what's constructed. The homeowner is typically charged up to $200 for each of these inspections and asked for verbal approval to release funds. The contractor is required to provide a lien waiver (page 129), and then he's paid for the completed work less 5 to 10 percent held for retainage (page 136).

Mortgage companies don't do a lot of construction loans. Only banks do. That's because construction loans are usually kept in-house until the project is at least 90 percent complete. At that point, the appraiser will provide the bank with a certificate of completion and the bank will "modify" your construction loan to a mortgage. Owners look forward to this conversion because a construction loan is typically offered at a 2 to 3 percent higher rate than a mortgage.

Banks don't usually check out a contractor's solvency, but neither do they approve loans on projects where the contractor wants a down payment. Some banks also refuse to pay for any change orders on projects. Those are the changes in the scope of work that result in cost changes—usually upward. On the one hand this is scary. What if something is left out of the plans that must be done and paid for later? On the other hand, if the contractor knows up front that the bank won't pay for change orders, he has a great incentive to make sure all the necessary work is covered in those plans and all the cost for it is included in the budget.

Pitfall

Do you think the bank is behind you, inspecting the construction work for quality and guarding your best interests? Think again.

Who They Are

When you walk into your bank and are directed to a loan officer, you may assume that this person is a salaried employee of the bank. This person would have only the best interests of you and the bank at heart, right? Well, times have changed. Since the 1970s, other entities have sprung up to compete in the mortgage market (you can even get mortgages online now), and most of these outfits have loan officers who work on commission. To compete, the banks have been forced to follow suit. This changes the loan officers' incentive. They get all or some of their income from commissions on the loans they make. The non-banks don't usually offer construction loans. If you need one, you will likely end up at a bank, but the same principles apply.

SITE BUILT
CONSTRUCTION LOAN INSPECTION

Borrowers:

Property Address:

Disbursements will be made according to the following percentages during construction. No funds can be disbursed for materials ordered or stored, only for work actually completed and installed in the building on site.

CONSTRUCTION CHECKLIST*	$ VALUE	DISBURSED	% OF WORK COMPLETE					
			1	2	3	4	5	6
Excavation, Backfill								
Footings, Foundation of Slab								
Concrete Floor, Basement/Garage								
Well & Pump								
Water Supply to House								
Sewage Disposal/Septic								
1st floor Deck								
Framing, Sheathing, Partitions								
Roofing/Exterior Trim								
Siding								
Ext. Doors, Windows, Combinations								
Insulation								
Sheetrock, Taped/Panel Walls/Ceiling								
Plumbing:								
Rough-in: Tub, Pipes in Walls/Ceiling								
Finish: Drain Supply Lines, Fixtures								
Electric:								
Main Power to House								
Rough-in: Wiring								
Finish: Switch, Recep. & Fixtures								
Heat:								
Rough-in: Wires/Duct/Piping								
Chimney								
Finish: Furnace, Fuel Tank, Heaters								
Interior Doors, Trim, Millwork								
Kitchen & Bath Cabinets & Counters								
Exterior Paint/Stain								
Interior Paint/Stain/Decorating								
Flooring								
Steps, Decks, Porches								
Walks, Driveway								
Topsoil, Grading, Seeding								
Kitchen Appliances								
Fireplace or Woodstove Flue								
TOTAL	$	$						

* Includes labor

_____   _____   _____   _____
Appraiser   Date   Builder   Date

A Day with the Loan Officers

It seems that loan officers on commission created a little crisis of conscience at a large bank. They were giving out lots of construction loans, but there was a backlash when a project didn't go well. Some customers pulled their savings from the bank, angry that the bank didn't support them well in their construction projects. Those customers now had the debt of that loan rolled into a mortgage and didn't like the finished product from the contractor. With that in mind, the bank asked me to come speak to fifty of their loan officers on the merits of good project planning.

I had trouble reading the audience. Why wouldn't they want projects well prepared and monitored? Wasn't the bank at risk if the projects failed? Then someone revealed that they got paid a commission when a loan closed. So if a loan officer protects you by holding up payment to the contractor who has performed below your standards, that loan officer might not get paid that month. You may have thought they were the keepers at the gate; that they would ensure the project was done right, stand by you, and dole out your money only if you were happy with the project, right? Wrong. In fact, one frustrated loan officer stood up and said, "Okay, say it's the end of the project. I've paid out all the money in that construction loan to the contractor except the last payment. The owners call and say, 'Don't cut that check. The new house is awful, and we have a lot of problems with the contractor.' What do I do?" I responded, "Well, what DO you do?" He said, "I pay it." I was shocked, and I'm sure those homeowners were too. The loan officer cut a two party check that both the owners and the contractor had to sign before cashing. However, the bank just washed its hands of this problem and left those owners alone to defend against the advances of the contractor looking for payment on a project they thought was a disaster.

While loan officers may still be benevolent and helpful, and want the best for you and your project, such characteristics are now more a moral choice than functions of their job. This dilemma gets harder for them every day. To be more attractive to potential customers, their competition may cut some of the requirements of owners and contractors. The bank that requires you and your contractor to present a tightly planned project with all the i's dotted and t's crossed may now be less appealing. The loan officers know this, and some even lobby hard for minimum requirements of you so that they can compete better. These folks are in a tough position, but based on these dynamics, they are not necessarily your allies.

The good news is, there are those loan officers who hold the customers' hands and lead them through the process step by step. Seek these people out. Any loan you receive that the bank disburses to a contractor is ultimately your money, since you're the one who has to pay it back. So don't go for the easy money. Let the loan officer know you want protection. You want support in this process and will comply with whatever requirements he thinks wise. Find out what services he will offer in return. What about that appraiser? Ask if you can get one with construction expertise. The loan officer knows this field better than you. He knows what makes a project succeed or fail. Rely on him as a resource, and make him make you get it right.

In the recession of 2008 we all came to understand just how severely our real estate economy had been undermined by banks playing fast and loose with loan regulations. Adjustable rate mortgages in the form of "no-doc(uments)," "zero-money-down," and "interest-only" loans let people buy or build homes they could barely afford, with the understanding that their monthly payments would adjust upward after a few years. This approach was predicated on the value of property increasing so homeowners could either sell at a profit or draw equity out of the property to pay the higher mortgage rates in their future. This made for low monthly payments relative to the size of the mortgages, and that helped fulfill the prophecy of a perpetually booming real estate market by letting house prices soar. It was a house of cards, and when it fell property values tumbled. Millions of homeowners were trapped in upside-down mortgages, paying off debt loads higher than the value of their homes. Foreclosures occurred at a rate never before seen in America.

Besides their own folly, what got homeowners into this situation? Banks and other lenders. Who were the foot soldiers of such an ill-conceived and short-sighted mess? Loan officers. All sorts of compensatory regulations have been put in place since then, but as long as loan officers work on commission, your best interest may not be their first priority. So, just make sure it's yours.

The Scary Money: Down Payments

The list of items required by a loan officer is a good one. You should require these things of yourself and a contractor even if a lender is not involved. How to do that is covered throughout this book. The banks' refusal to pay for down payments is telling. Many contractors ask for a down payment of anything from 10 to 50 percent of the project cost. This flies in the face of the golden rule for owners: Don't pay for any materials not yet delivered or work not yet done.

Contractors may say they need this money to buy materials to start the project. Yet they should be solvent enough and have a good enough track record in paying suppliers that they can get these materials on credit until you pay the first requisition. A down pay-

Pitfall

A down payment is an outlay of cash for work not yet done. Beware.

ment can also be seen as an act of good faith on your part. The contractor wants to see that you're committed to this project and can pay your bills. However, a good contract should persuade him of this and alleviate his concerns. In general, I would say a down payment is to be avoided. You will have nothing to show for this outlay of cash. If you choose to go with a contractor who will not start otherwise, either address it in the first requisition (page 170) or try this alternative: <u>You</u> pay for the materials.

CHAPTER 2

The Plan is the Thing
Making a Successful Project

This chapter shows how to get an airtight plan that will lay the foundation for a successful project.

- Task-Oriented: Your To-Do List
- Getting What You Need: How to Approach Your Design
- Sneaking Up On Your Design: Do's and Don'ts to Get You Started
- What's It Worth to You? Money and Design
- Beyond Eenie, Meenie, Miney, Mo: A Formula for Balanced Choices
- A House United: Working Together as a Couple

Task-Oriented: Your To-Do List

Once you've decided you want something built or remodeled, try to resist the temptation to pick up the phone and call a contractor. There are six things you'll need to have set up before anyone starts ordering lumber.

Define Yourself

Set up a process that best utilizes what you have to offer. Check out the players list (page 4) and contract structures (chapter 7) to understand what your options are. Then decide your role and level of participation based on your needs, your interests, your skills, your available time, your marriage or partnership, your temperament, and your lifestyle. In defining your own role, you are taking on an identity you will convey to others on the project. Will you lead this project alone? Will you hire help in design, cost estimating, or project management?

The Paper Trail

Information will be created, collected, and conveyed from the start of your project to its conclusion, and it can get like the game Telephone pretty quickly. So good record keeping is imperative, especially if any disputes arise later. It doesn't have to be fancy, just accurate. To set up a good filing system, use the subdivisions of the File Index on the next page that pertain to your project. Each of these topics will be covered in later chapters.

Plans: Whether they're just sketches you make or full-scale blueprints from an architect, the plans are the visual representation of the finished

66 The best laid plans... usually work. 99

project along with identifying dimensions, notes, and information that further explain them (page 26).

Specifications: These "specify" how the work is to be done, including standards of quality and what materials will be used. On a small project, you may convey this information through just your drawing with notes, but be sure you address it somewhere (page 26).

Schedule: You need a commitment to the timeline of this project. When will it begin and end? What are the significant work milestones, especially those that affect the progress of other work and payment for it? If the project deadline cannot slip, you may want to consider liquidated damages, charging a contractor for every day he goes past the deadline (page 131).

Contract: If you do nothing else mentioned in this book, get a contract (chapter 10)!

Getting What You Need: How to Approach Your Design

Reality will set in soon enough, so dream a little dream first. Get out all the ideas you may have before you start constricting them with thoughts of budgets and building codes. Some owners have been planning on building their dream house for forty years. Some have a file a foot thick of clip-

> *Get it down. Take chances. It may be bad, but it's the only way you can do anything really good.*
>
> —WILLIAM FAULKNER

FILE INDEX	
SECTION 1: MONEY	**SECTION 2: DESIGN**
Bank correspondence: written notes, phone notes, email, directives	Design correspondence: Written notes, phone notes, email, directives to architect, designers, engineers and suppliers
Loan application, loan agreement	Design ideas: clippings, photos, and scribbles
Construction budget	Architect or designer selection
Draw schedule	Meeting notes and directives
Change orders	Scope of work: considerations and decisions
Requisitions	Supplies and materials: brochures, cut sheets, articles
Lien waivers	Design-phase cost estimates
	Finishes selections: paint, countertops, carpet, tile, siding, colors, etc.
	Plans and specifications: schematics through finished drawings
	Contractor selection process
SECTION 3: PROJECT TRACKING	**SECTION 4: DOCUMENTS**
Contractor correspondence: written notes, phone notes, email, directives	Legal correspondence: written notes, phone notes, email, directives
Construction schedule	Contracts: architect or designer, general contractor, subcontractors, etc.
Job meeting minutes	Owner's insurance
Photographs	Contractors' certificate of insurance
Give-and-take list (see page 167)	Permitting: zoning, building inspector correspondence, permits
	Certificate of completion

pings and photos of everything they love about houses. For others it's a nearly secret passion they haven't dared express. Whatever has led you to this point, foster it, expand upon it, and let it reach the limits of your imagination before you start to rein it in. Out there, even on the fringes, will be some great things you can apply.

You have many resources available to you as you design your project. Even if you plan to hire an architect or designer, you may want to use some of the following resources to flesh out some ideas first.

Real estate open houses: Check the weekend real estate section of the newspaper, hop in the car, and see what's out there.

Your town's public meetings: Planning and zoning and design review board meetings are public. You can learn a lot about what others in your town are designing, pricing, and getting approved.

Bookstores and libraries: Camp out with a stack of books full of beautiful plans and elegant solutions to your design challenges.

Suppliers: Every store from the lumberyard to the lighting shop has cut sheets, brochures, and catalogs of its wares. More and more stores offer some form of free design or layout, especially with kitchen cabinetry and HVAC systems. Paint and wallpaper stores offer whole palettes of wall finishes that work together. Home Depot Expos offer design assistance with almost everything.

Home shows: Every year there are hundreds of home shows around the country. Each usually has a few hundred booths with contractors, suppliers, designers, and manufacturers displaying their talents and their products. Try to get a schedule in advance so you can attend some of the workshops and training sessions. Also be sure to bring a bag for all the catalogs and brochures you'll collect.

Magazines: There are 150 monthly design and decorating periodicals featuring everything from blueprints you can purchase to paint finishes you can replicate.

Television: More than 500 hours of programming per week are devoted to home design and construction.

The Internet: You'll find everything from product literature to whole house plans.

Be Careful What You Wish For

Distinguish between needs and wants as you design. Make sure all needs are included in your design and wants are prioritized for inclusion, deletion, or consideration later as the budget permits. Save even the wildest of wish list items for later consideration (page 165).

Your choices are infinite when you start, so design is more a process of deselecting than selecting. If you can come up with a general style with which you would like to be consistent, each design decision will fall into place much

> *To know one's own desires, their meaning and their costs requires the highest human virtue: Rationality.*
>
> —AYN RAND

more easily. Is it Colonial, Georgian, Arts and Crafts, Modern, Santa Fe, Post-and-Beam . . . ? Choose one and let that style guide the broad strokes of your design.

To thine own self be true. The more your space addresses your actual needs, the happier you'll be with it. People have a habit of including in their plan things that they think will make them live a certain way that will be better. Then they leave out those things that would address their real needs. For instance, if you include an exercise room, you will work out, right? Wrong. A music room will make your kids practice the piano. Not likely. The truth is, you are unlikely to change how you live, and so those spaces will go unused. Let your design address reality. If your kids drop their stuff the second they walk in the door, design for that. If your family watches a total of six hours of television a day, don't try to make the fireplace the focus of the room where the TV will be. If your husband's bathroom is kept off-limits to anyone with a compromised immune system, don't renovate with wallpaper and carpet.

Okay, so you're not living a storybook life. So what? Be honest and accept your own lifestyle. Do a needs assessment based on your current lifestyle and home. Monitor how you use your existing living space. Note what works for you and what doesn't. Do a time/cost-benefit analysis. How much time do you and your family members spend in each room, and what do you do there (cooking, dining, watching TV, bathing, entertaining, working at home, doing laundry, making a mess, etc.)? Now, can you really justify that $16,000 potting shed?

Foresight is free. A home is a vital place. Try to design so you don't preclude making changes you can anticipate now. Consider what life changes you anticipate over the course of your foreseeable time in your new space or home. Do you plan to add children to the family or

Insider's Tip

Don't miss the opportunity to get things later that you can't afford now.

have children moving out? Will you retire and grow old in this space that will need to meet your changing physical needs? Do you dream of an in-home business someday? What technologies are coming? What hobbies would you like to take up? Try to think of every possible eventuality. You can modify your designs slightly and inexpensively now to keep the door open for these possibilities later. For instance, you think that in ten years you might want to add an apartment for your parents. In the exterior wall where that addition would begin, you could include the framing for the door to that space, buried in the wall. You could install a T-junction and a shutoff in the water pipe near that future space, and you could make sure that the heating system you get today could handle the extra space in ten years. These modifications, if done ten years from now, would cost thousands, whereas today, as part of your first project, they will cost you almost nothing. So before you say no to yourself about everything you cannot afford today, consider building in the possibility for doing it later.

You're not building a time capsule. Avoid trends that will date your project or be incongruous with the rest of your home. Twenty years ago it was greenhouses; today it's those towers slapped on the corner of everything. You may love these architectural touches in the moment, but they are fleeting trends, and over time they will change from assets to liabilities. Try to express your love of things au courant in items that will be replaced over time through wear and tear, like fabric and furnishings, and leave your valuable structure out of it.

You learn something old every day. Visiting model homes or looking at stock plans from a magazine is a great way to start, but remember that these plans are popular because they suit the common denominators for both the owners and the builders. Don't let the homogeneity of American construction limit your thinking. Now's your chance to get the things that really suit you. Many of them come from the past. For my dream house, I will include a dumbwaiter to get the groceries to the kitchen from the garage below. I will have a Murphy ironing board that disappears into the wall. I will install blocking (2" x 4" horizontal framing) throughout the house at five feet off the floor for hanging artwork, knowing I'll always hit a stud for support. I will have a sleeping porch off the second floor like the one I so loved at my grandmother's house. What will you have?

Sneaking Up On Your Design: Do's and Don'ts to Get You Started

An architect friend of mine is fond of saying, "Good design is good design." I think to myself, "Give me a break! Is there anything more subjective than design?" However, I must concede there are some simple rules to approaching design that will certainly help it get in the "good" camp. Since you will either be designing your own project or working with someone who will help create your vision, here are some simple concepts regarding architectural design that you should bear in mind.

Best Foot Forward

Try to coordinate your layout and sight lines with your best architectural features. Maximize the impact of those items that you choose to make your house a home. Try centering the fireplace across from the entrance to the living room. Line up those door openings so you can see the bay window from two rooms away. Balance and symmetry are not trendy in custom design today, but they will always give your space a harmonious feeling and help keep your property resalable.

Is That What I Meant?

Be mindful that most design has occurred before and has become part of a style, a vernacular. Choices you make may have a connotation of another place, time, or style that you may not be aware of until you see the finished product. The open staircase sounded cool and you liked the earth tones. Who knew you were re-creating the *Brady Bunch* living room? Be careful.

Poor, inefficient design often has excessive traffic space that raises the cost of your building and offers little in return. Stringing a bunch of square rooms together with lots of hallways probably isn't the best use of your money or space. Open floor plans offer lots of flexibility and keep cost down. Remember, space can be defined by more than just walls. Furniture, soffits, floor finishes, and even plants and artwork can define spatial boundaries. Try to think of dual uses for floor space. Instead of having a long hallway to a walk-in closet, try lining a hallway with closets on both sides. You will achieve more storage space with less floor space and cost.

Tried-and-True

New materials, supplies, and equipment come on the market every day. Some are great. Some are not and they will be off the market in a few years, just when you would like to replace a broken part or find anyone who knows how to work on that thing. This is particularly true of heating and air-conditioning equipment. You may sacrifice one percent of promised fuel efficiency to get a tried-and-true system, but don't let a manufacturer cut its teeth on your project. Get things that the suppliers and the subcontractors say work best and hold up.

Don't Decorate Yourself into a Corner

Your project is a blank slate until the finishes are applied. They include paint and stain colors, wall textures, floor tile, carpet, countertops, cabinetry, hardware, and electrical and plumbing fixtures, etc. You will also be coordinating these finishes with fabric, furnishings, artwork, and other noninstalled decor items. This should be the fun part, right? Instead, it can become very hard for people, and here's why. Each time you select a finish, you reduce your options for the finishes yet to be selected. Say you choose a pickled stain for the kitchen cabinets. This limits your countertop choices, but you are still able to find one that works. Unfortunately, though, there is no floor tile that you like with that countertop. Whoops. You need to start over, and you haven't even gotten to the other five finishes in that room, or how they will transition to the next room. The solution?

Don't choose any one item in a vacuum. Make a list of all the finishes to be chosen. Consider the elements you already have, like that floral couch or your kid's bedspread. Collect samples for all of the finishes to be addressed. You will likely have a couple boxes of stuff loaned from the various suppliers. Now create your palette like assembling a puzzle. Try this piece next to that piece until you have a whole collection of finish items that work as one. Your contractor can help

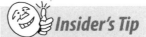 **Insider's Tip**

Don't make your interior decorating choices one item at a time. You'll end up frustrated with rooms that don't hang together.

gather the samples you need if you're doing this during the construction phase. However, you will get more accurate pricing on your project and relieve yourself of a lot of pressure later if you do this finish selection by the end of the design phase for inclusion in your specifications.

Remember that you are creating an overall wonderful effect. Like dressing yourself, this may not necessarily be achieved by getting your favorite individual thing in each category. Having your favorite carpet, for example, may preclude having your favorite wall color. Try to think of each space you create as a canvas on which you will paint the perfect room with fabric, art, furniture, plants, and the things you love. Don't let your finishes overpower your possessions (unless you're sure that's what you want). As my grandmother would say, "A floor should lie down!" She was right. What would you rather hear for the next ten years when guests enter your living room: "Wow, great carpet" or "Wow, great room"?

What's It Worth to You?
Money and Design

Most conversation about design begins and ends with money. You will try to determine the cost of what you want, whether that's a fair cost, and whether you can afford it and justify it. As you go through that process, keep the following truths in mind.

The joke about construction projects is that if you double the cost and triple the time you think it will take, you're halfway there. The starting point is part of the problem. Do not round down during the planning phase. If you find yourself thinking, "If we're lucky, it will only cost . . . ," stop and add 10 percent to your highest guess. This padded math will buy you a lot of peace of mind and save you from revising your plans over and over. If there's money left over, great—but I've yet to see that happen.

Owners often think that once they get their home done just the way they like, they will never leave it. This can make them do some cockamamie things to their home. Surprise! Statistics show that people who have built or significantly remodeled their home are likely

Pitfall

What you want in your dream house is not likely what others want in theirs.

to stay there an average of six years, only one year longer than those who have not. Don't do anything that will make this house undesirable to future buyers. Always think about salability and return on your investment as you choose where to put your money.

- Do not overdesign, overbuild, or overspend in relation to the land or surrounding property values. You don't want to have the best house in a neighborhood that limits your home's value.

- Your dream house may not be anyone else's. It is prudent to build your dream features within a more conventional, salable package.

- Regarding return on your investment, great kitchens, roomy decks, ample storage, second floors, and fireplaces will prove the best investments. Pools, saunas, hot tubs, and gazebos will not.

- Don't get carried away with even the "good investment" projects. If you put a $75,000 kitchen in a house in a neighborhood of otherwise identical houses priced at $325,000, you probably still have a house worth about $325,000.

- Cost ÷ Use = Value. Think bang for the buck on the money you will spend. We are all familiar with the living rooms that we peer into from the hallway but never enter. What percentage of that home's costs does that represent in terms of mortgage, taxes, maintenance, and utilities? Before you renovate the dining room used only at the holidays or build a huge porch in northern New England, give a little thought to the value gained.

- Again, today's trend is tomorrow's dated item. Remember avocado-colored appliances? Get what you love, but try not to build a place that someone will be calling retro in ten years.

Beyond Eenie, Meenie, Miney, Mo: A Formula for Balanced Choices

You have many design decisions to make and an almost infinite number of options. As you gather information to plan your project, making your way through the pros and cons can get overwhelming without guidelines. Consider these five things when making design decisions, and try to find the pattern in your decision style and that of your partner: Maybe you always tip the scales in favor of form. Your spouse may go for cost. Seeing these tendencies for what they are will help stop the swirling of information and bring you closer to successful compromise and a plan that really hangs together.

Form: How will it look? Is it historically correct or complimentary to the style of your home or future neighborhood? Will it appeal to future buyers?

Function: How will it work? How well does it suit the purpose? Will it appeal to future buyers?

Durability: What is the life span of this feature and the cost for its replacement? Would a less costly option meet the need as well, or does a higher capital investment now pay off in the long run?

Maintenance: How much and what type of upkeep will this feature require? Is that upkeep work that you enjoy or don't mind paying for, or will it be a burden?

Cost: Considering your answers to the above, does this item provide a good return on your investment?

> *A man builds a fine house; and now he has a master, and a task for life; he is to furnish, watch, show it, and keep it in repair, the rest of his days.*
>
> —RALPH WALDO EMERSON

A House United:
Working Together as a Couple

Building or renovating a house together can be a great experience, but any pleasure you derive from this process is always the by-product of a job well done. This pertains to anyone, but especially to couples. For many couples, this is the first time they will really work together. Differences and new dynamics of their relationship will come out. The decisions, division of labor, deadlines, and different styles of communication can all be sources of conflict. These conflicts will make you vulnerable to greater stressors and higher expenses if they are aired publicly for an architect or contractor to cope with. In short, conflicts open the door for chaos, and chaos is expensive. If you and your partner are not united in your approach to the project, it will cost you. For instance, the architect will have to charge you more if your wrangling over differences in the plan results in revision after revision. During the construction phase, you will pay for delays and changes brought about by misunderstandings and wasted time. And in ways you may never actually see on a bill, you will pay for being disorganized and difficult to work with.

Like everything else, a construction project succeeds or fails because of people, and you are the most important people in this equation. Look at it this way: The architect and contractor are not joining your family. You are joining their team as its leaders. But don't panic. Now that you know this, you can address it and create your own vision for roles that work to your respective strengths. Your odds of a successful project go way up if you and your partner conduct yourselves as a professional, confident, and united couple, indivisible by outside influences. Here's how to do that.

Negotiating taste is tricky business. When making design decisions as a couple, try to choose what each of you can tolerate rather than exactly what each of you wants. If you know you will have trouble coming to agreement, do not start with "Which one do you like?" Instead, try winnowing away the ones both of you don't like and considering a pool of three remaining options both of you could tolerate. An outside opinion is very helpful when you hit an impasse.

When you're working with others, you and your partner are a united front—even if it is a front. There should be no doubt in anyone's mind that your allegiance lies with each other first and foremost. This is easy to pull off until questions arise. As a couple, you will be asked to make many decisions based on lots of options presented to you by the people you've hired. Stop and think for a moment about whether that decision is simple or will trigger a lengthy discussion or worse. Take the heavy issues home to discuss in private after you have gathered all the pertinent information. This way you will always appear indivisible and professional. People will be less likely to try to drive a wedge between you for their benefit. I know this sounds dastardly, but it happens a lot.

When you render decisions, speak with one voice. Both owners should attend all pertinent meetings and speak freely. However, directives to anyone you are paying should come from one person, and everyone should know who that person is. It's a matter of professional courtesy and a good practice to avoid confusion. Have a heart-to-heart talk with your significant other about which of you should fill this role. The person you want is the one who best fits this description: a clear, unflappable people person. If you would like to choose who leads for all but the aesthetic decisions, that's fine. Just make that distinction up front, and share it with the whole project team. Then keep an eye on the schedule for the date when the decisions on finishes are due and the authority is passed to that person.

We've touched on all the things that bring order and success to a project: your tasks, design decisions, and good relations. The chapters that follow will address these topics in detail.

CHAPTER 3

Design as a Noun
Refining and Conveying
Your Vision

This chapter defines a reliable design and explores how you go
about creating one.

- Decisions, Decisions: Your Design
- Conveying Your Decisions: Construction Documents
- Building In Flexibility: Allowances, Unit Pricing and Alternate Pricing

Decisions, Decisions:
Your Design

After you have some sense of what you want to build, it's time to get it
down on paper. You have four options for doing this. You can do it yourself, buy ready-made plans, hire an architect for some or all of the services
offered, or work with a contractor to come up with a design. This chapter
will cover the first two options. Employing an architect is covered in chapter 4. Creating a design with a contractor is covered under the design/
build section of chapter 7. However, the tasks and much of the advice in
this chapter pertain to all four approaches.

This design phase is your best opportunity for preempting problems
before construction begins. Your goal in this phase is to define your
planned project to the last detail. Do not let your project evolve over
the course of the construction phase, making decisions as you go. If you
do so, you will never have control of your budget or schedule, and you
are likely to run out of money before your project is complete. Try to
make all pertinent decisions and remove as many variables as possible,
thereby lessening your exposure to risk. At the end of the design phase,
you should have plans and specifications that will convey your designs to
the contractor you select. Every item not conveyed properly before you
and your contractor have come to an agreed upon price can cost you later.
This is the time to really focus.

Conveying Your Decisions:
Construction Documents

The work you want to have done will become the scope of work, and it is
conveyed to a contractor through plans and specifications. They are to your
project what a cookbook is to a cake. The plans, also known as blueprints or
drawings, are like the picture of a cake showing the finished product, its size,

proportions, details, and decoration. The specifications are like the recipe, with ingredients and instructions for preparation. Together they give you the "what" and the "how" you need to make that cake, as your plans and specifications give a contractor the "what" and "how" he needs to execute your project. Add a contract detailing the "who," "where," and "when," and you have a complete set of construction documents to which everyone on your job commits himself (chapter 10).

Plans

What's enough in terms of design? The more detail you provide, the more clearly you convey your wishes and the less you leave things to interpretation. The more accurately the cost reflects that of the finished product, the more you reduce your exposure to risk. Of course, there is a point of

Sample Architectural Plans with Notes

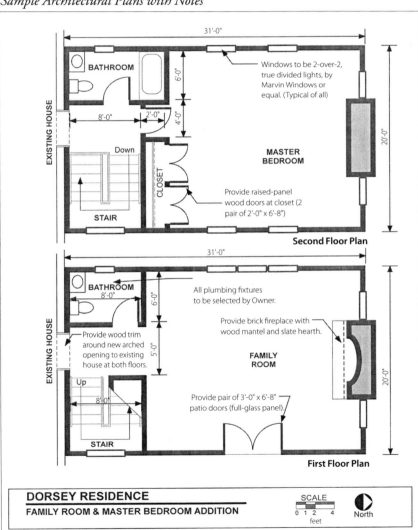

diminishing returns. You don't need to show each nail in your plans, but try to be thorough and not leave any big items to chance. As you lay out your project, be sure it tells the whole story, the who, what, where, when, and how of this project.

Whether your plans are hand drawings or a thick roll of blueprints, they should convey the visual image of what you want, and include drawings to scale with dimensions. A full set of plans would include a floor plan showing the bird's-eye view (page 25), and elevations showing the total project from all four sides. "Sections" and "details" can be added as needed. Sections are slices of elevations, showing the project from different points of reference. For instance, an elevation may show the entire south wall of a house from the exterior, while a section might be an interior view, also from the south, but just inside that wall. Details are drawings, usually made to larger scale, that show the assembly of specific framing or architectural features, like a beam tying into a post or a stair rail system. Plans also include lots of notes on dimensions, materials, and where the materials get installed. Pages of the plans are broken out for different subcontracting trades. There's usually a site plan, an electrical plan, a plumbing plan, and so forth. Imagine all these pages on transparent paper. If you were to layer all these plans on top of each other, you could see everything going into the project.

If you want to consider ready-made plans for a new home, that's a great, cost-effective way to go, or at least get started. There are more than fifteen thousand house plans along with cost guides shown in dozens of books, periodicals, and Web sites. You can order their stock designs for about 75 to 90 cents per square foot of house design. The latest plans for very high-end homes by some renowned architects can go for several thousand dollars. Either way, you'll get a thorough set of plans with exterior and interior elevations, a foundation plan, sections, and details, along with a materials list that you or your contractor can take to have priced. If you want to buy such plans, make sure they are appropriate to your climate or be ready to have some changes made. For instance, it's not wise to put a 4,000-square-foot, two-story house on slab in the North. You can have modifications made by a local architect, or you can even use the "customization service" offered by some of the companies that sell ready-made plans (page 197).

Specifications

The specifications are divided by trade and include instructions to the contractor and subcontractors. They spell out how you want things done. They tell the people doing the work what materials to order and how to build, assemble, install, or apply them. They also explain what standards of quality will be expected and how they will be measured. Below is a paragraph from the painting section of a set of specifications. Now, wouldn't this do a dandy job of protecting you from a lousy paint job?

If you're thinking about creating your own construction documents, you may want to consider *Guidelines' Quickspecs*. Guidelines is a company

Paint Specification

Mix and apply materials strictly as per manufacturer's instructions. Apply paint to thoroughly cover undercoat, and do not allow show-through, lap or brush marks, or any other defects. Vary the hue of succeeding coats slightly to clearly show coats are applied as required. Only coats of paint inspected and approved by the owner will be counted as completed. Sand defects smooth between coats. Defects are defined as irregularities visible to the unaided eye at a 5 foot distance.

that sells a CD-ROM form of complete specifications for all trades for around $200 (page 197). Of course, these are standardized specifications and so won't cover the materials specific to your project, but this is a great start for someone looking to create a homemade version of a professionally contracted job.

On a small project, specifications often look more like an extensive laundry list (e.g. install 200 sq. ft. of 1' x 1' x 3/4" gray slate on patio, install 6" x 3/4" pine baseboard throughout, install dining room chair rail at 30" above floor). That's fine as long as anyone reading it would know exactly what you want.

Performance specifications set a standard that a system must meet. Then the contractor or subcontractor proposes such a system. This is a broad and inexpensive design approach, and it works just fine. These specifications are typically used for septic, electrical, and HVAC portions of a project. You or someone assisting you would specify the level of performance of the finished system sought, and the subcontractor would propose a system to meet your needs. For instance, you might write a performance specification requesting: *A heating system with a 94 percent efficient boiler and two zones for a hot water baseboard system designed to keep your 2,000-square-foot house warmed to 70 degrees when it's 20 degrees below zero outside, and per BOCA and state code.* The mechanical subcontractor would review the plans, noting the size of rooms, the amount of wall and ceiling insulation, and the location and types of doors and windows. He would likely bring this information to his supplier, who would do take-offs, calculating what was needed to make a system that complies with your performance standards. The subcontractor would propose the finished system to you, showing all its equipment and components and where they'd be located in your project.

No two sets of plans and specifications are done alike. Some professionals do drawings with almost no notes and put all nonvisual information in the specifications. Some have so many notes on the drawings, I wonder what could be left to go in the specifications. Both approaches are fine as long as the pertinent information is covered. It's also okay for information to appear in both places as long as it doesn't conflict. In theory, if these documents are thorough, you could take them to any builder and get the exact same project executed.

Building In Flexibility:
Allowances, Unit Pricing and Alternate Pricing

What happens if you put your designs together in a great set of plans and specifications, then get it priced and the number comes back 30 percent over your budget? What if you just don't want to take the time now to specify every last detail of the wall and floor finishes before you get started? And what happens if you are renovating a great old house?

You can spell out what the finished product of the renovation should be, but not exactly how to get there because you just don't know what's in those walls or under that floor. You don't need to go back to the drawing board if you factor flexibility into your scope of work.

Pitfall

Locking yourself into design decisions that could change later can be risky and expensive.

There are three tools vital to controlling your budget and letting you build in flexibility and security while addressing portions of the work that remain uncertain through the design phase. They are allowances, unit prices, and alternate prices. The base bid is the price the contractor will give you to build according to your plans and specifications. He can also give you allowances, unit prices, and alternate prices with which you can later amend the scope of work and budget total without facing costly change orders or creating chaos.

Allowances

It is best to specify as many materials as possible up front, but in the real world, the selection of finishes often happens during the construction phase. During the design phase, suppose you know you need 225 square yards of carpet and you know it costs about $25 per yard, but you don't want to choose it now. Instruct the contractor to include in your price an allowance for $5,625 worth of carpet that you will specify later. Be sure that you create an allowance for the materials only and that the labor is included in the contractor's base bid.

Unit Pricing

Unit pricing refers to "units" of measure such as linear footage, gallons, tons, truck loads, etc. Unit prices are typically applied to work items that are difficult to precisely quantify. They are most appropriate for site work (excavation) or renovation projects. Use them for items you want priced in advance, in the event that the scope of work increases or decreases in a way you can't plan for now. You might want a unit price per cubic yard of ledge that will have to be blasted and removed before you can get a foundation in. You might want a unit price per square foot of rotted sills that need replacing or plaster walls that need patching.

Alternate Pricing

This tool is used like a bookmark you put in your agreement with your contractor that lets you adjust some portion of your work later at a cost you've agreed upon early on. You can have a work item or material in your base bid replaced by an add alternate or deduct alternate work item. You can accept an alternate price prior to signing the contract or inform the contractor that you might want to accept the alternate at a later date. For instance, you put oak floors in the scope of work, though you're really hoping you can afford cherry floors. Get an add alternate price for the cherry floors now. If all goes well and your budget is still in good shape when it's time to order the materials for the floors, you can opt for the cherry at the price given to you initially. Inversely, if you worry that you cannot afford the oak floors throughout the space, you can get a deduct alternate for vinyl floor covering in the kitchen and laundry room. If it turns out you cannot afford the original plan of laying oak floors everywhere, you can accept the deduct alternate to bring your budget in line.

If you're the creative type, the design phase can be the most fun part of the project. And now you know that phase has two elements: your vision for a finished project and a means to convey that vision so your contractor can see it clearly.

CHAPTER 4

Help with Your Vision:
When and How
to Employ an Architect

This chapter examines your options for design assistance, focusing on architects and how to best select and work with the right one for you.

- Do You Need a Professional? Considering an Architect
- The Yin to Your Yang: The Right Architect for You
- Everyone Pick Up Your #2 Pencils: Working with an Architect

Do You Need a Professional? Considering an Architect

To be called an architect, one must be licensed by the state in which he practices. Unlike designers, architects provide stamped drawings indicating their license to practice. Some municipalities, particularly in urban areas or where nature has upped the ante on design, require stamped drawings to address seismic, wind, and/or floodwater conditions. You can find out about your state's requirements through the American Institute of Architects (AIA) (page 33) or by checking at your town clerk's office (page 139).

Many owners who don't face such requirements assume that building a single-family residence or adding on a family room is too small a project to justify the cost of an architect. Instead, they opt for collecting all their ideas and working out the design with a contractor. This might well be the right approach for you, but before you discount what an architect can bring to your project, let's look at what architects really do, what you really need, and what they really cost. If you choose not to have an architect on your project, at least you will know what tasks you need to address by other means. I have been in your shoes over two hundred times and do plenty of successful design work for clients without benefit of an architect. Yet I would not build my own house without one because I now understand the value of the right services from the right architect, and I know how to use an architect's services in such a way that they will save me more than they cost me. Read on and then decide what's right for you.

A doctor can bury his mistakes, but an architect can only advise his clients to plant vines.

—FRANK LLOYD WRIGHT

What Architects Really Do

What image comes to mind when you hear the word "architect"? Do you envision a stylish guy at a drafting table, listening to New Age music and sketching expensive, artsy spaces? That's the image that comes to mind for many people, and it's not only misleading but also intimidating.

Now, in one sentence, how would you describe what an architect does? Most laypeople I surveyed said something to the effect of, "They conceptualize buildings." Well, that's only the first part of the first of the five phases of their work. So in reality, most architects get to spend less than 10 percent of their time conceptualizing anything. The bulk of the typical architect's time is spent creating the means for conveying those concepts to contractors and then managing construction projects to ensure that those concepts become reality. Their day-to-day duties include working with clients, code officials, engineers, and suppliers, and managing projects by working with contractors and clients to solve problems or interpret plans as their designs are being executed.

Though most architects may discuss your project and the associated costs for services as a whole, for purposes of calculating their fees and managing their tasks, architects divide their services into five phases: schematic design, design development, construction documents, bidding and negotiating, and the construction phase—and you can too.

Schematic Design: The Broad Strokes

You and the architect conceptualize and come up with the overall vision of the finished building in its broadest strokes to produce schematic designs. During this initial phase, you will meet often with the architect to convey your wishes, and he will guide you through options as, together, you lay out the parameters for the more detailed design that will follow. The tangible product of the schematic design phase is usually a few sketches showing various views of your future finished project and a rough cost estimate.

Design Development: Taking Shape

During this phase, you and the architect will work to crystallize your designs. You will be asked to bring more detail to your vision and select major components like windows and doors. Spaces will be refined, systems will be integrated and architectural details will be incorporated. The architect will build on the schematic drawings, refining all their components to create more detailed plans. The resulting products will likely be rough drawings done to scale including structural, mechani-

cal, and electrical systems with some specification of materials, finishes, and other highlights. He will submit a more refined cost estimate of the project at this time, reflecting the further precision of the overall plan as he adds function to the form laid out in the schematic design phase. This marks the end of the creative design portion of an architect's standard services. Once you have approved these drawings and accepted or modified the cost estimate, the architect can move on to the next phase.

Construction Documents: Making It Perfectly Clear

This phase is all about creating a means to convey the design to a contractor. The architect will create detailed plans and specifications. This phase can be more like putting a puzzle together, making sure all the elements and systems fit and function in the space.

Bidding and Negotiating: I Will if You Will

The architect will assist you in creating a pool of qualified prospective contractors. Then he will help to obtain competitive bids or negotiate a price and contract terms before awarding the construction contract to the selected contractor.

Contract Administration: Getting It Built as Planned

During the construction phase, the architect will try to guard the owner against defects and deficiencies in the work of the contractor. He will do this through the following means:

- Preparation of more detailed drawings as needed

- Review of the contractor's schedule of values (page 107), suppliers' shop drawings, materials, samples, etc.

- General administration of the construction contract, including site visits and job meetings to inspect and discuss the work and ensure that it is proceeding in accordance with the construction documents

- Review, revision, and approval of the contractor's requisitions for payment to ensure that you are paying only for completed work

- Preparation of change orders which act as amendments to the owner-contractor agreement by adding, deleting, or changing work items, their timeline, and/or their cost

The AIA makes this important distinction: "The Architect does not supervise construction. The contractor, and not the Architect, is solely responsible for construction means, methods, techniques, sequences and procedures." In other words, you, the owner, have a contract with the architect, and you, the owner, have a separate contract with the contractor. The architect and contractor have no binding agreement with each other. The architect can help you in monitoring the execution of that owner-contractor agreement, but if it hits the fan, the architect is not liable. After all, he isn't there at all times to witness all construction work, so he shouldn't be liable.

What You Really Need

So now you know how the steps of design and execution of plans are broken down and approached in the world of architecture. As you look back over the list of services architects provide, some may seem more essential to you than others based on the building project you have in mind. You may approach these services more like a buffet than a set menu, picking and choosing only those services you want in the quantities you want. The AIA has a contract for just this purpose called *B188—Standard Form of Agreement Between Owner and Architect for Limited Architectural Service for House Projects.*

Maybe you've seen the perfect home in a house plans magazine. If you purchase those plans and take them to an architect for minor revisions, you've just saved about 70 percent of the architectural fees and might want to spring for very thorough contract administration services by an architect during the construction phase. Maybe you want an architect's input only during the more creative schematic phase, and then you'd like to work out the budget and the plans with a contractor friend. Maybe you want complete designs and contract administration for just the framing of the building because you plan to do all the interior work yourself over time.

Whatever your project and whatever you determine to be your design needs, think about meeting with an architect to discuss your project and the variety of services that are available to you. It's likely the architect will not charge for this initial meeting and you will leave with a lot of free information and another perspective on your project. Go to www.aia.org to learn more about architects through the American Institute of Architects.

What They Really Cost

Generally, there are two ways you can pay for architectural services: by fixed fee or by an hourly rate plus reimbursables. Armed with an understanding of these payment structures, you can negotiate your own hybrid that will give you a lot of bang for the buck as you opt for only those services you need.

Fixed Fee

A fixed fee for architectural services is a lump sum based on a percentage of the construction cost, usually between 10 and 20 percent of the finished cost of your project, and it includes all the standard services. So if your home costs $200,000 and the architect's fee is 10 percent of that, the fixed fee for architectural services would be $20,000. This fixed fee is divided according to the following standard cost breakdown by services (see chart on page 34):

When an architect is determining a fixed fee, he knows that the price needs to cover every eventuality. The onus is on him to give you a price

SAMPLE ARCHITECT'S FEE SCHEDULE		
Schematic design	15%	$ 3,000
Design development	20%	$ 4,000
Construction documents	40%	$ 8,000
Bidding and negotiating	5%	$ 1,000
Construction phase	20%	$ 4,000
TOTAL FIXED FEE		$20,000

that he can stand by. That is his risk to deal with in a fixed fee structure. Look at it from his point of view. Anything could happen. He could end up with a fickle, bickering couple of owners, unforeseeable hours spent dealing with anything that arises, staff changes in his office, or a project that took on the world's worst contractor. However, if the project goes smooth as silk, you will not see any lessening of the fee. In the architect's world, it all averages out.

Also note that because his fee is based on a percentage of the finished construction cost, if the price of your project goes up through change orders in the building phase, he gets more money. There are two problems with this for you. One, what is his incentive to keep your costs down? None. And two, if those change orders are due to design errors, you may actually be paying him more for having done the job wrong than if he had done it right.

So the fixed fee structure represents one-stop shopping that covers any and all the services any project would need, but it has a couple of flaws. You may pay for risk of exposure to liability that never occurs, and if your construction project starts hemorrhaging money, so do your architectural fees.

Hourly Rates and Reimbursables

In this structure, you pay on a time-and-materials basis. Every month the architect bills you an amount that represents the number of hours he worked on your project times his hourly rate, which can range from about $90 to $250 per hour for residential work, depending on where you live. Reimbursables are the architect's expenses for mileage, copying, phone calls, blueprints, postage, etc. Most architects have a rate schedule for the per-item cost, and they can give you an estimate for the cost of reimbursables for your whole project.

Of course, this pay structure poses little risk to the architect. Whatever hours he works, he gets paid for. If the wheels start to fall off the project, he still gets paid fairly. Now you feel that you have all the risk, right? What kind of services are you committing to with a blank check for unlimited hours?

The Hybrid

A third option combines the best of both payment structures and lessens risk and cost to all parties. This is the option I most like to work with. It combines the two standard approaches into an "hourly rate with an upset limit." This is both an estimate and a cap on the price, based on some mutually agreed-upon assumptions about the architect's anticipated workload. If the architect works fewer hours than those estimated, you will pay less than the amount of the upset limit. If additional work arises that causes the price to go over the estimate, the architect will notify you in advance, and you can renegotiate. It doesn't sound much different than a fixed fee, but it gives an architect enough comfort by lessening the risk he incurs in an unbreakable commitment, and if all goes well, you can enjoy some savings.

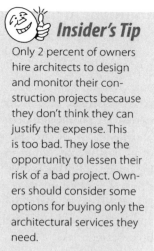

Insider's Tip

Only 2 percent of owners hire architects to design and monitor their construction projects because they don't think they can justify the expense. This is too bad. They lose the opportunity to lessen their risk of a bad project. Owners should consider some options for buying only the architectural services they need.

You might also modify the scope of the architect's services to suit your project. Just buy the portion of the standard services you really need. Bear in mind, though, that an architect is a licensed professional carrying liability insurance and has a reputation at stake in the community. He would much prefer to be involved in the entire project if his name and liability are at stake. Let him know you understand this, and be prepared to release him of liability on those items for which you're asking for minimal services.

Finally, you can get upset limit pricing for all five phases of the work, and break the owner/architect contract into phases too, with the proviso that if all parties are satisfied with phase 1, you'll move on together to phase 2. Again, this lessens risk to all parties and creates an added incentive for the architect to provide services in a manner that will keep you happy.

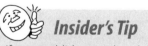

Insider's Tip

If you establish a good working relationship with the architect on an hourly fee basis, you may be amazed by how much money you can save by doing some of the legwork.

The first time I worked with my favorite architect, I would take little duties away from every meeting or phone call with him. When I got my bill for the schematic phase of a $1 million project, it was down from an upset limit of $15,000 to an actual charge of $7,000. Like any work, plenty of it is administrative legwork. If you are inclined to do so, you can offer to run down to the town clerk's office to pick up paperwork. You can run to suppliers to get catalogs on the fixtures and finishes you are considering. Just remember that in this case you are shifting roles a bit. So be careful to be an asset to the team. Carry these duties out professionally, and keep good records of your tasks and the time you spent doing them.

The Yin to Your Yang:
The Right Architect for You

Now that you understand the services that architects provide, imagine that you are writing a job description for the architect of your dream house. What skills might you want to list as necessary in a person expected to carry out these disparate services? You may come up with something like this: creative, artistic, detail-oriented, exceptional communication skills, ability to manage people and coordinate schedules, budget management, technical knowledge of all current materials, codes, and costs, working knowledge of all trades, including excavation, masonry, carpentry, plumbing, heating, electrical. This is quite a list, and it includes skills that you might not think of finding in the same person. The truth is, you won't. Architecture is both right- and left-brained. Each architect is stronger in some skill sets and weaker in others. It helps to think of their services as divided into three broad categories:

Artistic design: Vision of "form"—the aesthetics of design work. Use of shape, balance, light, symmetry, scale, materials, color.

Technical design: Making the "form" function. Design of solutions to address conflicts, making all the pieces work together: structure, traffic flow, site limitations, heating and plumbing systems, cost, etc. This requires knowledge of code, attention to detail, and a mind for solving real-world puzzles.

Contract administration: This is the monitoring of the construction phase of the project. For most people, it's hard to imagine that there would be anything to monitor if you have a contractor signed up to a detailed scope of work laid out perfectly in a nice set of plans and specifications. The operative word here is "perfectly." There are no perfect plans or people on either side. Whether done by you or a professional, a skilled and watchful eye will be essential as your plans are being carried out.

Few architects excel at all three of these categories, so try to match the architect with your needs. And what are your needs? When hiring anyone for any job, you are usually looking for one of two things. Either you're looking for someone to replace your efforts, as in the case of a nanny for your child, or you're looking for someone to do what you can't, as in the case of a tax accountant. In the case of hiring an architect, you are looking for the latter, so you need to think about what you're bringing to this party. Think about the right architect for you being a Fred to your Ginger, a horse to your carriage, a yin to your yang.

The Owner's and Architect's Ladders

Both the owner and the architect have preconceived notions about how a good and successful working relationship might look. You may not even know what assumptions you're harboring, and I know no architect who would confess in an interview that he was a bad match for the owners before him. It is incumbent upon you to figure this part out. The successful relationship will result in a balance between leadership versus deference, and receptiveness versus authority, that suits both parties. As you may already suspect, the classic bad match results in owners who have more interest in participating than they even knew, hiring an architect who couldn't care less about their opinions. If the design phase goes like this and the owners aren't happy with their treatment or the finished plans, they will be starting out the construction phase on the wrong foot.

Even the finest architects in the world struggle with this issue. Read the quotes below and ask yourself on which day would you like to work with the master?

"It is not an individual act, architecture. You have to consider your client. Only out of that can you produce great architecture. You can't work in the abstract."

—I.M. PEI

"Nobody would question Einstein about relativity, but everyone has an opinion about architecture. . . . Knowing you're right is not enough. . . . If you are right and believe in what you're doing, you have to be patient and take all the blows that come and continue to defend."

—I.M. PEI

Each person you bring into your project is a member of your team—essentially your employee. Be cognizant of the mix you are creating. The architect may be your first team member, and if all goes well, he will be your most intimate confidant for the duration of your project. This is not hard science, but here's a little help in structuring your intuition. On page 38 is the Yin to Your Yang Illustrated, showing the Owner's and the Architect's Ladders of work styles. First find the rung with the description of an owner that best matches you—not who you'd like to be, but who you are. If you're a control freak, admit it and embrace it now! Then look directly across from the chosen owner description to find the description of the architect that would best suit you.

OWNER'S LADDER	ARCHITECT'S LADDER
Total control over design. Just needs an architect to draw it up.	No control over design. "I am your tool, tell me what to draw."
Much control over design. Has a house design in mind but is looking to benefit from a professional's input, particularly for technical aspects.	Little control over design. Looks to owner for detailed directive on all design but offers some solutions to design conflicts.
Some control over design. May have magazine clippings, photos, design file with several themes to be considered. Looking for architect to bring owner through design phase, exploring options together.	Some control over design. Architect schedules regular meetings, seeks owner input and satisfaction. Sees owner as partner in design and offers many options during schematic phase.
Little control over design. Is open to considering any design from architect that meets broad requirements.	Much control over design. Will take broad directives from owner and then create and propose design.
No control over design. Has minimal parameters for design and wants to turn the architect loose to design as he will. More common than you might think, but this treatment is usually reserved for renowned architects.	Total control over design. Signs contract with owner, then designs what he thinks best.

Selecting an Architect

If you've decided you'd like to use an architect's services, hiring one is a pretty straightforward process.

Step 1: Who Are Your Choices?

Put together a small pool of architects to consider. You might spot a new building you like and ask who designed it. You might ask around and get good word-of-mouth advice. You can even put a notice in the local paper to seek out interested parties. You can take your chances in the yellow pages or call contractors who specialize in residential construction and ask whom they'd recommend and why. However you do it, commit to starting with a few people to consider, ask each of them the same questions, and take notes. Even if you think the first one you talk to is perfect for you, move on and talk with the other contenders. I guarantee you will learn a lot about architects, architecture, and how firms differ in their approaches to projects and owners.

Step 2: Interviews

Bearing in mind your own nature and the role you have carved out for yourself, try to find an architect who complements that role. Here are some suggested topics for discussion during the interview:

- Is this person an architect licensed to provide stamped drawings? If someone goes by the title "designer," it usually means he is not a licensed architect. Is he insured or able to obtain insurance for his design of your project?

- Find out about availability. How busy is this architect, and does he have ample time for you? Architectural firms are always trying to find the balance between feast and famine, having too much work to satisfy every client and too little to make payroll. From your vantage point, there's nothing worse than suddenly being a firm's least important client, so check this out. Ask about the current workload compared to staff availability and also about the foreseeable future. What work are they bidding or being considered for now? When will they know if they have been selected for that work? How would that affect the personnel allocated to your project? Just asking the questions will go a long way to helping keep you a priority.

- Who else from the architect's firm will be working on your project? If the person you are talking to is involved only in marketing and will not be the lead person on your project, you want to know that now and meet anyone you will actually be working with.

- Discuss fees. What's the hourly rate, and does this architect prefer working for a fixed fee, an hourly rate, or hourly with an upset limit? Most architects can and do structure their fees in all three of these ways, depending on the market forces and the client. Explore all those options and listen carefully to why they prefer one fee structure over the other. Also find out how much reimbursables will cost.

- Who would pay for corrective work in the event of design-related errors? Everyone makes mistakes, and architects are no exception. It's unlikely your plans will be flawless. If, for instance, the architect has made a dimensional error and the stairs cannot be built to code in the space allotted for them on the plans, a little chain reaction will begin on site. Work will halt, the contractor will look for a correction, the architect will work with you to provide one. The contractor will assign a cost to the correction and may have to return a custom-made handrail or take care of some other related hassle. This all costs money. Who pays for this problem? Owners often end up paying to fix design errors whether they know it or not. Those costs are usually much higher if they are incurred as change orders during construction. Two rules apply here that cover the architect. One, the owner/contractor agreement makes the contractor take on most of the responsibility for design errors. It requires him to verify all dimensions and conditions on site, bring inconsistencies to your attention, and execute the work in accordance with code and common practices, regardless of what the designs say. In other words, "Mr. Contractor, do as you should, not as I designed." Two, you will and should expect to pay for the correction of any oversights that result in value added to the project. For instance, if the architect forgot to specify a front door, you cannot expect to get one added for free. You need it, you have to pay for it. Regardless of how some contracts favor the architect, it's just a good time to ask the question about design errors. No one is infallible, so address the issue up front.

- How will the architect address design of the site, and the septic, heating, and other engineered systems? There are basically three ways an architect can address the engineered portions of your design. He can subcontract to engineers in some or all of the necessary fields. This is the most detailed and most expensive approach. He can do it himself if he is more of a generalist and can handle it. This is the midrange approach in both detail and cost. He can also write performance specifications (page 27).

(page 27)

- What ideas does the architect have for your project? This would be a good time to be quiet and let the architect reveal his true design leanings without any guidance from you. You will probably be excited about your project and want to gush about it. Resist this temptation and find out if he is a kindred spirit first. Let him go unfettered in any direction he likes. (If you are working as a couple, discuss your impressions with each other later.)

- What similar projects has the architect done? You would be surprised by which architects pursue which jobs, but the point here is that experience with your size budget and type of project is essential. It means that he has dealt with clients like you and with code people, contractors, and materials similar to those involved in your project, and he won't be learning on the job. Moreover, people tend to repeat the kind of work they enjoy and excel in.

- Look at the portfolio of the architect's projects. A picture is worth a thousand words.

Step 3: References

Getting a useful reference from a stranger is tricky business because the person you are talking to is a big variable in the equation. Maybe he's a pushover, maybe he's a hothead or hypercritical. In order to shed some light on this variable, be sure you facilitate the conversation. Don't just say, "So how was this architect?" Ask specific questions, and even if the reference goes way off on a tangent that may contain valuable information, always bring the conversation back to the questions on your list. Take notes. Call at least three homeowner references, preferably people whose projects resemble yours in budget and type. Try to find references other than those offered by the architect by asking, "What other projects was he working on at the same time as yours?" If they're not on the list given to you by the architect, chances are good that they represent a bad experience on the part of an owner, which you'd like to know about.

- Ask the reference detailed questions about his project. What was the budget, the building size, style, location?

- What was the architect's relationship with the owner, contractors, and building inspectors?

- Ask about change orders. What was the anticipated project cost and what was the actual final cost? (If this feels like prying, ask about the percentage difference.) Were increases in the construction budget due to the architect's design errors? Was much design-related problem solving necessary during the construction phase? How about attention to detail?

> *In my experience, if you have to keep the lavatory door shut by extending your left leg, it's modern architecture.*
>
> —NANCY BANKS-SMITH

What Your Contractor Can't Tell You

- How did the architect structure communication for this project? Design meetings? Job meetings? Phone calls? Was his door always open? How was input received from the owner and others?

- Is the owner satisfied with the finished product? What would the owner do differently?

- Would the owner choose this architect to work with again? Why or why not?

Goldilocks and the Three Architects

I have worked with dozens of architects, and it took a while to find the right type for me. I still work with dozens of architects, but it's a different stable from which I select now, having come to understand I need the type that's not too hot, not too cold, but just right for me.

Too Hot. Like many people using an architect for the first time, I was drawn to an architect who is very much like myself. We both fall on the visionary/artistic side of the design continuum. We got excited in each other's company, we agreed on almost everything, and we went on to be great friends. But she was not a good working partner for me in the owner-architect dance because we both focused on the same issues. The result was a lack of attention to detail in the plans. There were lots of brilliant design solutions I loved, but not the meat in the construction documents to get the job built that way without lots of hassles and changes made on site. When I went hunting for the next architect, I thought, "Okay, I can do the schematic design. I just need someone to get it all on paper for me."

Too Cold. The second architect was all about order and precision, and my approach backfired. I found him extremely hard to relate to and felt no encouragement to participate in my own project. It was as though I was expected to place an order, and then a design would appear that I would just love. There was no invitation to brainstorm, no working together to flesh out all the options. I needed give-and-take to know that the plans had evolved to the best possible conclusion. By the time I was hiring my third architect, I had learned a lot about my own expectations, working style, and needs.

Just Right. At last I found the perfect architect for me, and when I cannot hire him, I model my choice after him. He is a self-proclaimed nerd, open and affable. His strengths run more to attention to detail in the construction documents and a nerdy perfectionism in the field that is so sincere it's infectious. We brainstorm designs well together. I bring the aesthetic part of the design while he brings the technical. We each see entirely different things to focus on, but together we make a whole, with both form and function well covered. Every day during a design phase, I will phone him with what I call the Don't Forget List. I download lots of minute details that popped into my head in the shower or in the middle of the night. I never have to fret about those items again because when I open the finished plans six months later, every item I mentioned will have been perfectly addressed.

"*Move the chair.*"

—FRANK LLOYD WRIGHT'S RESPONSE TO A CLIENT WHO PHONED HIM TO COMPLAIN OF RAIN LEAKING THROUGH THE ROOF OF THE HOUSE ONTO THE DINING TABLE.

Step 4: Final Selection

It's decision time. Sit down with your interview notes and reference responses. Weigh the information, including your own subjective views and gut feelings. Assign values to the bits of information you have, and score it if necessary to pick the best person for you.

At this point, if a clear choice has not emerged, you may want to have the architects you are considering give you a proposal and cost for services. Be extremely ethical with this step. Do not share one architect's costs with another. Do not play one against the other by saying, "Well, we really like you best. Can you match this price?" Barring any changes in the candidates' availability, you should choose the lowest bidder of the best proposal.

When you have made your final selection, call the architect to award him the job and set up your first meeting and contract terms.

Everyone Pick Up Your #2 Pencils: Working with an Architect

Once you have selected the architect for your project, you will begin working with him to create your design. If he hasn't already done so, have him write up a scope of services spelling out the agreed-upon work, timelines for each phase of design, and the associated costs. Be sure to discuss and assign the following tasks as needed: surveys, permitting process, cost estimating, budget development, contractor selection, writing job meeting minutes, approval of the contractor's requisitions for payment, and the number of anticipated site visits. He should then draw up the owner-architect contract with any amendments that result from your discussion of scope, phasing the work, and the above items.

Set up regularly scheduled progress meetings. Always come prepared and take notes. If those notes include directives from you, it's a good idea to copy them to the architect. Keep a running list of these agreed-upon directives throughout the design phase. You won't believe how taxed everyone's mind will become with all the tiny details that mount up. You will need these notes later when reviewing the final plans before they go to the contractor.

Get the architect to the site right away to get those design juices flowing. For new construction he needs to get his mind around all your site has to offer in opportunities and challenges, lighting, natural formations, and the surrounding built environment. For renovation work, encourage him to open walls and lift floorboards to reveal any hidden conditions.

 Pitfall

Who owns the blueprints of your building project, you or the architect? Surprise! Not you.

Just like a photographer with his negatives, the architect owns the plans, unless otherwise stipulated. If you should decide at the end of the construction documents phase that you do not want this architect to monitor the construction project, you might not have access to what you have come to think of as "your" plans. So, now would be a good time to address this issue by asking the architect his policy for such an eventuality.

Don't be intimidated by the architect or suffer silently for fear of offending him when you do not like the designs. It's you who have to live in this house long after the architect has gone. Your sense of awe will fade fast if you are handed a big fat bill for designs you hate. Get used to giving a quick thumbs-up or thumbs-down as each design element arises, and move right along. But don't be shy about providing more photos, magazine clippings, sketches—whatever will get your vision across. Architects can respond only to what you tell them.

The schematic phase is about exploring. You really want to throw the doors open and consider every option. Once you get through this stage, the design work is all about refining and making that design physically and financially feasible. Encourage your architect to think broadly with you. Ask that he provide at least three different schematic drawings in response to your initial input and then walk you through the pros and cons of each. Otherwise, you might wake up six months into your project thinking, "I know what we should have done. . . ."

There's nothing more fun and rewarding than a good, creative brainstorming session that results in solid design solutions. You have the power to stop the conversation early, but you should hear the architect out. Ask a lot of questions. You will always benefit. Let your architect persuade you of things. Take advantage of his expertise, and soak up all the free information. You might just come out of a meeting with a much improved plan for the concept you brought.

When specifying materials, ask your architect which items are custom-built and which ones can be bought as ready-made stock and standard items. I have had a couple architects who were completely unaware that their designs included materials that deviated just slightly from those that could be bought at a fraction of the price. Look out for kitchen cabinetry, bathroom vanities, common versus high-end sizes, and details for handrails and moldings.

You're just wasting time and money if this project comes in way over budget once the plans are all done. Keep on top of cost estimating during the design phase. This is not necessarily your architect's long suit. He can hire a cost estimator during your design phase for very little. Encourage the architect to help protect your budget by using allowances, unit pricing, and alternate pricing (page 28).

At the completion of each design milestone, sleep on it. Take the schematics or the elevations or the kitchen floor plan and hang it on the fridge. Live with it for a while. Your subconscious will do the rest.

> *Home is where you hang your architect.*
>
> —CLARE BOOTHE LUCE

Pitfall

Not many owners can imagine what a building will look like by staring at blueprints. They can get the shock of their lives when they walk into the finished space.

Reading architectural drawings is a learned language, and you might need a little translation. It's very difficult for most people to look at 2-D drawings and imagine a 3-D space. This can result in great disappointment if, when a space is finished, it doesn't look a thing like you imagined it. Do whatever you must to create an accurate representation of that space that you can understand. Your architect can give you a virtual tour on his computer. You can make a model of your project. It doesn't have to be fancy. Cardboard and tape will work fine. You can also cut out and apply furniture to scale on your drawings. Computer software programs like *Punch Pro* or *3D Home Design* are great for owners and convert 2-D drawings to a 3-D tour instantly.

When the architect is finished with the construction documents phase, you will have plans and specifications for any contractor to price. Even if you all think you know every inch of those plans and specifications, insist on a meeting to have the architect walk you through those construction documents one page at a time. Bring your notes from all the design meetings, and ask to be shown where and how each design directive of yours is reflected in the plans and specs. If your questions trigger answers like, "The contractor will know he has to do that," chances are the work needs more specificity, and you should push for revisions of those points to get all the clarity you can. However, be aware that broad instructions like "Wire it to code" protect you more than detailed ones in work that is quite standardized.

I bet you're getting anxious to focus on *your* plans and specifications. Read on.

CHAPTER 5

Bang for the Buck and the Sixteen Divisions
What Can You Have and What Should You Worry About?

This chapter gets to the bricks and mortar of your design choices. It covers all the materials and tasks that can go into a project organized like the pros do it, using the "sixteen divisions." Within each division, the most common and costly construction pitfalls will be revealed, along with tips on how to avoid them.

- Divide and Conquer: The Sweet Sixteen Divisions
- The Devil's in the Details: Where to Focus Your Attention and Money
- And Another Thing: Other Considerations When Determining Materials and Scope of Work

Divide and Conquer: The Sweet Sixteen Divisions

Let's explore what you'll be spending your money on. What really scares you? Making the wrong choices, right? There's so much to learn and so much to choose from. Once you have an idea as to what your overall project will be, you will inevitably go from that broad concept to the more detailed definition of the labor and materials that will make that project come to life. That's the scope of work, and it's the result of hundreds and hundreds of decisions.

What do you focus on? What provides a good return on your investment and what doesn't? New materials come on the market every day. Which do you choose? I don't believe it's necessary or even feasible for you to become expert in each of the construction trades. No one is. However, you can be a savvy consumer of construction materials and services. You can learn where some of the classic potential pitfalls lie. And you can use the same system the professionals do to keep it all straight.

Your plans are a picture of all the construction work to be done. You may think of the work in terms of location, but those plans must be broken down by task and then by trade. An architect will break the work down by trade to create specifications. A contractor and his sub-contractors do it to create cost estimates and construction schedules.

For instance, if your plan shows the finished drawing of a wall of bookcases with a counter and a wet bar, the work it may take to achieve that project would involve rough carpentry, finished carpentry, electrical, plumbing, sheetrocking, and painting. That's six trades. As a contractor approaches those tradespeople for pricing, he must be able to spell out all the tasks for each of them on the project. This is usually done by employing the "Sixteen Uniform Construction Index Divisions." They, and you, can use the divisions to sort the work by trades and suppliers for description in specifications and budget management. Some people use twelve divisions as a standard, and each contractor has slight variations on what line items are put under which division. One contractor may have the cost of Dumpsters under General Conditions, while another may figure it into Site Work. However they refine the system, become familiar with it, since everyone on site will use it to measure progress and the amount sought for payment.

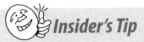

The Devil's in the Details: Where to Focus Your Attention and Money

We will use the standard sixteen divisions to explore your options for selecting materials and laying out the scope of work. Each section below includes:

- A definition of the division

- Tasks and materials that fall within the division

- Advice for working through your choices and avoiding pitfalls

These are areas of concern and risk that I've seen come up time and time again over the years. So here's your dose of foresight. Not all these divisions will apply to your project, but the ones that do should be addressed in your scope of work, budget, and payment requisitions.

Division 1—General Conditions

All project support and associated costs that do not result in the direct installation of materials.

Work

- General contractor's supervision of the project and his time for coordinating all labor and supplies

- Insurance: workers' compensation

- Insurance: builder's risk (if by contractor)

- Building permits and fees (if by contractor)

- Job site trailer, portable toilets, lifts, scaffolding, trucks

- Demolition, Dumpsters, trash removal

- Utility connection fees (if by contractor)

- Testing: concrete, water, soils, toxins (if by contractor)

- Cleaning

- Administrative expenses: office overhead, office staff, mail, phone, printing, banking

- Miscellaneous: any other costs to the contractor that facilitate the project but don't fall under labor or materials for tangible work

Advice

This division has items in it that can be paid by the owner or the contractor. To avoid surprise bills later, be sure to determine who's paying for what.

Division 2—Site Work

Exterior work involving excavation and site improvements.

Work

- Excavation: digging for foundations, sewers, drains, etc., and filling back in around the finished work

- Blasting and removing ledge or rock

- Preparing and shaping the land: tree, rock, and soil removal, creating ditches, swales, berms

- Site utilities: well digging, connecting to town water, sewer or septic, gas, and underground electrical, phone, and cable supply lines

- Installing and/or removing underground fuel tanks

- Site improvement: walks, patios, driveways, swimming pools, ponds

- Landscaping: grading, seeding, and planting of lawns, beds, trees, gardens

- Water features: fountains, koi ponds

- Irrigation

- Making roads, driveways, and parking areas

- Fencing

Insider's Tip

Once you and your budget get past work underground, you can breathe a sigh of relief.

Typical Materials

Precast concrete (septic systems, basement stairs, and entry steps), fill, gravel, topsoil, pipe, drainage tile, conduit, drains, culverts, asphalt, pavers, stone, concrete, fencing.

Advice

This division often poses the greatest danger to the solvency of a project. Nature can provide nasty surprises like rock ledge, high water, no water, bad soils, poor drainage, etc. If you have good plans for everything to be built on top of it, you should be able to breathe a sigh of relief once you have your foundation and utilities in. It is for this reason that I feel good about a project if I have spent no more than 40 to 50 percent of my contingency on this early stage (page 177). If you are not familiar with what's underground before you start, and the neighboring property owners can't assure you of what's under there, some advance work by a civil engineer may be money well spent (page 4). This is a great division for unit pricing to protect you against costly surprises (page 28). Don't sign a contract that says "no rock ledge removal included" or any similar disclaimer about underground conditions without a backup plan.

Pitfall

Your beloved plants, trees, and rocks are just in a contractor's way. Be very clear about what's to be protected and how.

A cleared site is much easier for a contractor to work on, but those natural assets are precious and can't be easily replaced if they are "accidentally" removed or damaged. In your plans, clearly locate all trees, boulders, and other existing natural formations you want to keep. Root systems extend out as far as trees' branches and are vulnerable to the heavy machinery and excess soil piled on them, so be sure to guard not only the branches from damage but also the surface of the ground under the drip line. Before work begins, walk the site with the contractor, tag those items, and make sure you all agree about what stays. Go back and update the contract documents if need be.

At some point early in the process of a new home or addition, the surveyor or the contractor will put stakes in the ground to mark the significant points of the building footprint. Site work tends to knock these over, so watch that your stakes are maintained so you don't have to get the surveyor back on site again.

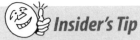

Insider's Tip

If you are building a new home on a wooded lot, you may have valuable topsoil to work with.

Topsoil is black gold. Work with your contractor or civil engineer to determine how many inches of topsoil are on your land and test it for its quality. It should be carefully stripped away from the work area and piled on site for later respreading. Guard that topsoil with your life. Ask the agricultural extension service or your local garden center how many inches deep the topsoil should be for your landscaping plans. If you have more than is required, you may be able to sell the excess to those less fortunate than yourself.

If you don't have sufficient topsoil, specify the desired planting surface and let the contractor calculate what you'll need and propose a price for it.

If you are putting in a driveway or other site improvement that requires a gravel base, you should verify that what you're getting complies with your plans. Try to be on site with a yard-stick to measure the depth of the gravel before it is covered up. Suffice it to say, I have never found anyone giving me more gravel than specified. If there's ever a debate about how much gravel base was put in, you can easily measure the materials separated by filter fabric.

Pitfall

If you ask for eight inches of gravel under your driveway and show up to find the driveway finished, how do you know you got an eight-inch gravel base?

Filter fabric is a great product you put between a gravel base and the soil above. Water flows through it to the gravel below, but it doesn't let the soil mix into the gravel and impede its ability to drain over time.

Footing drains that keep water away from your building will cost you next to nothing now. They will cost a small fortune if you have to dig that site up later to add them. They're made like a wrap sandwich. The excavator lays filter fabric down low at the foundation footings. On that he puts gravel, drainage tile, and more gravel. Then he wraps the fabric up and around the contents and backfills with dirt. The water that collects in footing drains should be "directed to daylight." There should also be clean-outs, vertical pipes that rise from the drainage tile to the ground surface for maintenance.

When installing a septic field and tank, make sure they are accessible and there's enough adjacent space if you ever need to install a replacement field someday. Ask the contractor to locate the field, the tank, and the tank ports accurately on the plans, including precise measurements from the foundation. That way, when you need a repair or tank maintenance you won't pay for someone to poke around your yard for hours looking for it with a metal shaft.

Many small contractors cannot offer much service in terms of landscaping. You may want to price and contract that separately, as most of it takes place well outside the contractor's scope of work. You may want to have it all planned out, though. That way, you can have any necessary land shaping and underground wiring and plumbing done under the general contractor.

Division 3—Concrete

Transportation, pouring, and finishing of concrete on site.

Insider's Tip

If you've got a muddy, steep site, you may not want to invite the concrete truck to it.

Work

• Poured footings, foundations, and floor slabs
• Fuel tank pads

- Pool construction

- Walks and curbs

- Interior architectural elements: floors, counters, mantels, lintels, etc.

Typical Materials

Forms, reinforcing steel (rebar), mesh, concrete, gunite (sprayed concrete) aggregate, tint

Advice

The focus here is on getting concrete of the right consistency poured over the right base in the right forms with the right reinforcement, in the right thickness, to the right dimensions, getting it finished as desired and cured properly to prevent cracking or buckling. The curing of concrete is not a drying process but rather a chemical reaction. Concrete

Pitfall

Concrete is like Jell-O. It can be stopped from setting only for so long, and if you just stir and stir and stir it, it may never set at all.

is sensitive to climatic conditions and time. It shouldn't be poured when the temperature is over 90 degrees or below 40 degrees. The curing process produces heat. On a very hot day, this heat can increase and cause the top to dry too fast and curl away from the wet concrete beneath. In weather that's too cold, the water in the concrete can freeze and stop the curing process entirely. This is why you may have seen contractors hosing down fresh-poured concrete in the summer and installing heaters in the winter. If you have the choice, just have it installed in optimal weather and forestall the risk of problems. To ensure its ability to cure, concrete should be poured within forty-five to sixty minutes of the time it leaves the plant. A good project manager will send back a truck full of wet concrete that's been sitting on site too long.

Concrete is specified at different densities for different purposes and under different circumstances and can be tested before it's poured. For instance, the concrete specified for a driveway in Arizona would differ from that specified for the foundation of a three-story home on a hill in Maine.

Put a vapor barrier under all foundation slabs to keep radon gas and moisture out of your building. You can use the same kind of plastic sheathing used for vapor barriers on walls, or ask for cross-laminated or reinforced polyethylene if you prefer the really tough stuff.

There are three ways to finish concrete: a "float finish" for nonaesthetic applications, a "broom finish" for a visually acceptable and skid-free surface, and a "steel trowel finish," which is machine-buffed to create a hard, polished finish.

Forms leave marks on concrete called form lines. If your foundation is exposed and you want a nice finished look, you can ask that those marks be rubbed off no longer than twenty-four hours after the concrete has been poured.

You can have tint added to your concrete for little expense to get a foundation color that complements the colors of your house.

If you have any concerns about drainage, it's easy to put in a hole for a sump pump as the concrete is being poured.

If you plan to have laundry facilities in the basement, note where the washer and dryer are going and ask for special attention in the troweling of the surface so that it's nice and level and your washer won't "walk" when it's on the spin cycle.

If you think you might want to finish off the basement as living space someday, talk to your designer and contractor about what things you should incorporate now so as not to preclude the easy installation of electricity, water, heat, flooring, walls, etc., later.

Concrete has become a big part of your faux finish options of late. There are masters of concrete work out there who can color and shape concrete to look like almost anything from a soapstone sink to adobe cornices.

Division 4—Masonry
Installation of brick, block, or stone.

Work
- Block foundations
- Chimneys, fireplaces, flues, and liners
- Walls, structural and veneer
- Steps
- Walkways

Insider's Tip

Picking natural products from small samples can be misleading. It's better to stop at a building whose materials you love and ask what they are.

Typical Materials
Interior and exterior brick, masonry block, stone, mortar

Advice
Block walls are not quite as strong as poured concrete because each joint is a potential breach in the system that's holding back moisture and soil. In addition, the block itself is more porous than concrete and can crack as moisture in it freezes and thaws. However, it's perfectly adequate for many projects and easier and less expensive to use than concrete in cases where getting a concrete truck on site is tough.

When selecting brick or stone, be sure you see a large assembled sample of it at the supplier's. When you are choosing natural materials, evaluating one small piece can be misleading. Due to all its flaws and color variations, you are likely to be surprised when you see the material in bulk.

For brickwork, consider mortar color, especially in historic buildings. Fresh mortar takes years to age and lighten to the color of old mortar, but if you request it, your mason can give the mortar that old look by amending it with lime.

Typical complaints about masonry work usually focus on one of two things. Customers are often dissatisfied with a bad stone or brick match to existing material. It's virtually impossible to match new to old materials, and the problem is only compounded when you see a whole wall of one next to a whole wall of the other. You may want to consider using an entirely different material that complements rather than clashes, as a close miss would. The other complaint concerns the quality of the tooling of the mortar joints. This is a quality-control issue, and you should inspect the work that first goes up in areas where masonry work is an aesthetic architectural feature. Work with the general contractor and/or mason to establish and hold the standard for tooling of the joints.

Division 5—Metals

The installation of metal construction materials.

Work

• Structural: framing

• Finish: decorative

Typical Materials

Steel framing and studs, I-beams, pipe columns, angle irons, railings, decorative grilles (e.g., radiator covers), fencing

Advice

Until recently, metal construction materials were limited to commercial and industrial buildings that needed the strength of steel to carry great spans without bearing walls. Their use is on the increase in residential construction as an alternative to wood products and to permit the large spans popular in open floor plans today. If you are building a living room

Insider's Tip

If you use metal framing, you can add in some wooden blocking for hanging artwork or shelving later.

with a second-floor loft on one end that's twenty feet long and you don't want to have columns supporting it from below, you may have to use a steel I-beam to carry a span that long. Leave this kind of work to the professionals. An architect or structural engineer should be involved in calculating the size and specifying the support and installation of such a beam.

Metal and wood expand and contract at different rates. Be careful your plans accommodate their happy coexistence.

If you're attracted to metal because it sounds more fire-safe, think again. Metal is not combustible like wood. However, it becomes highly unstable in the heat of fire and collapses. Wood remains stable until it's consumed by the fire.

Exterior metal railing comes in many styles, and much of it is preprimed and/or prepainted. I shy away from railing that is not, since no amount of preparation and painting in the field seems to stop rust on steel rails after a couple years, especially at the base and around any bolts where water tends to pool. Regarding its assembly, structural welding is not appropriate for visible metal such as handrails. Be sure to ask for a finish weld on the assembly of any metal materials that are supposed to look good.

Division 6—Wood and Plastics

The assembly of exterior and interior structural and finish carpentry.

Work

- Rough carpentry: framing, decks, subflooring

- Finish carpentry: trim, wainscoting, moldings, countertop installation, stair treads, banisters and railings, synthetic trims and architectural details

- Case work: shelving

- Cabinetry: kitchen cabinets, built-ins

Typical Materials

Dimensional lumber (e.g., 2" × 4"s) for studs, joists, and rafters, trusses, timbers; pressure-treated wood, plywood, finish lumber (e.g., 1" × 6"s); moldings, stair systems, wood laminates; synthetic wood replacements including plastics, plastic laminates, PVC, fiberglass, concrete, urethanes, solid surfacing

Advice

Lumber is not what it used to be. The standards or grades (Premium, Prime, Select, #2) are defined by the lumber industry and frequently changing downward. The grades are defined by how many flaws, such as knots, are permitted per board foot. That number and the size of the knots have increased over the years, and according to industry standards, 5 percent of the lumber delivered is permitted to fall outside its grade entirely. Since the removal of lead from primers and paints has made it virtually impossible to cover knots permanently, you should specify finish lumber as close to clear as you can afford and be sure to have all six sides of any boards, including cut ends, sealed with primer or urethane.

Another big concern is moisture content. When moist dimensional lumber dries, it shrinks. It can shorten, warp, cup, or twist, causing popped nails, sloping headers, squeaking floors, or even serious structural irregularities. Finish lumber does the same and can make your trim work look terrible, with gaping miter joints and cupped edges. You should discuss lumber standards with your architect and/or contractor, and ask how they plan to ensure the desired low moisture content. You may want to visit the lumberyard or lumber mill to check out your options. Learn and see for yourself what you can expect, and reference those standards in your contract. You should accept dimensional framing lumber with no more than a 19 percent moisture content and finish lumber with no more than 15 percent. Also ask for overlapping or scarf joints on all exterior and interior trim boards as opposed to blunt butt joints. That way, shrinkage won't create an air space between the boards. You may want to consider biscuits, little elliptical slivers of wood to link mitered edges and make them stable.

Trusses are prefabricated roof framing systems. They are cost-effective and efficient to install, but they include cross-members that will impede traffic in the attic space where they are installed. Many owners do not understand this and are very disappointed when they don't end up with a working attic for storage or future expansion of living space.

Timber framing consists of heavy, exposed timbers joined by driving pegs through mortise and tenon connections. It permits large, open spaces, since this system's support is based on point loads as opposed to the bearing walls found in conventional framing. Companies specialize in new timber framing as well as recycling old timbers from barns. The interior wall finish typically goes on the outside of the framing, leaving the beautiful timber-framed system exposed to the interior. Stress skin panels can be applied that are an entire wall system, including Sheetrock, vapor barrier, insulation, and exterior sheathing, in 4' × 8' sheets.

Due to new technologies and the lumber issues described above, synthetic alternatives to lumber are fast becoming industry standards. There are plenty of man-made products that may pertain to your project, including microlams, LVLs, Hardy Plank, Masonite, PVC trim, and so on. Choose where you want the look that only real wood can give you, but also consider some of the synthetic alternatives proposed to you by the experts. The main concern is expansion. Each material that goes in your project expands and contracts at a different rate. Have you ever pulled a towel out of the dryer to find it all gathered near the edge? This is because the trim edge shrank at a different rate than the terry cloth. If you are joining different building materials together, you have the same potential problem. The components of an all-wood house will behave roughly the same. Add a variety of synthetics and things can start to behave independently of one another. Talk to pros. Choose materials with a good, long record in the industry, and check the manufacturer's specifications and warranties.

Division 7—Thermal and Moisture Protection

Keeping heat and cool in and moisture out while maintaining good air quality.

Work

- Foundation waterproofing

- Insulation of foundations, walls, and ceilings

- Air barriers

- Vapor barriers

- Skylights

- Roofs

- Sealing and caulking

- Siding

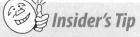

Insider's Tip

Getting water to flow away from your building is a bargain when you're first building, but an expensive mess later on. So spring for footing drains while the foundation goes in.

Typical Materials

Insulation, including polymer-modified asphalt, foundation insulating/waterproofing board, rigid, batting, and blown-in; air barrier wrap, felt paper, six to ten millimeter plastic sheathing, skylights; roof flashing, shingles, membranes, tiles, and rolled roofing; gaskets, sealants, foam, caulk; siding materials, including clapboard, stucco, shingles, adobe, and metal

Advice

Layers of materials around all sides of your home work to keep the building warm in the winter and cool in the summer. Starting from the interior of a wall and working your way out, there's the wall finish such as painted Sheetrock, then a plastic vapor barrier, wall insulation between framing, sheathing such as plywood or particleboard, an air barrier such as Tyvek or felt paper, and finally, painted or vinyl siding. Since the 1970s, a focus on energy efficiency has resulted in new materials and approaches to building assembly that enable us to make our buildings much more airtight than they were previously. This is great for saving on the heating and cooling bills, but it has brought about new problems with air quality, radon gas, mold, and exterior paint that won't hold.

Think of your interior space with that vapor barrier as a plastic bag. Now consider your lifestyle again in terms of moisture creation. How many people and pets are living and breathing in your home? How often do they bathe? How much water is boiled? Do you have fish tanks, plants, water beds, etc.? All these things create moisture and put it in the air. How will all that moisture escape the building? If moisture cannot get out of the building as vapor, eventually it will condense, turning to water. You can see this moisture as it condenses on the warm interiors of windows, but you cannot see the moisture that travels through the walls and condenses, running downward to create rotted sills or mold within the walls. Be mindful of this concern as you rely on experts to create a system that gets moisture out of the building, through the exchange of just the right amount of fresh air for stale air. This keeps your building healthy and still energy-efficient. Free consultation is available from utility companies and state weatherization programs. Many have financial incentives for homeowners. Call and see what they offer, including energy-use analysis, design assistance, and rebates for energy-saving lighting fixtures, water-saving devices, and insulation.

Pitfall

Some of the same manufacturers who were lauded for making our homes so tight and energy-efficient are now being pilloried for causing all the rot and mold out there. Let your building breathe a bit.

The mighty fall every day on this issue. You know how some great new drug comes on the market only to be pulled for its side effects? Some of these new synthetic products addressing energy challenges have side effects too. Some solve heat loss but could cause a ventilation problem. Some use less fuel but they're hard to maintain. There's no doubt we're headed in the right direction and most products are great. But manufacturers of some of these products are putting lots of disclaimers in their literature these days. Read them. For starters, neither air barrier wrap nor vinyl siding is waterproof. I just re-sided my house with good old-fashioned felt paper and cedar clapboards. I breathe easier and so does my house.

For roofing, you have many options now in terms of looks, life span, and function: three-tab asphalt or fiberglass shingles, ceramic tiles, wood shingles, slate, standing-seam metal, membrane, etc. Learn what roof systems are preferred in your climate. When choosing asphalt or fiberglass roof shingles, remember that the tiny pieces on the samples board do not reveal those that are mottled in coloring. It's best to look at photos of roofs in the manufacturer's literature to see how the entire surface will appear when finished. When monitoring the construction phase, make sure asphalt or fiberglass shingles go on within an acceptable temperature range. Too hot and you'll see the workers' footprints forever. Too cold and the adhesive won't seal, and the first good wind could snap your shingles.

Siding options include clapboard, shingles, board and batten, stucco, brick or stone veneer, and others in both natural and synthetic materials. If you're applying a natural wood siding, be sure to seal or prime it on all sides and cut edges before installation. You can attach it with stainless-steel nails for an extra few hundred dollars and ensure that those nailheads will never rust and streak the surface or wick moisture into your framing. But they will remain shiny, so if they will show and won't be painted over, you may want to go with galvanized nails. Consider using "wedges" to hold the siding slightly away from the sheathing. This permits ventilation behind the siding and helps prevent rot and peeling paint.

Synthetic sidings such as vinyl, aluminum, and pressed board are taking over the market. Each one has different manufacturer's recommendations for installation. Read them carefully so you can monitor the installation. For instance, vinyl comes with specific instructions regarding the temperature at which it is installed. It expands and contracts a lot. It's not attached firmly to the building but "hung," and the edges should not butt tightly under the trim. This permits the vinyl to flex. Ever see a building with the vinyl all buckled? That's because the pieces were installed on a cold day, and they butt into the trim. When a hot day rolled around, they expanded with no room to move, and *boing*!

If you are using vinyl or aluminum siding, the standard window and door trim and the "J-channel" that holds the ends of the siding are dead giveaways, letting the world know this is not a wood siding. Talk to your contractor and supplier about alternatives. New solid-vinyl products come in board lengths and can be cut and installed just like wood trim boards. You can also use real wood trim notched or rabbeted on the edges to receive the siding in lieu of J-channels. These kinds of compromises can give you the best of both worlds—a siding that looks like real wood but is almost maintenance-free.

Division 8—Doors and Windows
Building in access, light ventilation, and a view.

Work
- Window installation
- Door installation
- Installation of related hardware and security systems

Typical Materials
Interior and exterior doors and windows. Hardware including hinges, knobs, locksets, keying systems

Advice
Your choices are nearly endless. Sit down with a distributor, look at catalogs, manufacturers' cut sheets, and samples to weigh your form and function options. Don't skimp on the quality of doors and windows. However,

Pitfall

If new windows look wrong in an old house, it's most likely the flat muntins. Who knew?

you can enjoy some cost savings by choosing a window manufacturer who markets more to contractors than to owners.

Window styles include double-hung, casement, fixed, awnings, bay, and bow. Of these, only double-hungs permit the insertion of air conditioners. Beware of casements. Gravity is always at work, and so in time the sash may drop, making closure difficult. Regarding muntins, you can get true divided lights, which are separate panes of glass assembled in a muntin grid. You can also get imitation muntin grids that apply over large single panes of glass or between two layers of insulated glass, or both.

Window technology continually evolves to make windows more energy-efficient, attractive, and easy to maintain. There's double-insulated, low-e, and tinted glass, trim options, tilt-in sashes, less metal that radiates cold and heat, historic muntin bars, and prepainted wood. Different options are more or less appropriate for different climates. In general, the price you pay is determined by the thickness of the insulated glass and the number of options you want.

When designing window layout, people tend to want an infinite number of windows. For three reasons, you should show a little restraint. One, you will need wall space for furnishings and art. Two, a window, no matter how energy efficient, is still a hole in a wall and will never achieve the "R-value" of the wall itself. Lastly, Frederick Law Olmsted, the renowned landscape architect of Central Park in New York City, based much of his design on his belief that the anticipation of the view is at least as good as the view itself. But if you just must have that spectacular Palladian window at the end of the great room but cannot spring for it right now, have the framing installed in case that day ever comes.

Windows and doors can be a dead giveaway in a historic renovation. The differences between old and new windows seem subtle until you install them, so choose wisely. Present-day stock moldings on door and window muntins do not match the depth, breadth and style of the old. Some manufacturers specialize in historic details. I use a local man to make all my custom pseudohistoric-windows. It's a surprising bargain for a perfect effect.

Many of the options above pertain to doors as well. Doors prehung on their jambs are an industry standard now and not a bad idea. Look for doors with replaceable weather stripping for easy maintenance. When painting interior or exterior wood doors, be sure to seal all sides, and especially the top and bottom edges, with urethane or primer and paint to help prevent warping. You can also order doors with nice factory urethane or paint finishes that are warrantied.

Consider installing 36 inch wide doors. You or a future owner may need wheelchair access someday. Putting wide doors in at the building entrances and throughout the first floor, including the bathroom, will keep your place accessible. Thirty-six-inch doors also help widen the look of narrow halls and make furniture moving easier.

If you are building a space with more than a couple exterior doors, consider a keying system. For very little money, the hardware supplier will make the locksets and keys according to your specifications. Want the kids to have one key that opens everything but the toolshed? Go ahead, it's easy.

Division 9—Finishes

Application of any materials to rough-carpentry surfaces.

Work

- Wall finishes: soundproofing, Sheetrock (gypsum, drywall, plasterboard), blue board, green board, concrete board, plaster, veneer plaster, wood, wood paneling, ceramic tile, wallpaper, etc.

- Painting

- Ceiling coverings: acoustic, tin, textured

- Tile

- Flooring

- Countertops

Typical Materials

Soundproofing materials including resilient channel, sound board, batting insulation; Sheetrock, joint compound, ceramic and stone tile, grout, paint; flooring materials including carpet, wood or synthetic wood, VCT, sheet vinyl, linoleum, transition strips, vinyl baseboard; countertops in plastic laminate, butcher block, stainless steel, tile, or synthetics

Insider's Tip

I don't know why contractors don't start every project by telling owners a due date for the selection of finishes. But owners that don't have these answers when called upon will fail the pop quiz. So start this process early and wow your builder.

Advice

Although this work is the last to be executed by the contractor, finishes are often the most important and time-consuming decisions for owners. If you haven't chosen your finishes, the builder will come to you near the end of the project for all your final selections. And he'll need your answers immediately in order to complete the job (page 163). So make your choices early and avoid the pressure. Get samples of everything you need at once, including countertops, cabinets, carpet, vinyl flooring, vinyl baseboards, paint, wallpaper, etc. Your builder can provide all but wallpaper samples. Don't forget to consider fabrics and furniture along with these samples.

There's a large range of things you can do to achieve different levels of soundproofing. It's very cost-effective for the results you get, and well worth it if you have any vaulted space that carries noise upstairs to bedrooms or if you want some quiet space in an office or the master bedroom. Consider resilient channels, insulation, staggered framing, and subflooring materials with the experts.

The removal of toxins from paints, stains, and urethanes is reducing options for color, finish, and durability. The trend is to lessen the amount of toxic pigments, adhesives, and drying agents, and to get consumers to move from using oil-based formulas to water-based formulas. The upside is a cleaner environment. The downside is paint's having a lot of trouble sticking to things these days. Though it's hard to point the finger at paint alone, it's now common to see exterior finishes peeling badly within a year. If you are using exterior paint, be sure your specifications stipulate very good prep of surfaces and very good application of paint. This would include washing existing painted surfaces, scraping existing painted surfaces to the point of refusal, and applying primer and two coats of finish paint in weather conditions compliant with the manufacturer's instructions. For siding, preprime individual pieces on all six sides (yes, six), including all cut edges. Try to visit the site between each coat to ensure you are getting all coats of primer and paint on both the broad surfaces and the trim.

If you want someone to work on surfaces that have lead paint on them, be sure to specify in writing that the work, especially scraping, be done in a "lead-safe manner." This will require the painter to work in low-wind conditions and collect and dispose of all paint chips properly. That will prevent the lead paint from endangering people or property by getting airborne, and will lessen your liability. Call your state environmental agency for the pertinent regulations and language you need to include in your painter's contract.

When you create your color palette, try not to choose colors relative to each other on a paint chip. People who do this tend to end up with much bolder colors than they wanted. Instead, take a sheet of white paper, cut a small hole in it, and move it over each color to judge it independently. Also, ask a salesperson to show you where the reflective values are listed for the colors that interest you. This will tell you how much light bounces off or is absorbed by any given color. When in doubt, go a shade lighter. You can always add more pigment. Also be sure to stand back from any color sample you're trying to assess. Look at it from the distance you will be viewing it in the finished project. Paint stores have large color samples they can loan you, and small samples of paint, for only a few dollars. Materials such as countertops and roof shingles that look flecked close-up may make a solid color statement you didn't anticipate when viewed from a distance. So step back.

It's good to have the sheetrocker and the painter under one contract, or they can blame each other for imperfections. Try to be around for all three layers of "mud" and all three layers of primer and paint. This work happens fast so come by once or twice a day.

Do you really want a popcorn ceiling? You're more likely to find this as an option in a build-to-suit project (page 89). It's an inexpensive sprayed-on,

Insider's Tip

At the paint store, have a salesperson set up a file for you. They will record your entire color palette and all paint formulas you choose. This is very handy five years from now when you go to repaint and don't have a clue what paint you used on your porch doors. You can include wallpaper, vinyl baseboard, carpet, and any other materials you purchase from them.

textured finish that doesn't require painting, and permits for minimal taping of Sheetrock joints. In other words, it's cheap. However, it's nearly impossible to patch. If you ever have to do a repair on that ceiling, you'll probably have to spray the whole ceiling with popcorn again.

Regarding tile, please know you are not creating an impervious surface. Grout is porous. Hence, the infamous mildew. Mildew occurs from behind. Insufficient or inferior substrate is the problem here. Use moisture-proof or moisture-repellent substrate wallboard, like green, blue or cement board.

People regret tiling in places where they drop stuff, like kitchen counters and floors. Individual tiles crack. And on counters, you may long for a completely smooth surface once you've put in a tile surface with all its grout grooves.

On floors, use solid and thick enough subflooring to prevent motion that will lead to tiles cracking. Be sure to use floor tile, not the weaker wall tile, and consider the slip factor. Have replacement tiles on hand.

Natural stone is gorgeous, but it's a lifetime commitment that needs resealing with penetrating, not topical, sealers.

Regarding carpeting, go for long-wearing carpeting and pad for normal use. In the family room or other place where kids and pets may stain it before it wears out, go for the good pad, but save on the carpet and plan to replace it sooner rather than later. Be sure to specify how you want to make the transition from carpet to other surfaces, or you may end up with shiny little metal transition strips you hadn't planned on. Consider the light source in carpet layout. Carpet seams are more visible if they're per- parallel to a window.

Division 10—Specialties

Installation of accoutrements.

Work

- Bathroom accessories

- Handicapped accessibility hardware

- Pull-down stairs

- Attic ventilation

- Signage

Insider's Tip

Grab bars for handi- capped accessibility come in many great colors now. So no need to install the institutional look of stain- less steel.

- Mailboxes
- Fire extinguishers
- Flagpoles
- Shutters

Typical Materials

Towel bars, toilet paper holders, shelves, grab bars, medicine cabinets, shower seats, pull-down stair systems, louver vents, signs, mailboxes, fire extinguishers, window shutters

Advice

Make sure wall accoutrements can be attached through wall finishes to a vertical framing stud or horizontal blocking. Other than that, have fun shopping, and knock yourself out.

Division 11—Equipment

Installation of equipment.

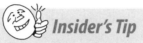 **Insider's Tip**

These are great items for alternate pricing (page 29) because they are ordered and installed at the end of a project.

Work

- Garage door openers
- Kitchen appliances
- Laundry equipment
- Central vacuum systems
- Safes

Typical Materials

Garage door openers, stoves, ovens, ranges, refrigerators, dishwashers, trash compactors, washers, dryers, vacuum systems, safes

Advice

Each midrange brand of appliances has a less expensive companion brand which is nearly identical but not marketed as strongly to the public. GE owns the less expensive Hotpoint, for instance. You can enjoy a lot of savings if you shop right. Superior insulating materials mean that appliances are getting lighter and can be front-heavy. To be safe and keep your Thanksgiving turkey off the floor, make sure you install the anti-tip clips that come with your stove.

Try to install dryers close to an exterior wall to lessen the length and number of turns in the vent hose. It's lint buildup in long, twisting hoses that causes fires.

If you install a washer above the basement level, consider putting in a shower drain. It's cheap prevention of floor damage in the event the washer overflows.

Install the canister for the central vacuum system in a place where it's okay to make a mess when you empty it.

Division 12—Furnishings

Interior decorating objects and systems.

Work

- Cabinetry

- Window treatments

- Anything not permanently attached to the building

Typical Materials

Kitchen cabinets, bathroom vanities, office cabinets, box valances, drapery hardware

Advice

Kitchen cabinets have a range of features. Look for four-sided drawers onto which the decorative drawer front is attached, solid wood doors and drawer fronts, strong drawer sliders, matching toe kicks, finish choices, European (invisible but only open 110 degrees) or barrel (exposed) hinges, and good assembly. Contractors and suppliers often offer the same quality as more expensive models available through upscale showrooms. No matter how spectacular your kitchen design is, consider the work triangle formed by the refrigerator, sink, and stove. If you can turn on your heels and take no more than a couple steps from one point of the triangle to another, your kitchen will be a model of comfort and efficiency. If one of those triangle items is to be in an island, give some thought to its being the sink instead of the stove, as is typical. Most of us spend more time at the sink, so putting it in the island can make you more a part of the kitchen's social scene as you face people instead of having your back to them. Appliances are often deeper than the standard 24-inch lower cabinets. So when designing an L-shaped layout, make sure all the drawers and doors of appliances and cabinets can open near the corners.

Refacing your existing cabinets is a great option for renovation if you like your current cabinet configuration and the boxes are in good shape. Refacing entails the removal of the outermost surfaces, doors, and trim, and replacing them with a whole new look.

Laminate shelving is great except under kitchen sinks. Cleaning products, trash, and plumbing under the sink are sources of moisture that delaminate the shelving. So before the plumber does his work, you may want to add plywood, stainless steel, or other material to the top of the laminate.

Be sure to get the toe kicks that match the cabinetry. Any other material used to face the base of your cabinets makes them look like they're floating and highlights irregularities in the floor surface.

Open soffits over cabinets are a great option for both storage and decorating.

Division 13—Special Construction

The creation of space that has a specialized function.

Work

- Bomb shelter
- Greenhouse
- Darkroom
- Home theater
- Saunas and steam room

Typical Materials

Regular construction, mechanical, and plumbing materials plus specialty equipment

Insider's Tip

Home theatres aren't just for mansions anymore. Your electrician isn't likely the source for great information on this. Start with the supplier of the equipment you want and they can supply the specifications for installation.

Advice

These specialty items often come in kits that can be purchased within or outside your general construction contract.

Division 14—Conveying Systems

Installation of equipment to move people and things.

Insider's Tip

If you want a conveying system later, be sure you account for that on your breaker panel now.

Work

- Elevators
- Wheelchair lifts
- Stair lifts
- Dumbwaiters

Typical Materials

Elevators, wheelchair lifts, stair lifts, dumbwaiters

These are highly specialized devices with a limited number of manufacturers. The Internet is a good source for researching your options.

Division 15—Mechanical Systems

Installation of plumbing, heating, air-conditioning and ventilating equipment, and distribution systems.

Work

- Plumbing
- Water heating
- Water filtering
- Bathroom fans
- Whole-house fans
- Heating
- Air-conditioning
- Air handling and ventilation
- Dehumidification
- Humidification
- Air filtering
- Fire suppression
- Solar energy

> **Insider's Tip**
>
> The world is getting hotter, so those of us in northern climates are catching on to what people from warmer climates have known for generations. Central air conditioning piggy backs very inexpensively on a forced hot air system. And a whole-house fan is a bargain, low-tech cooling device that the south's been keeping secret. However, if you consider installing one, you can't use blown-in insulation in the attic.

Typical Materials

Sinks, garbage disposals, toilets, showers, bathtubs, faucets, drains, pipe (copper, ABS, PVC, flex, cast iron), fans, water heaters, water filters, boilers, furnaces, heat pumps, ductwork, registers, radiant heat coil, condensers, air exchangers, dehumidifiers, humidifiers, air filters, sprinkler systems, fire dampers, solar panels and storage units

Advice

This division is constantly expanding as the result of new technologies. Focus on getting products and systems with established track records that offer high efficiency relative to their cost.

Insulate hot and cold copper plumbing pipes: the hot to prevent heat loss and save energy; the cold to prevent condensation in hot weather.

Consider putting a drain in your garage floor if it's permitted where you live and you promise not to pour oil down it.

Low-flow plumbing fixtures are required in some parts of the country. Some work better than others. Since most showrooms are not plumbed up to let you try these options, check with your plumber to find out which ones work and which ones don't. Toilets come in regular and "comfort height" at two to three inches higher at the seat.

Regarding bathtubs, cast iron radiates heat much better than fiberglass, but is costly. Moreover, many of today's fiberglass tubs don't give the option of steeping in more than eight inches of water. You can purchase steeping tubs for a premium in both fiberglass and cast iron, with and without air jets. If you're willing to accept the look of the old in your bathroom, a used, deep cast-iron tub from a salvage place may be a great option. If you go with cast iron of any variety, make sure your floor framing is designed to support it.

Mildew grows in bathrooms because of insufficient ventilation. Turning a fan on for a couple minutes is not sufficient ventilation, and it often doesn't get turned on at all. You can try to address this by tying your fan to a motion detector or a timer. You can also use highly energy-efficient fans that run silently for several hours a day.

Heating water through a heating coil on your boiler is very energy-efficient and provides unlimited hot water.

Your mechanical options in heating are hot water or hot air, requiring a boiler or a furnace respectively. The fuel source options are typically oil, gas (propane or natural), electricity, or wood. The more zones you can design into your system, the more control you'll have. Air-conditioning, air handling, dehumidifying, humidifying, and filtering options all tie into your heating system. If you're thinking of adding any of these systems later, be sure you design sufficient lengths of ductwork around the furnace so they can be incorporated. Also be sure the system's blower is sized properly for these possible additions.

Fire suppression systems (sprinklers) are being required more and more in residential construction. Along with the aesthetic and cost challenges they present, there's no easy answer for installing a sprinkler systerm in the top floor of a home in the cold north. The logical place to put the spinkler pipes is in the floor joists of the attic, with sprinkler heads in the ceiling below. You want that attic space cold, but the water in the system could freeze. You can put antifreeze in the lines, but if the system ever engages, you have chemicals to clean up. I have faith that this new residential market for fire suppression systems will spur on some brilliant entrepreneurs to come up with all the answers.

Division 16—Electrical Systems

Installation of all things electrical.

Work

• Electrical service

• Controls

• Lighting

• Receptacles

• Special systems: phone, cable, communication, computer, alarm

• Overhead fans, range hood fans

• Lightning protection

• Fire, radon, carbon monoxide detection

• Thermostats

• Entertainment systems

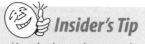

Insider's Tip

You don't need to spend any of your precious future shouting "Is it off now?!" Make sure the breakers on that electrical panel are beautifully labeled before the electrician leaves.

Typical Materials

Panel box, cable, wire, light fixtures, receptacles, switches, dimmers, timers, motion detectors, phone and cable jacks, intercoms, alarm systems, kitchen and bathroom fans, lightning rods, smoke detectors, radon detectors, carbon monoxide detectors, thermostats, doorbells, speakers.

Advice

Wiring for anything is relatively cheap. While the framing is open, put in all the fiber-optic cables, computer lines, phone lines, and stereo wiring you might anticipate using later. Choose your light fixtures well in advance, or specify a lighting allowance in the contract to give yourself time to choose. Regarding lighting, the issues are the appearance of the light fixture, whether it casts light up, down, or out, the amount of light, or lumens, it throws, the type of bulbs or lamps it uses, how energy-efficient the bulbs are, how expensive they are, and how frequently they need replacement. Always get fixtures with "UL approval" to comply with industry safety standards. Lay out your switches and choose controls for light fixtures by imagining coming home and getting into and through the house with light always before you.

According to the national electric code, you need to be able to reach a receptacle within six feet of any wall surface and have a receptacle on any wall section bigger than two feet wide. You can adjust the height at which they are located on the wall. I don't know where the standard eighteen inches above the floor came from. Customize the location of your receptacles, taking into account things like vacuuming, freestanding tables, and where the

Christmas tree will go. Quadraplex (four outlets) is the bargain way to go in kitchens, offices, and workrooms.

Put in plenty of jacks for phone and cable. You may not be as set on your furniture layout as you think.

If you would like a home security system but can't afford the full-blown version, consider a single motion detector in the downstairs hall tied to an alarm.

Consider installing an automatic set-back thermostat. You program it to call for heat or air-conditioning according to your lifestyle needs. It's great to wake to a warm house in winter and come home to a cool one in summer and still enjoy energy savings while you're gone. You'll cut fuel costs, especially if you're one of those people who forget to turn the heat down when they go to work.

And Another Thing: Considerations When Determining Materials and Scope of Work

Green Design

Starting with the energy crisis of the 1970's, engineers, architects and manufacturers began responding to the call by designing for energy conservation. Since then "green", as it pertains to buildings, has grown to mean minimizing your carbon footprint by using less energy (fuel) and water, living in healthy space, avoiding waste and minimizing your impact on the environment. I don't hope to address this topic fully here. However, I do deal with it every day and I would be remiss if I didn't try to give you the basics and point you in the right direction.

> *Buildings, too, are children of Earth and Sun.*
>
> —FRANK LLOYD WRIGHT

The federal government, states and municipalities encourage compliance with green design standards (4-Star, 5-Star and LEED ratings) through financial incentives. Start with your fuel supplier to access these funds.

There is an innovation explosion going on that's filled with brilliant thinking, but a market like this also draws failed experiments and is subject to changes in the very resources it's trying to conserve. I remember when the green approach was to install electric baseboard heating. Sounds crazy now, right? Fifteen years later we were being paid to pull it out again. It can get complicated. I recommend you educate yourself with books, websites and local resources first. Select what meets your green goals in descending order, starting with the simplest, cheapest and most effective, like foam around junction boxes. Then work as far down the list of options as you can afford and find worthwhile. Here's how to focus your efforts:

Design to Conserve
• Select products that have successful track records in the US. Then local subcontractors know how to maintain it and can get parts for it.

- Work with nature and site the building like the old timers did. Maximize natural light and solar warmth, create a buffer against the wind, create a positive grade for water run-off. Let gravity, sunshine, shade trees, rocks, all the natural elements, work for you to lessen your use of mechanical solutions like a pump or furnace. Once you start thinking this way, you'll notice some really silly houses. Minimize run-off and erosion by limiting the amount of non-permeable coverage of your land, like pavement.

- Consider alternative energy sources such as solar, water and wind power.

- When building new you can create systems that work on more than one fuel type so you can convert from one source to the other when it's advantageous (ie: wood and oil furnace).

- "Payback" is the monetary means by which we usually judge energy saving products. A good feature will pay for itself in energy savings in five years.

Selecting Green Materials

- Energy-efficient boilers, furnaces, heat pumps, air conditioning units, hot water tanks, appliances and light fixtures

- Low flow plumbing fixtures

- Insulated walls, doors, windows, floors, and ceilings countered by good air exchange and ventilation to keep buildings breathable, free of rot, mold and radon, and holding onto their exterior paint

- Recycled materials from wood, paper, plastic, rubber, and glass to make synthetic lumber, flooring, carpet, etc.

- Adhesives, coatings, stains, paints, caulk, foam. etc. that don't outgas toxins

- Wood that is not from exotic or endangered species

- Local materials to minimize shipping and support the local economy

Where They Sit Is Where They Stand

The people who act as resources to help you plan your scope of work can have differing opinions. The design team often recommends more gravel base, more concrete, more insulation, more everything, than the building team. Bear in mind their respective roles. The designer wants to have a superior job and to lessen the risk of liability. The contractor wants to keep his and/or your costs down. You can feel torn when both make compelling arguments. If need be, make a couple of calls and do a little legwork. Contact the town building inspector and the appropriate supplier for a third and fourth opinion.

It Only Starts out a Bargain

Watch out for the loss leaders. A loss leader is an inexpensive item on which manufacturers might actually take a "loss" in order to "lead" you into more expensive items required for an entire system. At Thanksgiving, the grocery store may sell turkeys at a well-advertised bargain price, but the stuffing, veggies, cranberry sauce, and pies are at their full prices. It's the same deal for some construction materials that are part of a system. For instance, ten-foot lengths of vinyl gutter are very inexpensive and might lead you to believe you can put an elaborate gutter system around your whole house for next to nothing. No such luck. The brackets, corner pieces, and downspouts will cost you plenty. In short, price all systems in their entirety.

Supply and Demand

Suppliers are a great resource for investigating your options for materials. In addition to whatever the pretty pictures will make you ask, be sure to ask how long each material has been on the market, how it's been received, and what its life span, maintenance needs, and warranty terms are.

Be mindful that you may not be offered the same discounted trade prices as your contractor. Your contractor may also get a 10 percent discount for any materials paid for by a certain date each month. And believe it or not, the supplier may actually give him receipts that have a markup in them. So a $100 item would generate a receipt for $115 without the markup noted. These are given under the premise that the contractor will hand these receipts to a client and say his markup is already in there. Wink, wink.

If you're inclined to have a change of heart after delivery, beware. Many suppliers will charge a restocking fee of 20 percent of the price of merchandise.

She Who Hesitates

Lead time is the time it takes to get your materials. Those that are in big demand, out of season, or coming from far away can take months to get on site. Stay ahead of this, especially on any allowance items that you are responsible for specifying during the construction phase, such as cabinets, carpeting, and light fixtures. Always ask and write in your notes how long a lead time you should allow, or these delays can bring your project to a screeching halt and you may pay dearly in both time and money to get your crew back on site. Allow lots of lead time for custom-made features like leaded glass, millwork, and work done by subs in much demand, like plasterers, slate roofers, faux finish painters, and any artisans of bygone crafts.

Submissive Behavior

If you are working with a contractor in a design/build (page 84) or negotiated (page 85) structure, he will likely suggest materials that he thinks are great. Don't just say yes, or even that you will check it out. Ask for a submittal. This is the manufacturer's info on the material. On large commercial jobs, the contractor must provide submittals on every single material that goes into a project, including all those specified in the construction documents. So your little requests are nothing. Always get submittals if changes in materials are proposed after the contract has been signed.

> *Watch an old building with anxious care; guard it as best you may and at any cost from every influence of dilapidation.*
>
> —JOHN RUSKIN

What Your Contractor Can't Tell You

Times Change

There's a vicious cycle of degradation regarding both craftsmanship and quality of materials. To keep labor costs down, more and more materials come ready-made, so fewer people on job sites have the skills of craftsmen of a couple generations ago. What used to be a standard skill in any given trade is becoming reserved for artisans. To ensure quality on the site, one must now use ready-made products or pay the high wages of the artisan. Consequently and sadly, I now have more faith in a prehung door already mounted in its frame than a custom-made frame hung on site. I also resign myself to paying through the nose to have a few roof slates replaced. In short, you must choose which architectural elements you think are worthy of the artisan's approach and cost. Maybe plaster walls aren't worth the fortune they cost compared to the bargain of Sheetrock, but you're willing to pay for hand-turned balusters for the staircase to get the look you want.

Regarding materials, changes in the industry have affected their sustainability. Lumber ain't what it used to be. Lead, asbestos, and other toxic substances, which we can no longer use, produced materials that had great longevity. The tightening of regulations to meet high energy-efficiency standards has contributed to mold and rot. This all pushes the industry toward synthetics. Laminates, plastics, and materials made of things you can't even pronounce are becoming the norm for construction, and many are now more cost-effective than the natural materials they replace. Vinyl siding is hard to beat in terms of cost over its lifetime. So is laminate flooring made to look like wood, and ceramic tile made to look like stone. This isn't necessarily a bad thing, but just as with the artisan's labor, it means you need to choose whether and where you have fine natural materials.

Something Old, Something New

My first love is historic preservation. Old buildings are our legacy, and due to cost and craftsmanship we couldn't build most of them again if we wanted to. There are resources available to you for repairing, renovating, or adding on to a historic building. Start with the department of your state government that deals with historic preservation. They can point you in the right direction for sympathetic design work, talented craftspeople, and even some funding opportunities. Best of all, they are kindred spirits if you love your old place.

Duh!

You'll need to specify and install large items, like a furnace, oil tank, appliances, and bathtubs. Note all dimensions of these items when designing your space and ensure you have openings and turning radiuses at stairs, doorways, and bulkheads to get these things in.

Once you see the materials and tasks all broken down by division, it's a lot to think about. Use those divisions as a mental filing system to help you categorize all your options, and just take one decision at a time. Now let's talk money . . .

CHAPTER 6

And the Grand Total Is…

Cost Estimating and the Budget

> This chapter breaks down the basics of how construction costs are assigned to your project and how you can monitor and participate in that process.
>
> - Follow the Money: How It Works on a Construction Project
> - Where'd You Get That Number? Four Methods of Cost Estimating
> - Crunching Their Numbers: Assessing a Cost Estimate
> - It's Alive! Your Budget as a Living Document

Follow the Money: How It Works on a Construction Project

As most owners conceive of and start a project, the issue of money relates only to affordability. There's a long list of numbers to determine, which can include land purchase, surveys, permit fees, loan fees, insurance premiums, closing costs, and so on. When it comes to the cost for construction itself, the owners often go to a contractor saying, "Here's how much money we have. What can you build us?" Eventually, they settle on what will be built for what price, and when they look back at the end of the project, those owners may think, "That was the last time I understood anything about where my money was going." This chapter will focus on the construction portion of your overall budget and help you understand what happens at the contractor's office—how he comes up with his pricing and what it is he's presenting to you.

The structure for monitoring your money is the budget. A budget is made up of hundreds of prices arrived at through cost estimates that are grouped together by the sixteen divisions (chapter 5) or a similar format used by the contractor. He will calculate many of these prices himself, and many others will be provided to him by subcontractors and suppliers. For example, a contractor will calculate the rough carpentry by determining the materials and labor necessary to do the framing of your house. This is based on the square footage of your project as dimensioned on your plans, along with all other specifications, details, and instructions available to him. He will have to take into consideration when the project is likely to start in light of current lumber and labor costs to ensure that this price will hold.

Anyone doing cost estimates knows that the more he breaks down the scope of work, the more accurate his price will be. He spreads out over every task in the project the chance of errors in his calculations and interpretations of the plans. Some of his numbers may be a bit high, some a bit low, but with luck and skill, it averages out to the right price. Imagine I asked you, "How much to make and bring me a cheesecake?" Shooting from the hip, you might estimate twenty dollars, but given the opportunity, you could better estimate the actual cost of ingredients, shopping, preparation and cooking time, mileage, and an acceptable profit for your efforts. After that, whether you came back to me with a price of fifteen or fifty dollars, you would likely feel confident about that number. If you specified a higher price for the cheesecake, you might not be competitive, and a lower price might cause you to lose money. By the same token, seeing your cheesecake cost broken down would give me much more information with which to judge whether that price seemed fair or not.

Good, detailed cost estimating is a contractor's lifeblood. For you, being able to understand and scrutinize prices you are given is essential to getting a fair price and feeling confident about approving or rejecting the base bid, change orders, and requisitions. The bulk of a contractor's cost estimating goes on early in the project before you sign a contract. At this stage, your contractor may or may not have an open-book policy with you, sharing his costs and calculations. However, even in the best planned and priced project, cost estimating will continue throughout the project to address change orders. It is reasonable to ask for breakdowns of those change orders, so learning how the contractor and others estimate costs can still be valuable to you. You can appreciate the challenge of this task, monitor your contractor's efforts, and negotiate with him intelligently when needed. If you really don't like a price, you can do some calculating of your own to help you assess it. You can also work better with an architect or professional cost estimator during the design phase, discussing pricing as an equal. So let's explore cost estimating and how it's done by the pros.

Where'd You Get That Number?
Four Methods of Cost Estimating

Cost estimating refers to the item-by-item pricing of individual tasks as well as the pricing of the entire scope of work. For instance, a cost estimate for siding an existing building might include all labor and materials associated with removing and discarding the old siding, and applying plywood sheathing, felt paper, and preprimed clapboards, for a total of $30,000. The cost estimate for that siding is added to the individual cost

We reckon hours and minutes to be dollars and cents.

—THOMAS CHANDLER HALIBURTON

estimates for every other construction-related task in the project to create a cost estimate for the entire scope of work. A certain percentage (+/–10 percent) of that total is added on for the contractor's profit and overhead to create the construction budget. To arrive at his numbers, a contractor uses one or more of the following four methods of cost estimating. He may use books or computer software, but they're all based on one or more of these methods.

Method 1: Order of Magnitude (Accurate to +/–25%)

This is the broadest approach to cost estimating. It's very close to an educated guess, but it's the place you will likely start. In initial conversations with almost anyone associated with your project, you will be thinking and estimating in these broad terms. For the professionals, the banker and the builder to name just two, it will be based on previous experience and extrapolations from published information. For you, it will be based more on your knowledge of the market. When you say, "The neighbors' house cost $250K to build, and ours will be about the same size, so it should be about the same price," you are applying an order of magnitude approach. It requires basic information like the size of the project and the type of construction. There is nothing wrong with this kind of pricing, but it's not the place to stop, because the devil is in the details and the details get pricey.

Example: A previous similar renovation project for an 1,850-square-foot space cost $100,000. This space is half again as big, so that's another $50,000, plus you want a fireplace for about $12,000. Just add these costs together to get a rough number:

$$\$100K + \$50K + \$12K = \$162K$$

Method 2: Square Foot Cost (Accurate to +/–20%)

Square foot cost is obtained by multiplying the area of work to be done by an established per-square-foot price for that work. This method requires a description of the work and the quantity of the work.

Example: The room to be painted is 15' × 15', or 225 square feet. The walls are 8' high. Painting costs 15¢ per square foot. To apply one coat of paint on the walls of this room, you would make the following calculation:

$$15' \times 8' = 120 \text{ sq. ft. per wall} \times 4 \text{ walls} = 480 \text{ sq. ft.}$$

$$+ \ 15' \times 15' \text{ for the ceiling} = 225 \text{ sq. ft.}$$

$$\text{TOTAL} = 705 \text{ sq. ft.}$$

$$705 \text{ sq. ft.} \times 15¢ \text{ per sq. ft.} = \$105.75$$

Method 3: Systems Estimating (Accurate to +/–15%)

Systems estimating is based on quantifying an entire construction system and applying dollar values to that system on a per-square-foot basis. Those dollar values are usually obtained through published cost estimating guides. This approach is often used to compare the costs of whole systems, such as wood-framed versus brick walls. It requires a complete definition of the work and a detailed design showing the various components in the systems to be priced.

Example: You're pricing the exterior walls of a 2,400-square-foot house. The exterior wall system specified includes 2" × 6" framing, Sheetrock, vapor barrier, insulation, plywood sheathing, cedar clapboard siding, and exterior stain. The pricing guide shows the cost of this type of system to be $9.40 per square foot. You have a total of 3,500 square feet of exterior wall. The price to build and finish those four walls would be calculated like this:

$$3,500 \text{ sq. ft.} \times \$9.40 = \$32,900$$

Method 4: Unit Price Estimating (Accurate to +/–10%)

Unit price estimates are a valuable component of certain types of budget estimating. This one's a little highbrow for most homeowners, but just so you know, most contractors use it for bidding purposes as they price work within each of the sixteen divisions. It is based on determining the quantities of materials and the cost of labor that can be attributed to a given unit of measurement of a material, such as lineal footage of installed baseboard. The value of materials is established by suppliers or published rates. Labor rates are established from published labor standards or the cost estimator's experience.

Example: 6" × 6" wooden baseboard lumber costs 95¢ per lineal foot (l.f.). A room requires 155 l.f. of baseboard. The standard labor rate to install baseboard is .033 hr./l.f. (or 1⁄3 hour of labor per 10 lineal feet). The labor rate for finish carpenters is $24 per hour. This gives you enough information to estimate the value of installed baseboard by using the following formula:

Material cost × quantity of materials

+ labor per unit of materials × quantity of materials × labor rate

$$95¢ \times 155 \text{ l.f.} = \$147.25$$

$$+ .033 \times 155 \text{ l.f.} \times \$24 = \$122.76$$

$$\text{TOTAL} = \$270.01$$

Good cost estimators usually use a blend of these methods depending on the level of information they have available. In most cases, you can count on a price being accurate and holding up only if the contractor has all the information he needs to estimate the work as you envision it. Without detailed

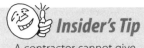
information, what else can he do but round up or guess wrong, and have to charge you for changes later as the work item becomes clearer? For example, let's assume you sew, and say I ask you to give me a price to make a jacket and stand by that price as fixed. With only that to go on, what are your options? You can refuse me. You can give me an outrageous number that will cover the cost of any jacket imaginable. You can give me a low price, get me to commit, and then charge me more later based on the information that evolves. These are the only options for contractors pricing in a vacuum. Now let's say instead that I ask you to make me a single-breasted blazer in wool gabardine with a silk lining and leather buttons in a size 12, due in two weeks. This is a lot of information, and if I am open to answering questions to give you even more, you will have all the information you need in terms of the design, materials, and schedule to give me an accurate price that we can both take comfort in committing to. As you look to your contractor for cost estimating, take into consideration what he needs in order to give you a reliable number.

Crunching Their Numbers: Assessing a Cost Estimate

How can you judge the numbers you receive? You now understand how a contractor calculates his costs. What he attempts to charge you is another matter. He can assign any amount he wants, and for some, "what the traffic will bear" is the rule of thumb. He can pad the labor and materials numbers he shows you, charge a massive profit and overhead, and you may not really see it on paper. He can provide false receipts or those that some suppliers provide with a contractor markup already added in. He can refuse to show you numbers. Even open books sometimes have another version in the back room.

I asked a contractor friend in California how he calculates his prices in a very hot market. He said, "I think of the highest number imaginable and then double it. No one blinks an eye, so I may start doubling it again." This is not an exact science you're working with here. You are at a disadvantage in terms of feeling certain you have accurate information, and you probably don't want to spend all your time sleuthing out the right number or trying to get your contractor to accept it. This is why you want to have as much of the project's ultimate cost accounted for and properly priced before you make any contractual or financial commitments. Then the contractor has an incentive to price things as low as possible to get the job. Once you have committed, that incentive for low pricing is gone.

Remember the first cost estimating method? Basically, "order of magnitude" is common sense. If your new neighbor from India told you he paid forty-five dollars for a pepperoni pizza delivered last night, you would know something was wrong. Based on what you know of the market and what you and others pay for pizza all the time, that number is too high. That's order of magnitude cost estimating and your best approach for assessing what's right. As you become more familiar with prices in the construction field, trust your gut more.

Seeing labor and materials separated is a big help. If you get a price of $1,225 to put in a window seat, well, who knows? Maybe that's fair. But if you know that the lumber and other materials are $550, the labor is $525, broken down to fifteen hours at $35 per hour, and the profit and overhead total $150, you know a lot more, and this price probably starts to look pretty reasonable.

Before you commit to cost estimates in any form—the whole budget or an individual change order—you have resources at your disposal for second opinions that will shed light on your situation and ultimately give you confidence that you are getting a fair value for your money.

Your architect or other design professional can provide cost estimates, but consider the source. Although he may spend a lot of time in and around costs, it is not his field of expertise, and he may be reluctant to give costs that are very specific. What's in it for him? Only your disappointment if he's wrong.

You can employ a professional cost estimator. Many people who have spent years in the field of construction go on to consult or offer such services as a sideline. Your architect or designer will be only too glad to work with one, as it takes some pressure off him. This service is usually offered very reasonably. Although the numbers you get are still just "estimates," it's a second opinion as to what's the right number

Pitfall

When you're out pricing materials for a construction project, it's next to impossible to get the low prices suppliers give to contractors.

for the work, and even more important, it is from a disinterested party and will give you a great tool for discussion when it comes time to refine and negotiate numbers with a contractor.

You can certainly get materials costs from any supplier. Some suppliers actually have designers and cost estimators on staff that provide prices to contractors that include labor estimates. It's part of the service and you can use it too. If you bring your plans to most places that sell plumbing and heating supplies, kitchen cabinetry, and framing lumber, someone there could likely sit down with you and help you get at least some broad numbers on your work items. Again note that your contractor likely enjoys certain purchasing perks you do not. First, he gets trade prices, which are the discounted prices at which suppliers sell to contractors and not you. Second, he may get a discount of 10 percent when he pays his bills by the tenth of each month. Lastly, he may be directed to more creative solutions and less expensive materials options.

It's Alive!
Your Budget as a Living Document

At the beginning of the project, the first thing I'm usually asked is "How much will it cost?" I hate this question. I am loath to give the first number. No matter what disclaimers I put on that number, no matter how much I couch it and warn against becoming attached to it, it's as though that number has been tattooed on the project before the designs are even started and the scope of work has been determined. It appears in budgets as though it's gospel and it is presented to the bank, the architect, the contractor, the city, the in-laws, everyone who may have any interest or reliance on that number. If it's said enough, everyone starts to accept it as fact. Well, the final number is actually a product of a lot of hard work, and that number is only final after the last payment has been made on the last requisition. Until then, a budget is just a tool.

Sample Construction Budget

CONSTRUCTION BUDGET — DORSEY HOUSE ADDITION			
DIVISION	**DESCRIPTION**	**DIVISION TOTAL**	**SQ. FT. COST**
1	General conditions	$6,500	$5.20
2	Site work	5,073	4.06
2	Selective demo	4,556	3.64
3	Concrete	5,414	4.33
4	Masonry	7,664	6.13
6	Rough carpentry	9,414	7.53
6	Interior finish carpentry	8,808	7.05
6	Exterior finish carpentry	7,730	6.18
6	Cabinets	1,850	1.48
7	Insulation	4,775	3.82
7	Roofing	9,836	7.87
7	Siding	6,800	5.44
8	Doors and hardware	5,800	4.64
8	Windows	4,800	3.84
9	Gypsum	6,016	4.81
9	Flooring	4,400	3.52
9	Ceramic tile	2,800	2.24
9	Painting	3,700	2.96
10	Specialties	795	0.64
15	Plumbing	11,500	9.20
15	Heating	12,834	10.27
16	Electrical	10,000	8.00
	Bare Cost Total	**$141,065**	**$112.85**
	Contractor's Overhead and Profit (15%)	21,160	16.93
	Contract Amount	**$162,225**	**$129.78**

What do you want from a budget? An accurate picture of what you'll be building and what it will cost you, right? Well, that's what you should get, but the sum of your estimates plus the contractor's profit and overhead—better known as the construction budget—is not a stagnant thing (page 78). No matter what you think now, you will not price the work just once and then be safely locked into that number. Try to see your budget as a tool of measurement instead: a living, breathing document that reflects your decisions, negotiations, shortfalls, windfalls, the changing market, and horse trading with your contractor. Everything that impacts the scope of work or the schedule will affect your budget.

So you're not an accountant. You don't necessarily need to do the budget preparation yourself or learn computer spreadsheet programs. You may hate such accounting duties. You may not have a computer or want to be bothered by any of this. Someone else in the project, such as the architect or contractor, can produce the physical copies and updates to the budget. However, the budget is your best tool, and there is no need for you to feel passive and let others set the tone that they'll spend your money while you just watch until there's a problem. One way or the other, you should understand the budget right from the beginning and make sure that it's accurately and frequently updated to let you know where you stand.

Who is privy to your budget and when? Budget information should be shared on a need-to-know basis. I don't know about you, but when I walk into a car showroom and the salesperson says, "What are you looking to spend?" the little hairs on my neck go up. People who have no business knowing what you are looking to spend on your project will ask you. Get used

to saying, "I'm not quite ready to share that information." Of course, many contractors would like you to tell them how much money you have and then offer you a certain scope of work for that amount. I have yet to find the need to reveal this information to everyone on a home design or construction project. It's on a case-by-case basis, but before you answer, just stop and think of who is asking you this question and why.

The Budget as a Tool for Goal Setting

Within seconds of thinking of building something, you will think about the money. What will it cost? What can we afford? Your answers to these two questions are your first budget. It may be very broad, it may be in your head or scribbled on a napkin, but it will loosely reflect what you think you can get for what you can afford, and that's a budget! Your next inclination will be to find out if your theories hold water. Good instinct. You ask yourself, "Can I really afford that much, and what can I really get for that?" As you seek answers in the world of financing, design, and cost estimating, bear these things in mind:

Which comes first, the budget or the design? Do you design to the budget or budget to the design? Well, both and neither. If you're doing it right, you will go along the same bumpy dual paths we all travel to get to a finished design at a fixed price. Think of two long lines that start far apart but meet in the end, off in the distance. One is budget, the other design. Design options such as size, quality, level of detail, and finishes will impact your budget, and the budget will constrain those design options back and forth, one step forward, one step back, until you have progressed down both paths to the point where they converge.

How many projects have you heard of that came in under budget? Nope, we humans are perpetual delusional optimists trying to get it all for as little as possible. For emotional peace of mind, try to build below your means and have a healthy, generous budget, even if it's not the one you share with the world. The easiest projects are those that are financially sound. So do not trim every ounce of fat off your budget before you start. A healthy budget should include accurate pricing of all the work to be done, a 10 percent contingency to address change orders and unplanned costs, and ample money for the work to be done after the construction phase, such as more tree clearing, landscaping, decorating, and furnishings. If at the end of your project you have no money for these things, what's the point?

The Budget as a Refining Tool

You could get someone to tell you that your initial crude numbers are right, you're smart, and let's start building this thing on a handshake or a very thin contract. Don't. Until you see numbers based on a detailed scope of work, you're in la-la land. It's okay early on to apply broad rules of thumb to pricing. Most people involved in home building and renovation throw around square-foot prices all the time. They can glance at a typical house type and give a square-foot price that includes all the sixteen divisions, all trades, soup to nuts. They can also think of work in terms of quick ratios. Overall, most houses come out to about 30 percent materials and 70 percent labor. Join them in this casual math, but don't stop there. As you refine your plans, set up that parallel path by refining your budget. In time you would like to have estimates and eventually maybe fixed prices on the work, divided by those sixteen divisions that will make up your budget line items. Begin filling in the numbers, first with guesses, then educated guesses, then bona fide cost estimates and eventually fixed prices. Save each version of the dated budget to create the first part of the project's financial record.

Your goal should be to get to the budget that reflects the "right" price. There's a horse race called the Hunter Pace in which an expert rider has run the course in advance of the race and set the "right" amount of time to run the perfect race. The jockeys then try to come as close to that time as

Annual income twenty pounds, annual expenditure nineteen nineteen six, result happiness. Annual income twenty pounds, annual expenditure twenty pounds ought and six, result misery.

—CHARLES DICKENS

What Your Contractor Can't Tell You

possible. This doesn't mean a breakneck pace that could kill the horse, or a stroll that lasts all day, but the right pace. Your goal should be much the same. You cannot have a contractor stay on a job if he's not making a profit. You cannot be engaged in a project that breaks you financially. You want as much quality construction for the least amount possible, right? The contractor wants the most money for the least amount of quality construction possible, right? Are these in conflict? Not if you come to the "right" price for the right scope of work.

If you're working with design professionals, the budget can be avoided for a long time during the design phase. There is not enough detail yet, and no one is even sure the project is going forward. This is fine for starters; just don't think that the first broad number is fixed or that a contractor will "work to that number" later, as your designer should be doing now. I cannot tell you how many bids I've seen come in 40 percent over budget. An outcome like this could render your architect's plans, and the time and money you dedicated to those, worthless. And the mad dash to bring the numbers in line while the contractor is still available to do the work can result in slapdash triage of your scope of work. The documents may end up with errors in them, or people may have different memories regarding the outcome of this frantic time. Keep cost-estimating as you design.

The Budget as a Sales Tool

The bank, the mortgage company, even the rich uncle who may be financing your project, all need some comfort. For them, your budget is like a business plan. It's proof that this project will work, that you can afford it. It should also help to assure them that the end product will be worth at least what you all have invested in it and could resell at or above that price. So you are now using this budget to sell this project to lenders, and they will give you invaluable feedback in reviewing it. Banks will require several things from your contractor, including a commitment to a fixed price. The bank will guide you through its requirements, but the most important one will surely be very much as described above: a construction budget broken down by divisions with corresponding costs.

The Budget as a Negotiating Tool

Do you like to dicker? No matter what contract structure you choose to work under, you will negotiate with your contractor for some or much of the work. Maybe his bid price includes painting at $10,000 more than another bidder. But for that, you would choose him. So you decide to talk it out and see if you can negotiate that $10,000 away. Maybe immediately after seeing the plans or pricing the work the first time, the contractor says, "There's room for savings here." Maybe you decide that while the walls are still exposed, you should add fiber-optic cable. You can't afford to pay much, but you've just learned he heats his house with wood and you're about to clear two acres of hardwood trees . . . hmmmm. Or maybe he asks way more for a change order than you think is reasonable. Whatever the reasons, you will be negotiating, and the budget and the numbers contained therein are your guiding light. They show you where the money is, where there's room to move things around, and which line items are inviolate.

Watch the pennies. Of course, when the project starts, you are all talking in big numbers to describe the costs associated with the project—like tens of thousands—but as the scope of work gets refined, so should those numbers. Though the other parties will hone their mathematical thinking to the tiniest increments, they may not be sharing that approach with you. That $5,000 discussion with you about your kitchen might well be more of a $4,813 discussion back at their office. As soon as the numbers start to be real, tied to a budget and pending invoices, bring the discourse down to earth and into focus. Show everyone that you think to the nearest dollar, not the nearest thousand dollars. You'll save money, gain the respect of the contractor, and set the standard for getting close attention paid to budget details. Fear not. No matter how casually big numbers are thrown around, the contractor is really counting to the nearest penny. Remember, his profit is only a small percentage of what you're paying for the whole project, so you can be sure that small increments of money mean at least as much to him.

The Budget as a Commitment

After choosing a contractor, whether through a competitive bid process or not, you will work to firm up the prices and the scope of work (chapter 8). When all parties are in agreement as to what work is being done at what price, the budget takes on a formal function. It becomes part of the contract documents and is attached to the owner-contractor agreement along with the project plans and specifications before the contract is signed. The attachments act as addenda to the contract, spell out what work you will get (plans), how it will be executed (specifications), and for how much money (budget). Copies of these contract documents will likely go to you, the lender, the contractor, and the architect if you have one. The contractor will have separate contracts with his subcontractors.

The Budget as a Monitoring Tool

Almost immediately after signing an owner-contractor agreement and giving permission to the contractor to start, money will begin to flow. Through the course of the construction phase, you may pay out money for the down payment, requisitions, and change orders. Begin tracking all financial activity right away and never pay out more than the work done to date is worth. Monitoring the budget through the construction phase is covered in chapter 14.

In these last pages, some of the monetary mysteries of a construction project have been revealed. You know how a contractor arrives at his numbers and how you can apply those numbers to your budget.

CHAPTER 7

Setting Up Your Deal
Contract Structures

This section reveals all the little-known options that owners have for structuring their projects, along with the pros and cons and an owner's best approach to each method.

- Who Knew You Had a Choice? Options for Contract Structures
- It's Alive! Your Budget as a Living Document

Who Knew You Had a Choice?
Options for Contract Structures

You can hire builders and contract for their services several different ways. Each way is reflected in a different contract structure. Each structure defines the roles of the contract parties as slightly or dramatically different from the next. Read on and choose which one best suits you and your project. Whether you want to write your own contract, use one provided by the contractor, or even do your project on a handshake, this chapter will help you understand what's at stake and how you can minimize your risk. You will find an appropriate contract for each of these approaches in chapter 10, so I take it back. Please don't do your project on a handshake.

> *There is more than one way to skin a cat. Just don't be the cat.*

What contract structure a builder is willing to work under is often affected by the building market. When the contractors are busy and have plenty of work, you may hear them say, "I never bid anything. I only do design/build or negotiated projects." This may be true enough when they are in demand and in a position to call the shots, but not likely true at softer times in the market. If you want to have your project competitively bid, you must determine whether such a response is a contractor's opening gambit or the hard truth about the time and place you want to build.

Here are the most common contract structures for residential building, along with pros and cons and helpful hints on how to maximize the pros and minimize the cons.

Competitive Bid

You and/or your architect give plans and specifications to more than one contractor (no more than five). Those contractors submit bids to you that reflect a fixed price for which they will execute the construction project.

This approach requires lots of up-front work for you and/or your architect: getting the design conveyed accurately through the plans and specifications down to the last detail, choosing contractors qualified to bid, and coordinating the bid process. See chapter 9 if you want to explore this approach further.

Pros: You are likely to get the best price for the work specified. Contractors will find gaps in the plans and specifications during bidding and may offer ideas on cost savings.

Cons: You may not end up with your favorite contractor. Some contractors may express a lack of familiarity with the selection, bid, and contract processes. This response may be genuine if you're approaching small contractors. You are really controlling the process with a competitive bid, and it's scary for inexperienced contractors to offer the firm commitments this approach demands. Contractors may ask you to disclose a lot of information prior to bidding. It is fair to tell them the number of other bidders, but don't share the names of bidders or the amount of your budget until the bids are in and you have negotiated a final price with one contractor. The contractors are not obliged to tell you anything about how they came up with their prices.

Best Owner Approach: See chapter 9.

Design/Build

The design/build contract structure is one-stop shopping from the beginning of the design phase through the end of construction. The contractor works with you to design the building project. The contractor also does cost estimating through this design phase. He ultimately offers a fixed price to execute the construction work. Some contractors provide in-house design professionals, some subcontract the design portion out to an architect, and some do it themselves.

Pros: That one-stop shopping is pretty irresistible. If you have gotten to this contractor by way of a good selection process, he enters the process as the chosen one. He knows you think highly of him and are ready to have him guide you through both the design and the construction phases. That's a lot of good faith to start a relationship with. The design phase is usually inexpensive. You get a contractor's perspective on design from day one, along with value engineering (finding ways to save money) and some degree of open-book negotiations (revealing his costs). The contractor will be familiar with the finished design and its costs well before construction begins.

Cons: This is the preferred approach for most contractors, since it gives them the most control. Typically, there are no checks and balances offered by a third party. Owners usually have high expectations of having all their needs met. However, the very nature of this all-inclusive approach is that you may walk into it woefully ignorant of how to get those expectations met. Basically, anything not asked for won't show up in the plans and specifications. You may get inferior design solutions that are less expensive to execute than what might be designed by a third-party professional. Designs may not be perfected, since the contractor presumes these plans will be only for his own use. This lack of clarity in the plans can lead to disputes later.

Best Owner Approach: If you amend the standard approach, you can have the best of both worlds: one-stop shopping and some control. First, don't work to a number. In other words, don't say to the design builder, "I have $200,000. What can I get?" You may get a $150,000 house. You should lean toward design builders who offer design services from professional architects or designers. You should enter into a design/build contract that is broken into two phases. The design phase and resulting plans and specifications should be separate from the construction phase. You retain the right to walk away with the design or stay with that contractor for the construction phase. Between the two phases, you should seek out second opinions on the designs and pricing you've received. Then decide if you want to go forward with that design/builder. You may be told that the designs will cost you more this way. Not true. You will pay for those designs one way or another. Design just seems free when its cost is being tucked into the construction phase.

Negotiated

For the negotiated contract approach, you should have complete or partial plans and specifications. After a good contractor selection process, you negotiate a fixed cost of the work with the selected contractor who will later execute it. It's used very often for high-end homes that are architect-designed. An architect may suggest a contractor deemed most appropriate for the project size and type, and with whom he has a good working relationship.

Pros: You can choose your favorite contractor. Like design/build, this approach starts with a lot of goodwill and offers value engineering and some degree of open-book negotiations. You have plans that were prepared independent of that contractor, so you have less risk of insufficient design that's inherent in the design/build approach. And since you own the plans, it's easy to walk away if you don't like the prices you're getting or anything else about this relationship.

Cons: Since the project is not being competitively bid, people sometimes go into negotiations with incomplete plans and specifications and the process can start to incur some of the risks of design/build. The architect may be lessening his workload by taking you to a contractor he trusts to fill in the blanks. Prices may be excessive. If you can't negotiate, you may feel like part of a one-way relationship with little control.

Best Owner Approach: Try to enter the negotiation with fairly complete plans and looking for a fixed price from the contractor. If you are using an architect or designer, it's okay to accept a little less detail in the designs, since the dynamics at work here are very different than in a competitive bid. However, you should ask for a reasonable degree of thoroughness so the contractor is doing mostly pricing and value engineering, not design. Whatever evolution in the design does occur should be tightly reflected in the finished plans and specifications before you enter into a contract.

Construction Management

The construction management (CM) approach originated on huge commercial projects where even big construction companies would be delighted to have just a small portion of the work, and where the owners did not want to pay a general contractor a standard markup on all that work. What they really needed was someone who would work for a fee and manage a bunch of contractors and their individual projects . . . and "construction management" was born.

These days, CM has come to be a catchall for many variations of standard approaches. In residential projects, it usually means that the owner provides plans and specifications. The CM takes bids from subcontractors and suppliers. Together, you and the CM review these bids, and you have the final say in choosing those to be involved in the project. You have separate contracts with each of these subcontractors. The CM then manages all these entities for an agreed-upon fee. The CM may or may not do the general construction work on the job. You may hear several other definitions of CM.

Pros: You can select your favorite contractor. This is an open-book approach, with almost all prices revealed. The CM represents the owner during the bid phase.

Cons: If this sounds a little messy, that's because it can be. You can't be certain that the prices you are seeing from subcontractors are their actual prices and that the CM isn't hiding or getting some portion of that money. Some contractors tout that they only charge a 5 percent fee as a CM. Then why would they do this work if they can get 15 percent as the profit and overhead on a more conventional approach? If you have separate contracts with each subcontractor, that's a hassle. The contractor bears no liability for their work, and he may even have trouble controlling them since he doesn't hold the purse strings.

Best Owner Approach: Beware. This is the "Trust me, I'm your pal" approach, and its many variations have grown out of the desire to lessen liability and gain favor with owners with the open-book policy. If your project has large subcontracts and not much general construction, I think this approach can be appropriate. For instance, imagine you are replacing all the wiring and plumbing in a large old house. A general contractor would only have to do some cutting and patching, and coordinate the work of the subcontractors. It may not be reasonable to pay a general contractor the standard markup on all the subs' work, so you would just negotiate a fee for his supervision services and helping you through the bidding of electrical and plumbing work. However, if you use a CM for a full-blown project, I would recommend a hybrid between CM and more conventional contract structures. Enjoy the benefit of the contractor's representation and an open-book process during bidding of the subcontractors' work. Negotiate his fee to manage the project and the cost of the general construction portion of the work. Roll all those numbers together into a guaranteed maximum price (GMAX) and sign a contract, now making him the general contractor with full responsibility for the entire project. You pay only him, and he answers to you with the subcontractors now neatly under his wing.

Modular Construction

A construction manufacturer constructs your building in a factory to be delivered to your property. These manufacturers are not just the double-wide builders. They usually offer several standard home plans. They even build from architects' plans. They produce entire small homes or build in modules (room sections) or panels (wall sections) to be assembled into homes of almost any size and shape. Some manufacturers have in-house designers to assist with your plans. Log cabin kits also fall under this category. Typically, you pay 10 percent up front and the other 90 percent upon delivery.

Pros: You can enjoy significant cost savings (10 to 30 percent), especially if you are using the manufacturer's standard materials in a simple plan. Any design work is done at a minimal cost and often deducted from the price of the delivered product. You can watch your house being built on the factory floor. Site-related construction issues such as weather and theft are averted. Their schedules are very reliable once you get on their calendar.

Cons: If you want a building with lots of custom or high-end features, you will not enjoy any savings with this approach. There is very little competition for modular companies in many areas. You will need a contractor on site to coordinate the work that is outside of the manufactured structure, including site work, a foundation, and tying in the utilities. Determining where the modular work ends and the contractor's work on site begins can be tricky in terms of liability. You must get the building permit. Getting the required building inspections to get a certificate of occupancy can be tricky.

Best Owner Approach: Use this approach if you want no bells and whistles in your home. The only real scheduling issue is getting on the manufacturer's list, but the on-site contractor must be ready to receive the manufactured building or modules. Talk to both the manufacturer and the on-site contractor about who's responsible for what, and reflect those lines of division in their respective contracts. You must suss out the inspection process for this approach within your town, since an inspector can't see work in progress. Some manufacturers have approval from their state and nearby states to hire third-party inspectors to get buildings and modules inspected on their factory floor.

Time and Materials and Cost Plus

The time-and-materials method is typically used for smaller jobs and for those with hidden conditions where the scope of work is not easily determined. The contractor or subcontractor charges you at an hourly rate for labor, including markup for overhead and profit plus the cost of materials. The contractor's profit and overhead are included in his labor rate, and he may mark up the cost of materials provided.

A variation on this method is known as cost plus. In this method, the "cost" is the contractor's actual costs for time and materials. "Plus" is the contractor's markup for overhead and profit. In the end, cost plus is basically the same as the time-and-materials approach.

Pros: Little preparatory work is required on your part. These methods are to your advantage in three circumstances: repairs, unforeseen conditions, and small jobs. If you come home from vacation to find your pipes burst or one day look up and see a rotted soffit under the roof, no one can determine what needs to be done without some investigation. So to ask a contractor for a fixed price at that time would be to your disadvantage. He would have no choice but to set a price that would cover any eventuality. On small jobs, like replacing your bathroom floor or cutting in a new doorway, an estimate would be helpful, but the work necessary to carry out one of the other contract structure options just isn't worth your time. So one of these approaches is the way to go in such cases.

Cons: You have almost no control and the contractor has little incentive to complete work in a timely fashion. The price can get out of control and is not determined until the work has been completed. You must monitor the contractor's time closely.

Best Owner Approach: There are six ways to gain some control:

- Make sure the contractor doesn't have too many crew members. You don't need Junior standing around getting paid fifty dollars an hour on a three-man crew when two would suffice.

- Ask for a definition of "time" up front. Does the crew charge for travel? Can they get all needed supplies in one trip? What other expenses can be expected?

- Ask the contractor to open what he needs to, diagnose the problem, and give you a proposed scope of work and an estimate. Negotiate it if need be. For instance, you might say, "That sounds a bit steep, but let's see what you get done the first day and revisit that estimate as we go."

- If you're doing a larger project or one that becomes larger than you thought after the initial diagnosis, you may want to stop and negotiate a fixed price.

- Monitor the time closely. You don't want to get a bill for double the labor time you roughly recall. Hang a piece of paper inside a kitchen cupboard and write the date and time the contractor arrives and the time he pulls out each day. Compare your tally to the bills you get (page 169).

- Lastly, you can offer to be their assistant in picking things up from the supply place and doing cleanup.

Build-to-Suit

Build-to-suit is a sales approach used by developers. If you buy their land, they will build you a house. These are typically not custom houses, but "customized" houses from a selection of their plans.

Pros: You get one-stop shopping, and most design work is done before the land is even purchased. Some developers offer financing, title insurance, closings, moving services, the works.

Cons: This is not the approach for anyone wanting a custom home. You have to take the whole deal. You cannot purchase the desired land unless you agree to have the contractor, specified by the developer, build you a house with his plans and his contracts. The most common complaint about this approach is the allowances. The model home you fell in love with has the highest end materials. With your approval, the developer includes in the overall cost allowances for things like kitchen cabinets, carpeting, and floor tile, which you will choose later. When you go to choose these items, you might find the sum included to pay for them is insufficient to get materials anywhere near the quality you expected. This leads to big up-charges and you feeling you've been had.

Best Owner Approach: Check with the future neighbors to see how their project went with this developer. Always ask the price of the home you first visited, the one with the great finishes. As much as possible, modify the designs and selection of materials to meet your needs. Have a lawyer review the proposed contract. Independently price out any allowance items (cabinets, carpets, tile, etc.) before signing to be sure your overall cost includes the quality of finish materials you anticipate.

Which of the seven contract structures best applies to you and your project? Pick that option and be willing to consider a couple more as you approach contractors to carry out your plans.

Once you have determined that the construction documents reflect everything you want done and included in your home, you are ready to find a contractor. Don't panic . . . Jesus was a carpenter.

> *Ask about your neighbors, then buy the house.*
>
> —JEWISH PROVERB

CHAPTER 8

The Second Oldest Profession
Selecting and Working with a Contractor

Whether you're creating a pool of contractors to bid in a competitive process or selecting one contractor to hire under any of the other contract structures, this chapter will provide you with a step-by-step approach for picking the right one for you. It then covers the inside skinny on working with a contractor.

- He Was Such a Nice Guy: Choosing More Wisely
- Welcome to His World: Working with a Contractor
- To Protect and Serve: Protecting Your Project and Serving Your Contractor

He Was Such a Nice Guy: Choosing More Wisely

What's the number one fatal mistake that owners make? They chat with a contractor or two and choose a relative stranger they think is a "nice guy." Now add to this relationship the issues of deadlines, taste, communication, quality of workmanship, invasion of their space, and more money than they've ever spent. Just what are the odds they will still think him such a nice guy after facing all this together? Okay, so "nice" isn't enough. You need to do a little work and be an informed consumer to get nice, competent, fair, timely, thorough, and dedicated. Here's how you do that.

> **Pitfall**
> Every construction horror story starts out the same way: "I thought he was such a nice guy."

Step 1: Create a Pool of Candidates

To gather a list of potential contractors, network. Talk to friends, colleagues, architects, the town building inspector, suppliers, real estate brokers, loan officers, and people whose recent construction work you admire. If you have to, resort to the yellow pages. Then call the Better Business Bureau, and screen the names you've gathered for anyone on their complaints list. Think long and hard before including contractors on your list who are friends, family members, or spouses of friends.

Step 2: Make Contact

Call the contractors on your list to see who would be interested in doing your project. Be prepared to share information about the project, but remember that this is preliminary contact with strangers. Keep it broad and simple. Tell them the size and nature of the project, the location, your general timeline,

> *"A man in the house is worth two in the street."*
> —MAE WEST

and what contract structure(s) you are considering. If they ask money questions, they're just screening to see if you're delusional about numbers. Any talk that makes you sound savvy will quell this concern... like "What's your work been coming in at per square foot lately?" Find out their level of interest, their availability, and whether or not they have all necessary licensing or certification required in your state. Have three to five contractors at the end of this process if you plan to bid the work competitively.

Step 3: Conduct Interviews

Meet individually with the contractors on your list, and ask each to bring a portfolio of his work. Remember, in the case of bidding, your goal is to get a final list of contractors, any of whom you would be glad to have on the job. If you plan to do your project under any of the other contract structures, the interview will be one of only two steps in your final selection. Be sure to cover the topics below with each contractor to really get to know how each will get your job done. Take good notes. Remember that you are being sized up too, and this is the first impression you will give to the ultimate contractor for your project. A good contractor will always see an informed and involved owner as an asset to the project. So don't be shy!

- What's the contractor's availability now and later? What jobs is he working on now, when will they be completed, and what are their budgets? You don't want to be the least significant job in a busy contractor's workload.

- Ask about his work crew. Are they on the payroll full-time? Get a description of this team. How many are on it? How long have they worked for the contractor? What are their duties, and who would be assigned to oversee your project? You probably don't want a paper contractor, who hires workers only as needed for each job. Better contractors have workers who will commit to them long term, and vice versa.

- Ask under what contract structure the contractor usually works, likes to work, is willing to work. In boom markets, most contractors would prefer not to bid competitively because they can get plenty of work without competing.

- What does the contractor think of the local permit process, and what is his current relationship with its players? Bad blood between your contractor and the permit people can be played out on your project.

- If you have plans, show them to the contractor, and discuss his vision for executing them. Note whether he shows interest in being understood by you and can communicate technical information. If he prefers talking over your head, fails to get his point across, or worse yet, gets exasperated trying to explain something to you, think where this could end up in the next several months.

- Depending on the level of detail of your plans and your preceding conversation, the contractor may have quite a bit of information about your project at this point. If so, ask, "What are your impressions? Do you see any problems?" You will get some helpful information about possible flaws in your design, scope, or anticipated schedule. More important, you can judge some of his skills in project analysis and organization. What is he worried about? What's the weak link and why? If he shares good insights with you, chances are he will do so throughout your project.

- Check out his portfolio to make sure it includes a list of references. Ask him to highlight the names of references whose projects are most similar to yours. Note how recent those are. Has it been a while since he's done your kind of project? If so, why, and is his crew the same as when he did those projects?

- Diplomatically find out a little about his personal life. You may not want a contractor on your job who's in the middle of a divorce or headed for heart surgery. Be quiet for a while too. You will be excited to discuss your project, but give the contractor time to reveal himself to you.

- Note your general impression of the contractor. Do you like him? Could you work well with him? Does he seem reasonable, flexible, interested in your input, respectful of both you and your partner?

Step 4: Call References

Contractor's references are the people most like you in this whole process. They've been in your very shoes. Talking with them is an essential step, and here's the important thing to know. The people you call for references are just as much a variable as the contractors you are asking questions about. If you just pick up  **Pitfall**

You're doing only half the job if you call a reference and just ask, "How did your project go?"

the phone and ask each reference, "How was this contractor to work with?" you will hear all sorts of good and bad stories, from all sorts of people, and you will end up with very little information with which to measure one contractor against another. You want to reduce the impact of your references' personality traits on the information gathered. The best way is by asking pertinent, identical, and concrete questions of people whose opinions matter to you. Here's how you do just that:

Whom to Call

- Refer to each contractor's list of references to identify a couple people who have had work done that bears some resemblance to your project.

- Find out about clients not on the list of names provided by the contractor and call them too. To do this, start with one of the references on the contractor's list whose completion was recent. Ask them what other projects the contractor was working on when he was doing their job. If that name is not on your list, things may not have gone so smoothly on that job and you should know why. Look up the phone number and call.

- The most valuable references may be those of professionals who work with contractors regularly. They can compare and contrast many of the

What Your Contractor Can't Tell You

contractors you are considering and give you a different perspective from that of a layperson. So call architects (even if you're not using one for your job), subcontractors, and suppliers.

What to Say

Introduce yourself and explain that you are calling for a reference and have some very specific questions. Tell the person he is welcome to add any comments when you're through with your questions.

Explain how this information will be used. Promising not to share it with anyone else might make the person feel more free to comment honestly. These are litigious times, and people fear being sued or getting a nasty phone call if they give a bad reference. If you're getting the cold shoulder, just move along to the next reference. Note your impression of the reference too. Is the person reasonable, persnickety, cranky, easygoing?

Questions to Ask

Write the following questions on a couple pieces of paper with enough space between them to write your answers. Photocopy and fill out one set for each reference contacted.

• What project did you work on with this contractor?

• What was the original construction budget or per square foot cost?

• What was the final construction budget or percentage of change of cost?

• Describe the quality of work.

• Was the site kept clean, safe, and organized?

• Was the project completed on time?

• How was the working relationship between all parties?

• Were any crew members a particular asset or a detriment on the project?

• Did the contractor pay his bills?

• Were any liens filed on your property?

• Would you work with this contractor again?

• If so, would you have any conditions for doing so?

• Other comments

If all you're hearing from references is "good," "great," "liked him," dig a little deeper or get a few more references. This might very well be a great contractor, but no one is perfect. If you do go forward with this person, you should know his weak points even if they're tiny, so that you can be prepared to work around them.

Step 5: The Chosen Ones

If you complete steps 1 to 4, you've got a lot of valuable information on which to base a sound selection, and you're moving along like a pro. Now you need to weigh this information and other considerations that enter into your decision.

If you have a big pile of interview notes and answers from references, you can reduce the information to a more manageable format in a couple of ways. You can create a database with the contractors' names on the vertical axis, the questions on the horizontal axis and the answers in the intersecting fields. This will give you a one- or two-page matrix for easy comparison at a glance. If you're feeling very nerdy, you can set up a little scoring system. First, look at all the questions in the horizontal axis and assign a percentage value to each based on their respective importance to you. The percentage values of all the questions should add up to 100. For example, maybe you don't much care when the contractor is available to start, but the quality of his work is imperative to you. You might assign 5 percent to his response regarding availability and 10 percent to the references' input on the quality of his work. Now score the responses: 1 = poor (or no); 2 = fair (or not sure); 3 = good (or yes). Multiply each by the percentage assigned. Compare the totals, and see how they sit with your general feelings about how the contractors compared with one another.

As you review answers and weigh impressions, keep in mind that contractors present themselves very differently, and sometimes the good guys finish last. Some very honest souls may sit there and annoy you by scratching their heads over your plans and picking them apart. Others may put you at ease instantly with a warm smile and lots of compliments . . . and good looks don't hurt. Some contractors are intimidated by the socioeconomic chasm between you and them. Help each contractor state his case, and listen carefully to the real content of his words. After all, is construction really a field that should hinge on charm? The curmudgeonly fretter might be just the guy for you.

Ever heard this old adage? "If you want something done, give it to someone busy." Good contractors are often busy and are worth waiting for. Idle contractors . . . you gotta wonder. So don't discount the ones that are booked up, and don't jump at the chance to sign up with someone just because he's available immediately.

Be wary of contractors who try to drive a wedge between you and anyone: your designer, your spouse, the city inspectors. If during the interview, a contractor has a tendency to bad-mouth others in the process or is just dying to tell you why your plans stink, he may be a divisive character and you may be the one he's bad-mouthing later.

A project is only as good as its people. If your references convince you that their project was a success because of a "super-duper super," be sure that person is part of your project, and right through to the end.

> 66 *The employer generally gets the employees he deserves.* 99
>
> —WALTER GILBEY

What Your Contractor Can't Tell You

You may have a contractor in the running who was recommended by your designer or architect as someone he works well with. When is it a benefit and when is it a drawback to work with an architect and contractor who have worked together? Generally, it is a benefit. The upside is that they have an established relationship. They can speak shorthand. They trust each other and probably think well of each other. They will cut each other slack, do favors for each other, and you will benefit. But remember, this is a triangular relationship. You hold the money and they hold the knowledge. They are likely to work with each other again, but not with you. Make sure you are comfortable with your role in this: that you feel like a respected member of the team and not the odd one out.

It's a free country, but I say, hire a friend for a thing like this only if you're willing to run the risk of damaging or even losing that friendship.

If you live in an area where licensing is not required, the market conditions influence what constitutes a "contractor." In a hot market, everyone seems to move up a notch. A day laborer is a carpenter, a carpenter is a contractor, and a contractor is a developer. Keep an eye out for the newcomers. You don't want them cutting their teeth on your project. They might well not know how to manage crews, handle inspectors, give you accurate numbers that hold up, or face the day-to-day stresses of the job once it's under way.

Beware of fast growth. While all big contractors started out small, this transition isn't for everyone. Getting into the big leagues requires a growth spurt. A contractor has to hire on more crew, buy new trucks, get a bigger office, and usually take on more debt. The nature of his work changes a lot too. He goes from being a worker to being a manager of people and money. Some guys were made for this transition, and some, it turns out, were not. If a company is to fail, this is likely when it will happen. Find out how long the contractor's business has been this size. If he's in a growth spurt, talk it out with him and be sure you're comfortable that he can handle it. If you smell panic or desperation, don't take pity, take flight!

Insider's Tip

If a contractor's business is growing fast, approach with caution.

> 66 *Hire a young carpenter, but an old physician.* 99
> —CHINESE PROVERB

Step 6: Qualifications

Now that you know whom you are willing to have work on your project, there are still some hard facts you must gather. A lender will require a couple of these things too. When you have chosen your finalist (or finalists in the case of bidding), ask him (them) to submit responses and necessary paperwork regarding the following questions (if need be, blame this request on your loan officer):

- Does the contractor carry workers' compensation insurance (page 123)? If so, he should be prepared to give you proof of that with a certificate of insurance before work starts on site.

- Lenders do not usually ask for a contractor's financial statement or a guarantee against his failure on the project, such as bonding or a letter of credit. For them, a contract is enough, and it probably is for you too. But talk to your lender or lawyer about these tools for additional protection if you'd like to consider them. One of the best measures of a contractor's financial stability is suppliers. If he has a good record for paying his bills, chances are he has a flush bank account and uses the payments he gets from clients to pay his bills as he should. So if you didn't call suppliers as a reference already, you may want to for this purpose.

- Has the contractor been sued? If so, when, where, by whom, and what was the outcome? Many contractors have been sued, so don't let a yes answer necessarily remove one from consideration. Hear him out and investigate if need be.

- Have the principals of this firm ever declared bankruptcy? To me, this is a bigger red flag than having been sued. Remember, bankruptcy is a last resort for the insolvent, a way of gaining relief from debts. If the answer to this question is yes, you'd better hear a very compelling explanation if you plan to go forward with any comfort.

- Have any of the principals of this company operated as principals under another firm's name? If so, what name(s)? If someone drops out of your process once he hears this question, good riddance to him. If a company has gone bankrupt, lost its good financial standing, or gained a bad reputation for any reason, it may hang out a fresh, new shingle so that the bad references die with their old business name. I know one bunch that operated under three company names in five years. As soon as they'd get a few complaints made to the Better Business Bureau, they'd pick another name.

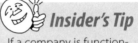

Insider's Tip

If a company is functioning under a different name than it once did, you'd better find out why.

- Has this contractor placed liens on properties (page 129)? If so, how many? Describe the circumstances and how these liens were resolved. These liens are part of the public record at your town or city clerk's office. Feel free to check out the facts and if possible, call the lienee as a reference.

If your preferred contractor satisfies your request for qualifications and those of your bank, you're ready to make your final selection. Congratulations. Now don't you feel more at ease than you would have if you just picked the "nice guy"? You are ready to move forward with whichever contract structure you have chosen.

Welcome to His World: Working with a Contractor

You need to understand who you will be employing in this critical role. So now we go inside the heads of a general contractor and an owner, to illuminate the dynamics behind this unique relationship.

What Drives Him

Two things drive a contractor: money and his reputation. A contractor prospers in four ways:

- From what he charges for his labor

- By marking up others' labor

- By marking up materials he supplies

- By collecting a percentage of the total construction budget as his profit

How he chooses to charge for these four things is the first half of the equation that makes up his financial standing. The other is outlay of funds. Running a job costs money. The contractor must pay a hefty price for insurance for himself and his crew. He has overhead that includes everything from his ad in the yellow pages to the rental of space heaters. And he pays others to work. For him the game is to maximize the efficiency of all his time, resources, and people on a job site to keep costs down. In a fixed-price deal, if he does this, he will get the profit he carried. If he does not, and the project becomes inefficient, added costs will eat into his profit.

A contractor gets work based on his reputation. If he produces quality work in a timely fashion and keeps subcontractors, suppliers, and owners thinking highly of how he's done it, he will get more work.

What Worries Him

In coordinating a project, a contractor is juggling many variables that may impact on his income and his reputation. His plan for doing it is a fragile thing, dependent on the action of others. On the money front, the cost of materials changes every day. If he is committed to a fixed price, he must pray he can get those materials for the costs he carried. Delays of every kind can eat a big hole in his profit. Slow shipping of materials, sick crew members, and changes in the scope of work triggered by you, an architect, or an inspector can all mess him up.

Ethical dilemmas worry him. When he's negotiating or competitively bidding a project, he knows that good guys finish last. If he prices every bit of work shown and that which must be done but is not shown, his price will be higher than that of someone who chooses only to price what's shown on the plans and charge you later for the rest.

You, the owner, and those representing you are a big worry. Your expectations, your relationship, your communication, your budget, your timeliness, your standards, and your ability and desire to settle little disputes and pay him are all a crapshoot at the outset of a project. How this all plays out could affect both his income and his reputation.

> *Nothing astonishes men so much as common sense and plain dealing.*
>
> —RALPH WALDO EMERSON

What Worries You

Owners' worries change over the course of the project. Initially, owners worry most about what they can afford. Then they worry about making decisions with a spouse or partner. Then comes choosing people for the job and wondering what all the horror stories are about. They know that lots of people have troubles on construction jobs, but don't know why or how they can preempt that. So they worry about being taken advantage of. They are rarely prepared for the volume of decisions they have to make, and they tend to worry about getting everything done in a way they won't regret later. If one spouse is more responsible for the owners' participation in the project, that spouse hopes the other remains supportive and thinks he's doing a good job. Toward the end, most owners worry about stamina and patience, as they just want the project to be over.

The good news is you can remove much risk and lessen most of these worries through good planning as laid out in this book. You can have a budget, a clear shared vision, and most decisions made before you even meet a contractor.

A contractor does have opportunities to take advantage. Not all will be revealed to you. You have no way of knowing for sure that the prices you receive from him reflect his actual costs plus a reasonable profit. You have to go on faith much of the time, and ultimately, you are forced to take it or leave it when it comes to prices. Some people really don't enjoy this part of the process. So how do you know you can trust this person? Past behavior is the best indicator of future actions, and people tend to be quite consistent in their treatment of others. So rely on those references. They will paint a fairly clear picture of whom you're considering for your contractors.

 Pitfall

The contractors who take advantage of owners are usually the same guys who stiff their suppliers and have subcontractors who won't work with them again.

To Protect and Serve: Protecting Your Project and Serving Your Contractor

Some of my best friends are contractors, but I would be remiss if I didn't try to explain the culture they bring you into. Throughout this book are statements that may seem conflicting. One minute I say how well you need to treat a contractor to be an attractive client, and the next I suggest how to keep from being robbed by one. As strange as it seems, these positions are not mutually exclusive. You must find a balance, a certain level of detachment, and do both. I was at a job site just after O.J. Simpson's ride in that white Ford Bronco back in 1996. The crew was in hot debate about whether O.J. was a good guy or had killed his ex-wife. I asked "Why can't he be a good guy AND he killed his ex-wife?" to which the job super brought down the house with "Amy, you've spent way too much time with contractors." I didn't come by this odd perspective by osmosis. For the first several years that I worked as a construction manager for owners, I was frequently shocked to find people I liked and respected trying to rob my projects. Over time I came to understand each of us is a product of our circumstances. These guys didn't pick up a hammer one day and say, "I think I'll go rip people off." No, they entered a profession that's competitive, where risk and the margin for error are high, the margin of profit is low, the contracts are tough, costs change every day, and clients run the gamut from being hyper-demanding to missing in action. In time most contractors come to believe they need to take profit when they can, and there the rationalizing begins.

We all do it. Did you ever take Post-its from the office? Then you're a thief too, and I'm sure you have a perfectly good rationale for taking them. A contractor's self-talk can sound like this: "I so underbid this project." "These people don't know what they want." "I'm doing so many extras they don't even know about." String this rationale together over many years, many projects, and many contractors, and you see a whole culture based on getting the most for giving the least. Ultimately, contractors are both victims and perpetrators in this unique culture of theirs and the virtuos find it hard to survive.

As I was writing this very section, a project manager for a large construction company called to tell me he was leaving the big job he landed at a big firm only two years ago. He will go out on his own now as an independent contractor. When I asked why, he said, "Because I want to be able to face my friends and neighbors at Little League games. I'm getting paid a fortune for doing half as much as I did on my own before, but I can't sleep nights with the stuff they make me do." It's doubly sad because the company he's leaving used to be renowned in this area. It was the darling of the industry. It did elegant, interesting work and was led by a sweetheart. But this man wanted to grow, and so he partnered with a more mercenary contractor to help him do that. They're making tons of money now, but they don't have many friends or repeat customers. Yes, it's hard to stay in this business and be a righteous soul.

Insider's Tip
Construction contracting is a world in which good guys finish last.

I call the policy I have adapted to live in this culture "no first strike." I will do everything in my power to be a good owner. I will give timely decisions, pay for work done, communicate clearly, even bring the coffee to the crew on cold days. I will accept mistakes, help resolve problems, be fair, and bend over backward to try to make everything go as smoothly and efficiently as possible for the contractor. There will be no first strike from me—but if I catch a contractor trying to cheat me, that's it. I stand ready to invoke the nastiest clause in the contract I have at my disposal, to shut that job down if I have to, and to make sure I give honest references to any potential future customers. Nice, huh? No, not at all, but as tough as it sounds, it's also fair, and I don't even have to explain this position. They can see it. I can live with that, so can the contractors, and the projects come through better for it.

A Piece of Work

For my first five years as an owner's representative, I found myself hurt and angry when I realized that a contractor with whom I had worked for months was robbing me. When caught, he lied or didn't care or somehow revealed a crookedness in his dealings with me that left me crestfallen. To make matters worse, I would then have to fight with this former friend to negotiate a solution, and I always got the bad end of those deals. These contractors genuinely didn't seem guilty. I had to find a new mindset if I was going to survive in this business. After much observation with as much objectivity as I could muster, I came to the following conclusions: No one thinks he himself is a crook. Even if his hand is all the way at the bottom of that cookie jar when the lights are thrown on, he will have a good rationale that makes it possible for him to sleep nights. Accept the premise that a contractor's job is to get as much money from you while doing as little work with as few materials as possible. Yours is to get as much work and materials out of him for the least amount of money. And the trick is to do this in an atmosphere of fun and mutual respect.

If these things sound mutually exclusive, let cartoons be your guide. Remember the cartoon with Wile E. Coyote and the sheepdog? Not the roadrunner, but the sheepdog. They would meet each morning at a tree with a punch clock. They would punch in and say kindly to each other, "Morning, Bert" . . . "Morning, Sam." Then Sam would spend the day trying to steal sheep by any elaborate means necessary with the assistance of Acme products, and Bert would spend the day catching and walloping Sam. At the end of the day, they would punch out at the tree and say, "G'night, Bert" . . . "G'night, Sam," and go their separate ways to rest up for the same thing the next day.

Believe it or not, this is the mind-set I've adopted. I am the sheepdog, and the contractor is the coyote. We can be the best of friends, but I remember what motivates him and what motivates me and guard my interests. I can try every other approach that owners have tried forever—beg, be tough, offer my jugular, berate, whine, hope, throw tantrums, make nice—but this is the mind-set that works. Now you are ready to read the story of a good contractor. People are usually horrified that I think of Jerry as such. This is what separates the experienced from the inexperienced owner.

A few years back, I replaced another owner's representative on a job building nine duplex homes. I inherited Jerry as the project's general contractor, and I was anxious to meet him, having heard he was "a piece of work." We met in the job trailer that fall day, and there was no mystery about him. Jerry was a happy-go-lucky, unabashed thief. He seemed the type that had a smile for everyone he robbed. The good news was that our roles were clear. My job was to keep him from taking all the money and leaving us with a bad project. He was the coyote, and I was the sheepdog. We were both happy in our roles, and I was delighted by the lack of subterfuge.

At every turn, I caught Jerry pilfering from the project. First he removed acres of topsoil worth a fortune. Then he started substituting inferior materials for those specified. I caught him more often than not, and we would negotiate a solution, but the conclusion of the job was a classic. Three of the nine buildings on the project were complete, and I went to the site to inspect them. The buildings were to have double-hung windows, meaning both top and bottom sashes would slide up and down. When I tested the windows, the top sashes were fixed in place. Jerry had substituted single-hung windows for the double-hungs specified. When I asked him what happened to the windows, he said there was a twelve-week delay in shipping the double-hungs and that the windows he installed were in stock and still met code requirements for fire egress. This changing of specified material in the midst of a job is a huge breach of an agreement, and yet it's done, or at least attempted, on a regular basis by brazen contractors who think you're not watching closely. The windows were fine for our needs, and so it was now only about money. I said, "So when were you going to tell me this, and what are the savings to me?"

He answered, "Nothing. There's not a dime's worth of difference between the singles and doubles. I could just get 'em on time for you to move people in here."

I bit my tongue and moved on to the next building, where I had the same conversation with the project super, Jerry's second-in-command. When I asked, "What are the savings to me, Mike?" he said, "Nothing. There's not a dime's worth of difference in cost." I thought, "You guys should have rehearsed better so you didn't say the same thing."

I returned to my office, called the supplier, and posed as the owner of a fictitious project. I got the prices for both types of windows and found that Jerry stood to pocket $18,275. A dime's worth of difference, my Aunt Fannie! Now I had the ammunition, but how to use it? Over the years, I had come to dread such confrontations. People never see themselves as thieves. They rationalize their behavior to themselves a hundred different ways. So when a good owner catches a contractor in the act, it's like holding a mirror up to him, and he may not like the reflection. I did not want a scene, and I wanted the project to benefit. Timing was everything. I was willing to live with the change in the windows. If I revealed the cost problem immediately, I would face several more weeks of Jerry trying to cheat me out of the money I recouped. No, he was feeling rich, smart, and content. I would wait. So I sat tight, made a little plan, and braced myself for the feathers that would fly in two months. The time passed without incident. At the last job meeting, we went through every item on the agenda, including Jerry's submission of the final requisition. Just as everyone was about to push their chairs back from the table, I said, "Hold it, there's one more item." I laid my notes on the window pricing in front of Jerry and said, "You tried to rob me of $18,000, Jerry."

I said nothing more and just waited. I was ready for the screaming to begin, maybe a table to be flipped, definitely a lot of defensive ranting on his part. Instead, Jerry looked at the notes, then tipped back his chair as he clasped his hands behind his head. A slow, gentle smile came across his face. He looked me straight in the eye and said, "I can't believe you caught that. How long have you known?"

"Two months," I said, smiling squarely at him.

"Damn, girl!" he said, wagging his head.

So as not to mess up our clean paperwork, Jerry proposed we leave the final requisition as it was, and he wrote me a check for $18,275 and hugged me good-bye that day. Two weeks later, Jerry was found severely beaten. Word on the street was that it was done by some of the subcontractors he had failed to pay. So I guess he was an equal-opportunity thief and not everybody's favorite contractor. But he will always be one of mine.

To Protect

Sure, like everyone in business, contractors range from pussycats to sharks, but if you treat them all like pussycats, what might happen to you? If you're more circumspect and guard against the sharks, what could it hurt? If you end up with a pussycat, great. You won't know that for sure until the last requisition, though. Others may take exception to my point of view, but many people have projects that fail. I have colleagues, other construction managers for owners, who have a long list of contractors with whom they would never work again. The only thing their projects have in common is themselves, so they are doing something wrong in their approach. Out of the dozens of contractors I've worked with, there's only one I wouldn't work with again, and I enjoy a reputation of being tough but fair.

On a day-to-day basis, when working with a contractor, you protect your interests in four ways: Be prepared, watch the store, keep chaos to a minimum, and always keep the financial incentives in your favor.

There's an old saying used on job sites by workers who have just executed something poorly. With a little giggle, they say, "You can't see it from my house," as they walk away from a bit of inferior work. This is not likely to happen if you have a presence on site. When the work's under way, watch the store (page 164). I went to a meeting of property managers recently. They revealed that those who have a presence on site, even only once a month, have half the repair costs to their apartment stock as those who don't. It's the same for construction or any practice. People perform better when they are accountable. Even if you don't know what you're looking at, they don't know that. Be there.

Chaos is profitable to contractors who know how to capitalize on it. Things can start swirling and divert attention and money to places they shouldn't be. Don't rise to the bait. Stay cool. Try to keep down the drama and be the calm in the storm. And as a couple, if you think kids can divide and conquer, you won't believe how clever grown-ups can be that way. Stay united even if it's only an act on site.

Pitfall

Chaos is very profitable
... but not for you.

When people tell me they can't get their contractor to show up toward the end of a project, I know right away that they have likely paid out too much money too soon (page 136). You must keep a financial incentive before him until the bitter end—especially for the bitter end, because the work then is annoying and the financial reward minimal. Did you ever try calling a dog that won't come? Didn't you wish you had a treat to entice him with right about then? Not so different.

To Serve

This is the part about being the best owner and team player you can be. Beyond the duties mapped out for you in your contract, you do this in three ways: Empathize and support, respect allegiances, and be a benevolent squeaky wheel.

Let the contractor know you are the very embodiment of the informed owner who is an asset to a project. This may take some doing, but with what you learn in this book, you should be able to convince him that this is so. Let him know you understand and respect the issues that drive him and what he worries about. You want him to make a profit. You want him to be able to keep his costs down and his productivity up. You want him to look good in the eyes of his crews and other potential customers. You want to give him the world's best letter of reference at the end of this project and make him the guest of honor at the housewarming. A good contractor is worth his weight in gold. Create an environment where he can thrive.

You wouldn't believe how many people are directly or indirectly involved in a full-scale project. Even a small renovation may bring twenty new people into your life. Be mindful that most of these people came by way of the contractor. They are his professional peers and will be for years to come. Respect the allegiance between these parties. Especially try not to get between a contractor and his subcontractors or suppliers once a project has begun.

We're all human. People have foibles and weaknesses that you may be able to help offset with your strengths. The contractor is juggling a lot of things that require technical skills, communication skills, organizational skills, and administrative skills. The chance of finding someone who excels equally in all four of these areas is unlikely. Though your roles are pretty well-defined on any project, you may find, as I have on every project I've ever participated in, that there's something you can bring to the party to help fill in the gaps. When you spot a gap that worries you, be a squeaky wheel about it, but offer help if you can. Maybe you really facilitate groups well and you can gently reframe things said in job meetings until people come to consensus. Maybe your contractor's desk is a mess and you can work with his administrative person to keep the paper trail flowing. In other words, don't expect he will be perfect at everything. Pitch in, but don't overstep.

A contractor has so many details to focus on minute to minute, day to day, maybe you can help bring the long-range focus into play. Look two weeks out and ask if everything's still on track for next month's deliveries. Will hunting season put a dent in the crew? Is there anything he needs from you to keep moving? Can you help out in any way?

Some of what you've learned about selecting and working with a contractor may be frightening. The truth be told, I like and trust everyone in my current stable of contractors. But these good relations are made possible only by remaining ever mindful of our respective roles. Do the same and you'll come to like and trust your contractor too.

CHAPTER 9

How Low Can They Go?

Bidding the Project

> If you're considering the competitive bid approach (page 83), this chapter will show you the process for getting the lowest price for the best work, just like a pro.
>
> - You Talkin' to Me? Should You Bid Your Project?
> - Package Deal: Getting Your Bid Package Together—the Four Elements
> - Going Out: What You and They Need to Do—the Four Stages

You Talkin' to Me?
Should You Bid Your Project?

When bidding out a project, an owner seeks prices for a predetermined scope of work from more than one contractor, through a competitive process. Prior to starting the bid phase the owner should complete the interview and reference steps outlined in chapter 8 to create a pool of three to five bidders. The goal is to award the bid to the best-qualified contractor offering the lowest price for the same services as the other bidders.

For over twenty years and in both boom times and bust times, I've debated the merits of the various contract structures (chapter 7) with my colleagues. With few exceptions, I have not found a better method than competitive bidding. It gets the design team to define a tight scope of work in a timely fashion and you gain comfort that you've obtained a qualified contractor's best price.

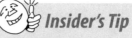 **Insider's Tip**

Of all the contract structures available to you, it is the competitive bid process that is most often used by professionals and is required when public funds are used on a project. Why? Because it's hard to beat for benefits to the owner.

Being unfamiliar with this process, you may first think it's a lot of work and a scary process that holds risks. It is a lot of work, and you must be organized. I would not recommend doing this alone for the first time unless you are confident and ambitious and have the time to dedicate to it. What makes it daunting is that this process requires you to get all your design work done up front, then get those designs into a bid package that any builder can understand. It then tests the validity of your assumptions about cost in a competitive forum. However, whether through this contract structure or any other, you will have to address these issues at some point. It's safer to make the decisions and face the budget realities at this early stage and with your wallet closed.

The size of your project will have a lot to do with whether or not you want to bid your project and how many of the steps discussed below you want to carry out to the letter. If you're thinking only about replacing your front door, a full-blown bid process would be excessive because your risk is too low to justify the effort a bid process calls for. However, you could certainly apply some of the concepts. You may want to find your door of choice and ask a couple recommended carpenters to give you a price to purchase, deliver, and install it. If, on the other hand, you are having a whole house built or a significant addition or renovation done, think seriously about bidding out the work. The professionals often draw the line at $25,000, bidding out all projects they anticipate costing more than that.

Any licensed architect and many other professionals in the construction industry (page 4) can run a competitive bid process. This chapter will spell out all the steps necessary for you to monitor their work or even carry out the process yourself.

Pitfall

It's not the high price that kills a project, it's the deceptively low one.

While a high price may be a painful shock and stop your project or some portion of it at the outset, it is the too-low price that puts your project in jeopardy during the actual construction. That number, whether given to you by way of oversight or trickery, will first lull you into a feeling of comfort. But no contractor can or will give you the quantity and quality of the work agreed upon once he knows he's losing money. He can't! This is when a project goes off the rails and you cannot get it back on track without money, and usually plenty of animosity. Nope, you want the right price, that magical number you can both live with . . . just barely.

Package Deal:
Getting Your Bid Package Together—the Four Elements

In order to put a project out to bid, you need to create a pool of contractors and give these "bidders" certain information about your project and an understanding of when and how they are to perform in this process. The information you pass on is called the bid package, and it contains four elements: plans and specifications, contract, instructions to bidders, and bid form. Everyone's tasks (owner, architect, and contractor) are carried out through four stages: going out to bid or disseminating the information, the bid period, bid day or getting the bids back, and bid analysis and awarding the contract.

Plans and Specifications

Your plans (page 24) could range from a sketch you made in a notebook to a fifty-page set of blueprints from an architect, depending on the size of your project and the level of detail you choose to allocate to them. The point is they're visual and include dimensions and notes explaining what you're looking at.

The level of detail for your specifications can vary from just the notes on the plans to a full-blown specification manual. They instruct on installation, assembly, and application of construction materials and set the standards for quality.

Contract with General Conditions

Be sure to talk to an insurance agent before you send out the bid package so that you can include any requirements in your contract. You will want to address workers' compensation, builder's risk and homeowner's insurance (pages 123-24).

Instructions to Bidders

This section of the package tells the bidders all they need to know about the bid process. It typically includes:

- A summary of the scope of work (e.g., 500-square-foot addition with vaulted ceiling) and reference to the construction documents

- An outline of your desired schedule, including project completion date

- The length of time contractors may be held to numbers they submit on the bid form. The contractor may not withdraw his bid until that date.

- How your selection of a contractor will be made. "Lowest and best bid" is a customary description.

- Good times to call you with questions, and information on access to the site (location and times) for construction

- Where to pick up the plans and specifications and whether or not the bidders have to pay for or return them

- Bidders are to report any errors or ambiguities they find in the construction documents. Then an addendum will be sent to all the bidders with the appropriate revised information. All such comments and questions must be submitted at least one week prior to the bid due date.

- Bids are to be based on the information conveyed in the construction documents. If a contractor wants to propose a substitution for any materials specified, he must propose this prior to submission of his bid. If approved, the change in material will be included in an addendum and distributed to all bidders. No other substitutions will be considered.

- Of course, win or lose, the contractors are dying to know what the other bidders submitted for numbers. This is addressed in one of three ways that you describe up front in the instruction to bidders. You can have the bidders join you and reveal the numbers to all as you open each bid. You can open them privately and not reveal the numbers to anyone. I like the third option of opening them privately and emailing a summary of the numbers to the bidders the next day. The facts don't change, but the drama is lessened with this third option. You can better absorb the information you received, verify it, make your selection, and then share the information.

- It is your intent to award a contract to the lowest bidder. However, you have the right to reject any bids. Your selection of the bidders is based on the information you gathered about them. If that information remains accurate, you'll likely want to accept the low bidder's number and select him as your contractor. But if circumstances change—if he's losing that superintendent you wanted, if he files for bankruptcy, if he takes on three huge new jobs during the bid phase—you have the right to cut him loose and accept another contractor's bid.

Bid Form

The contractors you have chosen will submit a proposal to do the work for a stipulated sum or base bid. They will also answer other questions to spell out their commitment to you in terms of cost, schedule, personnel, and how changes to the scope of work will be priced. It's easiest if you produce a bid form with blanks for all these responses, to go out as part of the bid package. The information on the bid form of the contractor you choose will become part of the contract you sign with him. The bid form should include space for all of the following responses that are pertinent to your project:

Base Bid: This is the total fixed price of all the work shown and described in the plans and specs.

Schedule of Values: This breaks down the base bid (preferably by the sixteen divisions) showing how much the excavation will cost, how much for the electrical, the doors and windows, etc. If you can get them to list their profit and overhead as a separate item, excellent! As you might imagine, contractors tend to bury the profit and overhead, scattered here and there under different line items, and you cannot identify it. Actually, what the contractor is looking to pocket on this job is his own personal concern, but it sure makes analysis of those line items easier if it's separated out.

List of Proposed Subcontractors: Within the general contractor's base bid and broken out in the schedule of values will be several numbers from subcontractors (trades). This list will tell you who they are.

Proposed Construction Schedule: Usually in bar graph form, this shows dates from start-up to completion of a project, highlighting all trades and major milestones (page 134).

Proposed Draw Schedule: This outlines the size of anticipated requisitions and when they will occur. You will need this to satisfy any lender involved and to monitor the contractor's progress. It should correspond to the milestones on the proposed construction schedule (page 137).

Allowances: These are amounts of money you would like the contractor to include in the base bid for materials you have not yet specified (page 28).

Unit Prices: These are most appropriate for renovation projects and should include units of work you want priced in advance in the event that the scope of work increases or decreases (page 28).

Alternate Prices: These are items that you would like priced separately that can alter the base bid scope of work later (page 29).

Pitfall

If you start a project without first determining how changes will be approved and calculated, you're just asking for it.

Change Order Formula: A change order is the mechanism for amending the contract. It can reflect a logistical change of no financial consequence. It can reflect a downgrade in materials or a decrease in the scope of work resulting in a decrease in the contract amount. However, most often it reflects an upgrade in materials or an increase in the scope of work resulting in an increase in the contract amount. Request the labor rates for the general contractor's crew members and for each of the subcontracted trades (painting, plumbing, masonry, etc.), and note on the bid form that these rates will be used to calculate both add and deduct change orders—that is to say, both (a) additions to the scope of work and (b) tasks that will be deleted from the scope of work. Also get a number for the contractor's profit and overhead he will be applying to change orders. It's fair for this to be higher than the profit and overhead in the base bid (15 to 20 percent is common).

Signature: The contractor signs the bid form under a statement of "bidder representation" that should read something like this: *"The Bidder has read and understands the Contract Documents as they relate to the work for which this bid is submitted. The Bidder has visited the site, is familiar with its location and conditions, and has correlated all observations made there with the work required in the Contract Documents. The bid is based on all materials, labor, equipment, and systems required by the Construction Documents without exception."*

Going Out:
What You and They Need to Do—the Four Stages

To move forward, or "go out to bid," you should now have a pool of contractors ready to bid the project (page 91) and a four-part bid package as described above. Get out the calendar and make a bid schedule, which includes:

• When and where the bid packages can be picked up or when they will be sent to the contractors

• The date and time of the walk-thru when the contractors can look at the building or site with you and/or your architect or designer

• When and where the bids are due back

Call the bidders you have selected to participate, and notify them of this schedule. It's best to distribute the bid package on a Friday and schedule the walk-thru for the middle of the next week after the contractors' workday ends. An early walk-thru helps keep them from procrastinating by getting them focused on the project right away. Make the bids due back to you two and a half weeks later on a Monday. This gives busy builders three weekends to work on their bids and get questions answered. Making the bids due on one set day will minimize your coordination work and be fair to all parties.

Your Ethics

This process is all about getting you the best price possible. For a contractor to really want to "sharpen his pencil" and take the time to look closely enough at your project to give you his best number, he needs to trust the process. So you need to run a trustworthy process. Your goal is to create a level playing field and give everyone a legitimate chance at scoring. Let each party have the exact same information in order to give you a price that is one of only a few variables you are considering. Ethics comes into this process right away. Each contractor needs to know and believe that your intentions are honorable, that he is really under consideration, and that this process isn't a waste of his time and considerable effort. After all, you could be using him to verify a price from your cousin who already has the job. You could just not know what you're doing and be easily swayed by the other bidders. Any number of things could happen that could leave him out in the cold, and he fears being abused by an ill-run bid process. So your job in this process is to set dates you stick to, respond to questions accurately and timely, keep all parties apprised of the same information, and make your final contractor selection based on the information given you. Letting the contractors know that you appreciate their position and will run a fair bid process will go a long way to quelling their fears and getting you good prices from enthusiastic bidders.

Their Ethics

There are several ways a contractor can try to gain an advantage in this process. He can bad-mouth the other bidders, try to offer cost-saving changes to the scope of work for your ears only, or find flaws in your plans that permit him not to price things now that he can charge you for later. An honest contractor is

> **Insider's Tip**
> The ethical contractor is at a distinct disadvantage in a competitive bid situation.

actually at a disadvantage in a competitive bid process. Imagine you are a builder bidding a project and you see an error in the plans. You have two options. You can tell the owner, who will tell all the bidders, and you lose your advantage. The other option is you keep your mouth shut, give a bid number that does not include the missing work, and then charge a big fat change order later to get that work done. Which is the ethical thing to do? Tell the owner about the error, right? And which will give the contractor the better chance of getting the job? Not telling the owner about the error, right? Just stick to your plan and the information in this chapter, but keep an eye on how the bidders play the game and keep an ear out for flaws in your bid documents. Here's a true story about a very smart contractor. By the way, a nicer guy you never did meet.

A Very Good Boy

Mark was a construction manager for a good-sized construction company. He got a set of construction documents to bid on. Like any good contractor in that position, he knew everything he needed to know about the architect's strengths and weaknesses as soon as he unfurled those plans. It was clear that this architect knew little about site work, especially the materials for it. The architect had specified some crazy high-end gravel not indigenous to the area. Obviously, he had gotten it out of some resource book. This stuff would cost $22,000. The local stuff would provide drainage just as well and cost about $3,000. The specifications indicated that during the construction phase, the architect wanted submittals for all materials. Once he approved them, the materials could be purchased by the contractor.

Mark thought long and hard about this opportunity and the risk involved. All the contractors bidding were seeing the same thing he was seeing, and he knew they were mulling over their options too. It was like a game of chicken. If he carried the cost of the specified materials in his bid, he could lose the bid to someone who didn't carry that cost. If he didn't carry that cost and carried only $3,000 in hopes that the local material might be approved, he might win the bid but lose his shirt later if the architect caught him. The architect could insist on the specified material or accept the change but ask for the $19,000 difference back. Mark could also come clean and tell the architect that he had specified needlessly expensive gravel and that there was a big savings to the owner if they switched to the local stuff. The architect would be grateful for the help, make the switch, and inform all contractors bidding on the job. Mark would lose his advantage.

Mark finally settled on splitting the difference. He carried $10,000 for the gravel. That is to say, of the total bid of $320,000 that Mark submitted for the project, $10,000 of it was for the gravel. If the architect made him use the high-end stuff or give back the difference, it would cost him $12,000 of his profit. But if the architect accepted the local gravel without incident, Mark would pocket the $7,000 difference between what it really cost and what he carried.

Mark's company won the bid as the low bidder. When he saw the other bidders' numbers, Mark suspected he was the only one who dared try this.

Once on the construction site, Mark got a sample of the cheap local stuff and put it in a baby food jar. He attached an approval slip for signing and then waited for the perfect opportunity. About five days into the job the architect showed up in a foul mood, looking like he hadn't slept. Mark heard him arguing with his wife on the cell phone. As Mark saw the architect slip in a mud puddle, he knew the time was right. He ran out there, cheery as could be, thrust the jar of gravel and a pen in front of the architect, and got a signature of approval on that submittal slip with no discussion at all. When he told the story back at the office that afternoon, his boss said, "Oh, you're a very good boy!"

Bid Period

Once the construction documents are out to bid, two things should take place to help the bidders submit reliable numbers: a walk-thru and a question and answer period.

Walk-Thru

The walk-thru is an opportunity for the bidders to see the site to be worked on, whether it's a vacant lot or your current home in need of renovation. All bidders come at the same time and join you and/or whoever is helping you with this process. I love the walk-thru, watching the bidders size each other up, jockey for position, and reveal different points of concern. You can make attendance at the walk-thru mandatory if you think that it's essential and that their bids might not be accurate without it. If you are building a new home in an established development where these contractors have worked before, a mandatory walk-thru is probably not necessary. If you are building an addition that juts out between massive trees you hope to save, you may want to require their attendance so they can really appreciate what you're trying to have done, and you'll be confident that the bids they submit reflect that.

Questions and Answers

Starting at the walk-thru, the contractors will have questions. They will point out things that don't comply with code, things that may be more costly than needed, or tasks that seem missing in the scope. They do this not only for your benefit but also to protect themselves from being asked to do work later that wasn't included in the bid price. From now until shortly before the bids come in, you must collect these questions and provide all bidders with the answers as quickly as possible by way of addenda. For instance, one contractor may call and say, "Your plans show no handrail on this deck, and I think it's too high off the ground on the north side to allow that. You want a rail there or not?" You or your architect might call the city building inspector to come up with an answer to that question. Since answers actually change your scope of work, they are put together in an addendum to the contract and distributed to all the bidders in time for them to take those changes into consideration in their bid. You may well have to put out more than one addendum.

Bidders' Considerations

What affects how each contractor prices your work?

You – Essentially, a contractor enters into a short-term partnership with relative strangers each time he does a project. To date, some of those partnerships have been successful for him and some have not.

The contractor will size up all parties and the reputation of all the other players, you included. His assessment of all risk will affect his decision to bid and the bid number itself. It is for this reason that referrals from your architect, building inspector, and like-minded friends and neighbors are so helpful. However, if he's smart, he will not rely on the social connection alone. It's a good starting point for all parties, but like you, he is looking for a mutually beneficial business relationship here, not a new best friend.

Him – Who is the contractor? Is he cautious? Is he an "artiste"? Is he in demand? Is he desperate for work? Is he in a life transition? Is he a small contractor, or is he a big one with a big new office building and lots of staff to support? His personal and professional situation will have much to do with his ability and desire to stay in your bid process and what kind of numbers he gives you.

Insider's Tip

You are a big factor in the pricing you receive from a contractor. Put on your game face.

Them – How many other contractors are bidding this project, and who are they? Most contractors do not want to spend much time preparing a bid if their odds of getting the work are very low. Instead, they will either drop out of the process or "throw a number at it," contributing a sky-high price that takes no time to prepare but will cover them for almost any eventuality. If ten people are bidding the work, their odds are low. Your goal is to get a minimum of three competitive bids. Since some contractors may drop out of the process, a pool of five bidders is a good number to start with. The contractors are likely to know one another and their respective natures. They know each other's capacity for work, quality of work, and behavior during a competitive bid. If a contractor sees a pool of bidders against whom it's pointless to bid, he will likely walk. So through your selection process, try to get apples and apples, comparable contractors.

What – What's the project? Some projects are clean and simple and take little oversight to manage. Some are complicated with lots of custom details. Renovations have hidden conditions that create unknowns until walls are opened.

What's the current market? It's simple supply and demand. If you are trying to get a builder during a building boom, you will likely pay more for his services and wait longer to get him. If you are trying to get a builder when the building market is in a slump, you might get the best contractor in town to do a better job than you dreamed of at a very fair price.

Where – The contractor will have to cover his travel costs and those of his crew members, subcontractors, and suppliers. Contractors farther away from your property will be at a disadvantage bidding against those who are nearby, depending on the price of gas relative to the size of your project. Then there's the location of your site as it affects the work itself. It can cost you more to build on top of a mountain with no roads or in a dense urban area with no room for site set-up or storage than it will on a flat, open building lot on the edge of town.

When – Three dates will affect your bid: when you go out to bid, when you want the project to start, and when you want the project to be finished.

When you go out to bid, try to avoid holidays, deer season, Mardi Gras, the week before the kids go back to school, whatever local events may make it tough for a contractor to find the quiet time necessary to prepare your bid.

If you are in a hot building market, try to create a slight advantage for yourself. Consider what time of the year is slower. In the fall, contractors in the North are rushing to get the work done, but they have an eye out for two things: They need work to keep their crews busy indoors through the winter, and they'd love to find a great project all planned out for early next spring too. Try going to bid in the fall if you can offer them one of these desirable slots for the coming seasons. It results in good, aggressive pricing by them and savings to you.

> **Insider's Tip**
>
> When you're considering when you would like the project to start, in addition to meeting your own needs, think of the market and the seasons.

How soon you require a project to be finished has a big impact on a bidder. The need for speed makes a contractor use his resources differently. A builder knows how he wants to use his crew and can best assess the optimal pace to maximize profit. If you say your project should be done in three months, for instance, he could assign two crew members while he himself manages your project and another at the same time. If you say it must be done in two months, however, he might not feel comfortable managing the other project simultaneously. He needs an extra crew member for speed and so puts himself on the crew. Now he's getting no income from the second project. Even though he's swinging the hammer at a higher hourly rate than earned by the carpenters he hires, this scenario will cost him, so it will likely cost you. Thus, if you have the luxury of time, state in the construction documents that the completion date is to be agreed upon by the owner and contractor later. Let the contractor propose the most cost-efficient schedule. Negotiate as needed, and before you sign a contract with the selected bidder, lock in a finish date and add it to the contract.

How – How can a builder approach the work? Just how much control does he have over the site and setting his own general conditions? How much control does he have over pace and how he uses his crew members, the mess they make, the noise they make, the hours they work? A contractor needs to mobilize and manage people at a certain pace, buy and store equipment, and have utilities, phone, water, and bathroom facilities available. He understands that you may have restrictions in the contract such as work hours, where he can park, daily cleanup standards, and space limitations. Be aware that any impediment to speed or efficiency costs the contractor and must be reflected in the general conditions portion of his bid to you. Require what you must to keep this project manageable for you, but give as much as you can for the sake of your own budget.

Bid Day

This is a very exciting day. If you're doing a big project with very hungry contractors, be ready for a little hubbub coming your way. Though you are just waiting around to get envelopes with the completed bid forms in them, a whole host of last-minute pricing and horse trading is going on with those contractors. You may get last-minute questions and very-last-minute bids. This is because the subcontractors are sometimes reluctant to give a price until they understand every detail and know the contractor is so close to the time the bid is due that he cannot use that price for haggling with the subcontractors' competitors ("Bob will do the plumbing for $6,000. Can you beat that?"). They may receive prices from subcontractors by cell phone and be writing numbers on the form as they arrive at your house. Don't let it worry you. This is their problem and they are used to it. Just try to stick to whatever rules you laid out about deadlines to be fair to everyone.

Bid Analysis and Awarding the Contract

At this point, the contractors have submitted their bids to you, giving you all the pieces you need to compare and contrast the bids and award a contract. Check the math and make sure the schedule of values totals the base bid numbers. If the bids are high, use deduct alternates to reduce the total contract amount. If the bids are below your budget, you may want to use the add alternates to upgrade to your preferred choices (page 29).

If the bids have a wide range of prices, this could indicate vagueness in your construction drawings. Talk to the bidders to better understand how they were interpreting the plans and specifications and to find out if some clarification is needed before you choose a contractor or sign a contract.

Compare the individual prices in the schedules of values. Compare one contractor's site work to another's, one's rough carpentry to another's, and so forth. It's interesting reading and will reveal a lot about how each contractor and subcontractor sees the project. If one bidder is dramatically low, his schedule of values may reveal (page 107) why in a way that gives you comfort or gives you pause. It's also the starting point for negotiations (e.g., "You are the low bidder, but your plumber's price was twice that of this other subcontractor . . .").

Review the proposed construction and draw schedules for suitability with your timeline. Negotiate a project completion date, and put it in the contract.

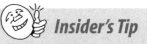 **Insider's Tip**

Don't start a project with a contractor who's already grumbling about money. It tends to lighten the wallet.

Review the bids in light of your reference and interview results, and all the terms submitted on the bid form. Hopefully, you will feel comfortable awarding the job to the lowest bidder, but unless you have specified otherwise, you have the right to choose whomever you please at this point. Some people would advise that you take the next-to-lowest bidder, believing that the lowest bidder will always be looking to recoup what he "left on the table." I don't think this is ethical, but remember, your pursuit is for the lowest and best number. If that low bid seems too good to be true, it probably is.

Recheck the availability of your selected contractor and that of his key crew members. Contractors are bidding work all the time, and you may not want to be the smallest and least significant of three projects he just landed all at once.

Make sure the contractor you are about to select is still happy with his bid. Without implying that you might pay more, ask him flat out, "Are you still comfortable with your numbers?" and then let him explain why or why not. Most contractors will say they are happy with their numbers, and you have just put them on notice that you don't want to hear a lot of whining for more money later. But occasionally, there's a problem. Remember, a contractor's goal is to give you a number by which he can make a profit and one that is one penny lower than the next bidder's. Even if you do not reveal the bids, he may well know the other bidders' numbers and be miserable that you are about to award him the project. Reconcile this or let him go. You want a contractor that's happy going in.

The contractor you are leaning toward has spent a lot of time thinking about your project by now. This would be a good time to talk about value engineering and any other thoughts he may have on improving the project in terms of bang for the buck or the scope of work. First ask if he sees anything missing from the scope of work, something he did not include in his price that must be done. This will help you avoid a nasty surprise change order the first week of construction, not to mention getting off on a hostile foot. Imagine how you'd feel if this contractor came to you a day after you signed the contract and said, "I need $3,000 more for tree removal. That wasn't mentioned in the plans, so I didn't price it." Ouch! Then ask where he sees room for improvement or savings. Weigh what he says, negotiate any changes in price that result, and amend the documents accordingly.

Set a date for discussing final terms and signing a contract. Then schedule a preconstruction meeting for a week or so before you want work on site to begin (page 150).

If all this hard work has been done, you now have the lowest possible price on a well written contract signed by a well qualified contractor ready to execute a well defined scope of work. Well done!

CHAPTER 10

Cover Your Assets

Contracts, Insurance, Liens, and Other Commitments

> This chapter covers the boring but essential paper trail that protects you against the worst-case scenarios.
>
> • If You Only Knew: Where Laypeople Go Wrong
> • Whose to Use? Construction Contracts
> • Don't Build Home Without It: Must-Haves
> • It Couldn't Hurt: Optional Additional Protection

If You Only Knew: Where Laypeople Go Wrong

This could be the biggest investment of your life, and it's a litigious world out there. If you take only one thing from this book, let it be this: *You need a contract!*

When asked where homeowners go wrong with contracts, lawyers who represent them in construction litigation say the following are the most common problems:

- Using a very limited contract provided by the contractor

- Starting the project before the design process is finished. This leads to chaos and ever-increasing costs.

- Insufficient allowance amounts for the many materials that owners will select later

- Defective workmanship. The owner relies on the contractor to monitor his own work and that of his subcontractors and is disappointed in the finished product. By this point too much money has been paid to the contractor, and the owner has little recourse. If a lender is involved, owners think that the lender's inspections address quality. They do not. The lender's inspections are only to confirm the percentage of work completed as submitted in the contractor's requisition for payment, not necessarily whether it is completed well. Owners would be wise to involve an independent property inspector or architect in the monitoring of the construction phase. It's a bargain for what you get and what you prevent.

> *"A verbal contract isn't worth the paper it's written on."*
>
> —SAMUEL GOLDWYN

- Moving in before the work is complete. This makes for unhappy homeowners and contractors. The project completion date gets murky, as do the warranty start dates and determining who is responsible for the condition of the space.

- No retainage clause in the contract and no retainage held through completion of the project (page 136)

Whose to Use?
Construction Contracts

Forcing the issue of a contract is tough for some homeowners. They feel as though they are making an accusation against the contractor they're hiring before the project even begins. Most small contractors will hand an owner one sheet of paper with a short laundry list of tasks he's offering to do for a certain price. He would like a signature at the bottom so he can start work. There is little or no detail on materials to be used, how the work will be done, warranties, payment schedule, or the owner's rights. Owners sign these things even for projects over $100,000. They are usually very sorry they did. A good contract lays out the rules and guards both parties against great loss. I like to think I'm putting the onus on paper, and it liberates all of us to work with a safety net that lessens our fears and permits us to focus on the project at hand.

Pitfall

If you're thinking of signing a little scribbled agreement the contractor gives you, don't come crying to me.

There are several ways to obtain a construction contract. You, an architect, or a contractor can provide it. If the contractor provides it, he will either write his own or purchase one from a source like the Association of General Contractors (AGC). An architect will provide an American Institute of Architects (AIA) contract. If you provide the contract, you have many options. You can get one from the AIA or the AGC or have an attorney write one. You can create your own with computer software like Family Lawyer by Quicken, or use Nolo's books or online help in preparing contracts. And you can buy standardized contracts from an office supply store.

Don't Reinvent the Wheel

Each of the professional groups has contracts that favor its respective group. Over the years, these groups have worked together to bring more continuity to their contracts, but the fact is the AIA got there first and set the industry standards on which most legal precedent has been based. They have almost ninety documents available that cover every contract structure and project administration task you can imagine. Most contractors are familiar with AIA documents, and lucky for you, they favor the owner.

Insider's Tip

There's a great resource at your disposal. You're free to use what you like, but in my research I found nothing to beat the AIA documents for easy access, thoroughness, and owner protection.

> *Here are the articles of contracted peace.*
>
> —WILLIAM SHAKESPEARE

You must purchase and use original, standardized documents in order to assure their validity. AIA has made this easy. Up until recently, AIA sold hard copies of their documents only in bulk, since they are used primarily by professionals. They have now created a great way you can access individual copies of all their documents. You can go to their Web site (www. aia.org), go to *Contract Documents*, then to *AIA Contract Documents on Demand eShop*. There you'll find all the basic documents you need for a pittance. In addition to contracts, you'll find the paperwork for managing your project, including forms for processing change orders and requests for payment. You can also buy hard copies of their broader range of documents from your local AIA chapter, listed on www.aia.org.

The Contract Form to Match Your Approach

Below is a table indicating which AIA contracts are appropriate with each of the contract structures described in chapter 7.

CONTRACT STRUCTURE	APPROPRIATE AIA CONTRACT(S)
Competitive bid or negotiated	A101—Standard Form of Agreement Between Owner and Contractor—Stipulated Sum, with A201—General Conditions of the Contract for Construction or A105—Standard Form of Agreement Between Owner and Contractor for a Small Project, with A205—General Conditions of the Contractor for Construction of a Small Project or A107—Abbreviated Standard Form of Agreement Between Owner and Contractor for Construction Projects of Limited Scope for Stipulated Sum (General Conditions Included)
Design/build	A191—Standard Form of Agreement Between Owner and Design/Builder
Construction management	A101/CM—Standard Form of Agreement Between Owner and Contractor-Stipulated Sum, Construction Manager-Advisor Edition, with A210/CM—General Conditions of the Contract for Construction, Construction Manager-Adviser Edition or A121/CM—Standard Form of Agreement Between Owner and Construction Manager Where the Construction Manager Is Also the Constructor Also see A131/CM and B141/CM for other construction management options
Modular	Not applicable
Time and materials	A114—Standard Form of Agreement Between Owner and Contractor Where the Basis of Payment Is the Cost of the Work Plus a Fee Without a Guaranteed Maximum Price
Build-to-suit	Not applicable

If you go with the Standard Form contract, you will need to purchase the companion document for general conditions too. It outlines the roles and rules for everyone on the job and contains many clauses regarding owner's rights. If you go with the Abbreviated Standard Form, the general conditions are rolled right into that contract. The Abbreviated Standard Form should be fine for most residential projects.

Many contractors will offer their own contracts. They may be perfectly fine, but get a copy of the comparable AIA contract (e.g., A101—Standard Agreement Between Owner and Contractor) and compare for yourself.

How do you impose the contract you want? Simple. Since the project starts and ends with you, the best way to avoid having to consider contracts you don't want is to make your contract part of the construction documents up front. That way, you can familiarize yourself with its terms on your own timeline and amend it to suit your needs. Then any contractor negotiating with you or bidding on your project has all three things needed to know everything about what you're expecting: the plans showing the finished project to be executed, the specifications outlining how he is to do that work and with what materials, and the contract laying out the rules and legal obligations of all parties.

For small repairs done on a time-and-materials basis, you will likely not need a contract. For small projects with a fixed scope of work, you could also get a standard contract at an office supply place and amend it to your needs. However, the best rule of thumb is this: Don't go into a project on just a handshake for any amount more than you are willing to risk losing. Even a handwritten agreement outlining the basics and signed by both parties is better than nothing.

If you choose to use AIA documents and you do not have an architect on the project, you may have to alter the document slightly to remove or reassign references to an architect. You can make these changes right on your computer if you download the documents. The related clauses are pretty straightforward, so this isn't too hard. However, if you want to do more than replace "architect" with "owner" in some clauses regarding decision making, remember that the AIA documents are tried-and-true in U.S. courts. You don't want to rewrite individual clauses too much and run the risk of losing their protection. If you need to make changes to a document, do it through supplementary conditions.

Those are added clauses that refer back to standard clauses and amend them. If a lawyer is helping you with the contract documents, try to use one who has experience with construction documents, or inform your lawyer that you would like the standardized document clauses left intact as much as possible.

The Best Benefit of Contracts

The biggest benefit of having a contract is not usually the way in which it protects you if things go wrong, but rather how it prevents things from going wrong in the first place. It's the process of preparing the contract, of talking through all the issues with all parties and addressing the ugly stuff up front, that really sets the project on course. Those who cannot make it through this process with a contractor may even find it more valuable than those who can. I know several homeowners who were looking forward to their project with delight until they whipped out the contract and found the contractor unwilling to sign his name to the very things he had promised to do.

Some say a contract cannot protect you from a bad contractor and you don't need one with a sainted contractor. But until you go through this process, you cannot tell one from the other, and if he's human, your contractor is likely somewhere in the middle.

No, you probably don't want to go to court over a clause in the contract. I haven't gone once in my work on more than two hundred buildings. That's because a contract is the result of a lot of shared work that binds. It is also the big stick if things go wrong. It brings people to the table to negotiate solutions. Without it, you may end up hearing, "That's not what we agreed on," or worse yet, "Try and make me."

Don't Build Home Without It: Must-Haves

Whatever way you go about getting a contract, there are a few things it must include. Here is a list of those items. Detailed information about each of them follows.

- Contract parties

- The scope of work

- Cost

- Schedules

- Rules for change orders

- Insurance

- Warranty terms

- Contractor guarantee

- Customized clauses

- A few choice words

- Means of dispute resolution

- Signature page

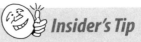

Insider's Tip

I've never once had to resort to pulling out a contract and reminding a contractor of what he signed up to. Nor have I ever called in an attorney on a job that had a contract... only on those that didn't. Funny how that works.

Contract Parties

List the names, titles, addresses, and phone numbers of all parties on the contract. Use only these names to fill in any blanks on the standard contract forms assigning duties and authority. This defines the relationships on the project: who works for whom, who pays whom, who directs the contractor, who chooses design elements. Include any pertinent license or registration numbers of the professional parties.

The Scope of Work

Your contract must refer to a clearly defined scope of work (page 24) detailing all tasks and materials to be used. Reference the following in your contract, and if they are small, staple them right to the contract: (a) plans, showing the finished product in detail, and (b) specifications, describing how the work will be done and with what materials.

A partial scope of work is not good enough and may in fact be worse than none at all. If the scope of work does not accurately address everything in your upcoming project, signing a contract for a fixed price may turn out to be more like the starting place of your unanticipated expenses. You will be locked into this number and likely receive lots of up-charges for work not reflected or properly detailed in the plans and specifications. It is this kind of shoddy advance work that creates project horror stories. All parties are bound and committed and the project is under way but on shifting sands. Be sure you are on firm footing with as many tasks and materials as well-defined as possible before you sign anything. Anyone in the field should be able to look at those documents and know just what materials need to be purchased and what tasks need to be done.

If the contractor provides these plans and specifications, you can have them reviewed by a cost estimator or independent construction inspector to get suggestions on adding clarity. This is money very well spent. At the very least, if you plan to commit to one of those little laundry lists of tasks written up by a contractor, make sure it's as detailed as possible to protect you. For instance, if the description presented to you reads "12 feet of built-in cabinets," you will want to amend it to detail all materials to be used, including lumber and paint grades, any demolition and rubbish removal required, rough carpentry, finished carpentry, hardware, wiring, paint and cleanup, deadline, and cost. Oh, and of course you will need to attach a drawing with all dimensions detailed. Now everybody knows what's expected, and you've lowered your risk of problems immeasurably.

Cost

In a fixed-price contract, the lump sum is agreed upon by you and the contractor. This could be the base bid that resulted from a competitive bid process or the numbers arrived at in a negotiated or design/build process. If you are using a time-and-materials or cost plus structure, the cost may not be fixed up front, but you can get standardized contracts for those structures too, and they include the terms for calculating the cost of the project over time.

If you are giving the contractor a down payment (page 13), be sure this payment is reflected in the contract.

Outline any unit prices, allowances, and/or alternate prices with a description of the work and price agreed to (page 28).

Schedules

Insert the start and completion dates of the project. Attach and reference the construction schedule, as covered in detail in the next chapter. Note any other agreed-upon milestones such as when the heat goes on or when the kitchen is operable. Also note time-sensitive responsibilities of any parties such as when the owner must select carpet. The construction schedule indicates the intent of all parties. It's like an estimate, but it is not binding. By law, time is not regarded as a "material provision" in a contract. If you want to better ensure the completion date, you will have to include liquidated damages (page 131).

Attach and reference the draw schedule (page 135), showing when and what the contractor will be paid and what work he will have completed prior to each payment.

Rules for Change Orders

No matter how tight the design and perfectly the scope of work is described in words and drawings, I haven't met the project yet that didn't include some changes to the scope of work during the construction phase. Each such change, no matter how minor, alters the terms of the contract and so must be addressed formally through a change order (page 171), which indicates any change to the scope, the project cost, and/or the schedule.

Your contract should include two things regarding change orders. First, it should contain language indicating that no work outside of the original scope of work should be executed or will be paid for without prior written approval from the owner. Second, the contract should contain a formula for calculating change orders. You will need to negotiate this with the contractor, and the formula should be his cost of labor and materials plus

Pitfall

Once your project is under way, you ask the contractor to add another set of steps from the deck to the lawn. He says it will cost $4,000. Why? Because he can.

an agreed-upon amount for profit and overhead (15 to 20 percent is fair). See if you can also negotiate an open-book approach to change orders, wherein the contractor shows you receipts for his costs. The same math should apply to both add and deduct change orders, but this could really take some wrangling and trust between the parties. After all, what if you decided to wipe out large portions of work? That would represent a loss of income to the contractor and not be fair. Moreover, for contractors who are not looking to gouge you, change orders are a hassle. They require a change in the contractor's purchasing, coordination, and scheduling. This is why the contractor is entitled to calculate his profit and overhead on change orders at a higher rate than for the rest of the project.

Insurance

Let's face it, stuff happens. Most homeowner's policies offer some coverage associated with minimal maintenance or repair that's likely to take place on your property at any time. If you're doing work beyond that level, get the following insurances in place. If you have a construction loan, the lender will require

Pitfall

If the contractor isn't insured and someone is injured on the job site, they're coming after you.

these and be able to walk you through them in greater detail. Otherwise, meet with your homeowner's insurance agent and lay out a plan to make sure you and the contractor have the following.

Insurance for the Contractor

Get copies of the "certificate of insurance" for each of the types of insurance you will be requiring before any crews begin work on your property. These are the three that offer you relief from nearly all potential hazards:

Workers' Compensation and Employers' Liability Insurance: insures against injuries to workers and protects you against workers making claims against your property insurance. Without it, you are deemed the statutory employer and could be liable if anyone working on your property is injured. Workers' compensation for the subcontractors is a bit trickier. This insurance can make up 15 percent of their payroll expenses, so some smaller outfits go without. Discuss this with the general contractor and your insurance agent to determine if you want to insist that everyone on the job has workers' comp.

Commercial General Liability Insurance: insures against damage to property. If a hammer falls off a scaffold and goes through the pool liner, a claim would be made against this type of policy. It also covers the damage to property as a result of defective work, but it would not pay to rectify the inferior work itself. For instance, if the new roof leaked into your living room, this insurance would pay to replace the water-soaked couch, but not to remedy the leaky roof. Lastly, it covers injury to nonworkers on the job site, including you. Ask that you be listed as an "additional insured" on the contractor's policy. This means that you are included in the protection against claims as well.

Business Automobile Insurance: covers any damage or injury caused by the vehicles of the contractor or his crews on your site. If a worker backs into the new foundation or, God forbid, hits the neighbor's child, he's covered.

Insurance for You

Builder's Risk Insurance: can be purchased by you or the contractor and covers an unoccupied property as it evolves from a building site to a finished space. Specifically, it covers materials in transit and on site from fire, theft, vandalism, and collapse. Either you or the contractor can purchase this, but you should specify that in either case the contractor will pay the deductible. This keeps the responsibility for mishaps where it belongs, on the contractor. Whoever purchases this policy will be expected to update the insurance agent on the progress of the project.

Homeowner's Insurance: can be used as an alternative to builder's risk insurance and is fast expanding in definition to cover both renovations and new construction projects. You can purchase this policy at the beginning of the project and add a rider for "theft of building materials of an unoccupied space" and you will end up with the same coverage as builder's risk with a few additional advantages:

- You don't have to buy a homeowner's policy after the project is done. You already have it. That's one less thing to do.

- You don't have to remember to update the insurance agent on the status of the project as you might with builder's risk.

- In the real world, people often start moving personal property onto the site before the project is complete. Builder's risk would not cover loss or damage of this property. The homeowner's policy will.

- It's cheaper!

In the case of an expansion to or renovation of a home that will remain occupied, you don't even need the rider. Just increase the amount of coverage to cover the anticipated increased value of your property. Be sure to verify and discuss these options with your insurance agent and let the agent know this coverage is for a construction project in progress.

Any lender will require builder's risk or an enhanced homeowner's insurance policy on the property and will insist on being included as an additional insured. If the contractor asks to be listed as an additional insured, think twice. If a claim is made against the policy, any payment made by the insurance company will be done through a check with all the insured parties listed. If this claim or other incidents on site lead to bad blood between the parties, you cannot cash that check without the contractor endorsing it too.

Warranty Terms

Warranties are a pretty simple concept we are all familiar with, but there are some important things to consider about warranties on a construction project.

Installer Conflicts

Warranties are great on discrete items like a boiler that fails in two months. It can get trickier for items in the scope of work that take more than one subcontractor or supplier to address. For instance, flaws in the taped Sheetrock joints cannot be seen well until the paint goes on. When it does, if you complain about the finished product, the sheetrocker may blame the painter or even the framer, and the painter might blame the sheetrocker. If you use a general contractor who has hired all these parties, you have no worry. Your contract is with the general contractor, and he has to provide you with an acceptable finish regardless. If you hire subcontractors directly, think about where their work overlaps and see if you can prevent a warranty conflict. I always get my sheetrocking and painting done by the same subcontractor.

Supplier Conflicts

Another warranty conflict is that between the contractor or subcontractor and the supplier. Most materials are warranted for one year, and several individual materials such as roofing materials and synthetic siding have extended warranties that may be decades long. All materials warranties have caveats attached to them regarding installation. If manufacturers can show that their materials were not installed according to their instructions, they can wriggle out of standing by their product. For instance, if your roof shingles start to blow off a month after they were installed, the supplier might well and rightly point to the roofer for shoddy installation not complying with the manufacturer's instructions. The roofer does not agree and refuses to pay for more shingles. You get caught in the middle. This is yet another reason for good monitoring and solid language about manufacturer's instructions in your contract. If you wrote down the date those shingles were installed and then called the National Weather Service, you might learn that it was 35-degrees from the time the shingles went on until the time they started blowing off. It was too cold to activate the tar sealant that holds the shingles down, and so the installation did not comply with the manufacturer's instructions. The roofer would be at fault and have to uphold the entire warranty for labor and replacement materials.

Keeping Warranties Useful

The clock starts ticking on a warranty once the item is in use, not necessarily when your whole project is done. Here's how you track your warranties and maximize your chance to take advantage of them in the event of failures.

- Collect or have the contractor collect all warranties, manufacturer's instructions, and maintenance information included with the materials arriving on site. File them in a safe place off site.

- Note the dates that the big ticket items go into use; the windows and doors, boiler, furnace, water heater, appliances, etc.

- If you see the slightest problem with any of the items under warranty, write a dated letter about it to the contractor right away and make a copy for your files. That way, the problem is on record before the warranty date passes.

- Pull out next year's calendar and schedule a warranty walk-thru eleven months after the completion of the project. This will cover all finishes done toward the end of the project, and most contractors will honor a warranty on the other items that were in use prior to that as well. Write up any defects. You need not propose solutions, just state the problems, send them to the contractor, and schedule a meeting to discuss the necessary repairs.

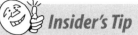

Insider's Tip

It's a good idea to tell the contractor at the beginning of the project that you'll be doing a warranty walk-thru the year after the project is complete. This can't help but make him pay close attention and keep his standards high.

Contractor Guarantee

Warranties are on materials. You also need a more sweeping guarantee from the contractor. A one-year guarantee on all labor and materials is standard.

Customized Clauses

The boilerplate contracts draw firm distinctions between people's roles. You should try to honor these distinctions in order to keep the contract valid. For instance, the contractor is usually responsible for providing all materials and directing the crew members and subcontractors. If you want to provide materials, amend the contract to reflect that. If you want to insert a specific subcontractor into the project, amend the contract accordingly, and be sure to cover who is paying for and supervising that person. If you just disregard the contract clauses on roles, you might invalidate some of the other clauses that protect you on cost and quality control. If you amend any clauses to any existing contract document, be sure all parties put their initials next to those changes.

Standardized contracts are just that, standard. They cover almost everything, but in terms that are not specific to your project. They have blanks you must fill in regarding the parties' names, project cost, payment schedule, and other items. Now is the time to customize the contract to suit your project and your lifestyle. If you find yourself saying, "I hope the workers don't swear around the kids," go ahead, address it in the contract and allay your fears. Some areas that are typically addressed in contract amendments are working hours, access to the space, conduct, noise, parking, and cleanup.

My favorite amendment concerns the punch list (page 182). It's customary to hold back 200 percent of the value of the piddling final touch-up work ("punch work") from payment of the last large invoice. For instance, the contractor gives you a final request for payment of $25,000. Still to be finished are touch-up painting, replacing a broken switch-plate cover, and ten other tiny things totaling $500 in value. You would "hold" 200 percent of the value of that work, or $1,000, and pay the contractor $24,000. This is supposed to create an incentive for the contractor to come and finish. It doesn't do much because 200 percent of nearly nothing is still nearly nothing. So I hold 1,000 percent of the value of that work. Using the example above, I would hold $5,000 and pay only $20,000 until every little work item on that punch list was polished off. Those projects get wrapped up fast and everyone's happy. If a contractor questions the clause, just say, "What, you don't intend to finish in a timely fashion?"

A Few Choice Words

If you are not using a standardized contract, be sure to include the following powerful phrases regarding quality control and protection:

- "The Contractor shall install all materials and supplies in accordance with manufacturer's instructions."

- "The Contractor shall execute all tasks in a workmanlike fashion."

- "Time is of the essence."

- "The Contractor indemnifies the Owner against any liability cost or expenses arising out of personal injury or property damage resulting from negligence of the Contractor or any of his Subcontractors."

Though some of it sounds colloquial, this language above carries weight in court, and when a contractor signs a contract with this language included, you are further safeguarded.

Pitfall

If something goes wrong, you always have the option of suing, right? Yes, but more often than not, a lawyer will recommend you settle because it will cost you too much to take the dispute to court.

Means of Dispute Resolution

Contracts lay down the rules. So what happens if someone breaks them and a dispute results? You and your contractor need a way out of trouble if your project goes awry. Each of you needs an avenue for enforcing the contract clauses in the event that goodwill and your signatures aren't enough. You have three options—litigation, arbitration, and mediation—and they all have advantages and disadvantages.

Litigation

Suing the contractor or other party is always an option if you don't waive the right to it by committing to one of the other two options (arbitration or mediation). On the downside, you may spend more to litigate the problem with a lawyer, expert witnesses, and court fees than you would to just pay for the remedy. In fact, many courts offer mediation as the first step in the litigation process. Some states are even setting up out-of-court alternatives to construction disputes, since litigation costs make viable financial remedies unavailable to the homeowner. Second, juries are not made up of professionals in the construction field and may find the technical details hard to understand. On the other hand, juries are more likely to side with homeowners.

Arbitration

Arbitration is a faster, less expensive process than litigation and is done by professionals. An arbiter is like a "private judge." Typically, arbiters have expertise in law, architecture, and/or construction. They hear both sides of a dispute and render a binding decision. It's important to note that in arbitration, owners seldom receive cash. It's more typical for the contractor to be required to fix the problem in a case where the arbiter finds in favor of the owner. If you're headed to arbitration, this may be a hard pill to swallow, since you probably won't want that contractor back on your project. So don't set a torch to all our bridges with him.

You will have to pay an arbitration filing fee and possibly pay the arbiter for services. You may still want to hire expert witnesses and a lawyer to help represent your interests, but overall this process is still less expensive than litigation. Contact the American Arbitration Association or JAMS/End Dispute for more information on arbitration.

Mediation

Mediation is not binding. In this case, the parties agree to have their dispute heard by a mediator acceptable to both. This person's goal is to facilitate conversation on the disputed matter and bring the parties to a resolution. The mediator is much less likely to say "You're right and they're wrong." A typical criticism of this process is that a mediator needs to get you to a mutually agreed-upon resolution that may require compromise that the owner is not happy with.

Mediators come in three kinds: the "social work" mediator, who is likely well trained in the art of mediation but less well versed in the technical matters of construction; the "professional" mediator, who has expertise in the field of construction; and the "legal" mediator, who has more expertise in the law.

It's a hard call and one that's best made in hindsight, but I would recommend arbitration as the best means of resolution in most cases. If you choose to insert an arbitration clause into your contract, be sure to check out the statutes in your state to ensure that you have the right language. It differs from state to state, and you want to ensure that your clause is valid for your location.

Signature Page

You and the contractor must sign and date the contract. You can also have it notarized. Before work begins, make sure all parties have copies of it.

It Couldn't Hurt:
Optional Additional Protection

Very small contractors or "tailgaters" will not likely include the following clauses in any contract they create. Some may not even be familiar with them or able to comply with them. I would not build anything of significant cost without these. Read on and see if you want to include them in your owner-contractor agreement to mitigate your risk. If you do and the contractor doesn't, you may want to rethink your contractor selection.

Liens and Lien Waivers

This is the darker side of following the money. A lien is a nasty little device whose bark is usually worse than its bite, but it can still leave a mark and should be avoided. Here's how a lien works. Anyone—and I mean anyone—can go down to the town clerk's office and file a "writ of attachment" or lien on someone else's property. It's a way of making a claim against someone they feel owes them money and has refused to pay. Typically, this first step must be followed up within sixty to ninety days with the commencement of legal action by filing a writ of attachment or order of judgment at the local courthouse. Otherwise, the lien is voided. Either way, until the lien is removed, you do not have a clean title to the property. If a lien is on your property when you go to convert your construction loan to a mortgage, you cannot do it. Nor can you sell a property until a lien is lifted. And the biggest surprise of all is that most towns don't notify you if a lien has been placed on your property. It could just sit there like a little time bomb.

So who puts liens on properties during a construction project? On a project that isn't going well, a distinct possibility is an aggrieved contractor who wants you to pay for something you have refused to pay for. However, what's more common is subcontractors or suppliers who have not received payment from the general contractor. That's right. You may have paid all your bills, but the contractor may not

Pitfall

Even if you have paid the contractor everything owed, how do you know he's paid the suppliers? If he hasn't, they could slap a lien on your property.

have paid his, and those people he has not paid will go for the deep pockets of your project in hopes that you will pressure the general contractor to pay them.

This brings us to lien waivers. A lien waiver is a one-page document signed by a general contractor, subcontractor, or supplier saying that he has received satisfactory payment and therefore waives the right to place a lien on your property that includes the amount just paid him. On large-scale projects these are signed by at least the general contractor in exchange for each and every requisition paid. Large subcontractors and suppliers are asked to sign as their work warrants and at the end of the project before final payment is made. If you have a loan from a bank for your project,

CONTRACTOR'S, SUBCONTRACTOR'S, AND
MATERIAL SUPPLIER'S RELEASE AND WAIVER OF LIEN

Contractor/Subcontractor/Supplier Name _____

Address _____

Phone _____ Email _____

For and in consideration of the receipt of $_____, in payment of labor and/or materials furnished, the receipt and sufficiency of which are hereby acknowledged, the undersigned does hereby waive, release, and relinquish any and all claims, demands, and rights of lien for all work, labor, materials, machinery, or other goods, equipment, or services done, performed or furnished for the construction located at the site hereinafter described, to wit:

Project name/location _____

For (owner's name) _____

As of this date _____

The undersigned further warrants and represents that any and all valid labor and/or material and equipment described on behalf of the undersigned have been paid in full to the date of this waiver, or will be paid from these funds.

Total paid to date on this contract/material purchase is $ _____

Print name of contractor/subcontractor/supplier _____

Signed by: _____   _____
                       Duly Authorized Agent   Witness

Balance due on total contract after above draw $ _____

This lien waiver may not be applicable to the laws of your state.

the bank will likely have the contractor sign a lien waiver before each payment, and certainly before the last payment is released. If you do not have a loan officer insisting on this, use your discretion but at least get a lien waiver signed by the contractor and the largest supplier before you make the last payment, and call the subcontractors to see if they are all paid up and happy. Then call City Hall to ensure no liens have been attached to your property. *Then* cut your last check to your contractor.

I know a couple who built a house with cash, so no title search was done upon completion of the project to convert a construction loan to a mortgage. When they went to sell their house seven years later, they learned they hadn't had a clean title all that time. There was a lien on their property, and the contractor just sat in wait until the day they tried to sell. They could pay him and sell the house immediately or bog down the works by disputing his claim and risk losing the buyers for their house. They paid the contractor, but were none too happy about it. The embarrassing truth is that this happened to one of my brothers and his wife . . . proof positive that no one listens to the little sister.

You are now forewarned about this tool that can be filed quite capriciously. It should give you even more incentive to plan wisely, act fairly, and monitor the flow of money.

Liquidated Damages

I think it's best to build plenty of wiggle room into your schedule. Delays happen, and if you insist on a finite day for completion, you'd better have flawless plans because you may pay dearly for any changes in the scope of work that need to be completed within that time frame. In short, you may end up being the one who pays for such precision timing.

On the other hand, life is filled with deadlines beyond your control—when school starts, closing dates, job changes, etc. So if the finish date of your construction project is imperative, there's a tool you can include up front in your contract agreement called liquidated damages.

Liquidated damages are usually a per-day cost levied against the contractor for each day he goes beyond the scheduled completion date. The cost must be based on real financial loss caused by this delay, such as rent elsewhere, travel expenses, or additional fees charged by the architect. These numbers must be estimated in advance and included in the contract up front. For obvious reasons, contractors hate liquidated damages. If you include them, you may want to offer an incentive clause for early completion that works the same way. You would pay the contractor for each day between the time he finished early and the original completion date agreed upon. You can also offer a fixed bonus amount for on-time or early completion. It's nice to have a carrot as well as a stick as a good-faith gesture when applying liquidated damages. Also be sure to enumerate exceptions to the liquidated damages clause, including weather conditions, illness, and other things out of the contractor's control.

See? There's no need to go on blind faith. Just like the pros, you can protect your interests through easily accessible contracts, insurance, and other legal tools. Get the documents you need before you build and everyone can breathe easy.

CHAPTER 11

Believe It!
Time Really is Money
Schedules

This section explains the impact of time on your project costs and how to monitor it by using schedules.

- Tick Tock: How Time = Money on a Construction Project
- More Than One Way to Tell Time: Types of Schedules
- What Was That Other Thing? Additional Things to Track

Tick Tock:
How Time = Money on a Construction Project

We all know that time is money and that the cost of labor time is calculated into anything we purchase. In construction, people seem to talk little about time at the beginning of a project, and it's all they can talk about and assign costs to by the end. Therefore, it's helpful for you to know all the ways in which this equation comes into play on your construction project so you can be mindful of its impact on you and your budget from the get-go.

Labor

Other than you, everyone associated with your project will be paid for their time worked. Architects, engineers, and designers charge for design time, which includes meetings, drawing, cost estimating, and project management. The general contractor charges for all time spent coordinating and overseeing your project, including phone time, travel time, office time, and time on site. His crew members and all the tradespeople charge for their time executing the scope of work.

When anyone commits to you by way of a lump sum, it is predicated on certain assumptions about the time it will take to do the work. If you alter that scope of work, you open the door to a recalculation of the time equation, including any underestimating that took place initially. It's yet another reason to start your project with a well-defined scope of work, so that you don't have to alter it and expose yourself to recalculation. If you must make changes, always ask about the impact on time.

Your own labor is not free. While you may be your best bargain on the job, keep tabs on your own time. Measure your value on the job against other activities you may be giving up. In other words, don't be a hero.

The difference between dreams and goals is a timeline.

—DR. PHIL MCGRAW

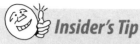
If your time would be better spent at Little League games, staying late at the office, or recharging your batteries with a vacation, see if you can hire out some of what you're doing, pay for delivery from the nursery, or let the contractor pick up the roof shingle samples. Give yourself a break!

General Conditions

The contractor has every reason to get as much work done as quickly as possible. Help him do this by holding up your end on any time-sensitive decisions, granting access to the site, and lessening the time he spends on anything you can do. However, be sure quality and thoroughness are not being sacrificed for speed. Any owner who understands this balance is really speaking the contractor's language.

General conditions are costs to the contractor, and ultimately to you, that facilitate the project but don't fall under labor and materials for tangible work (page 46). They include storage of materials, rental of equipment like scaffolding and lifts, administrative services, phone bills, trucks, insurance, site trailer, portable toilets—everything it takes to run the job. After a project has been under way a bit, any good contractor can tell you how much this job is costing him to run per day. If his number of crew members remains stable, each day that the project goes on costs him that amount whether it's a productive day or not. As soon as he possibly can, the contractor wants to drop these costs, as they eat at his profit. For the most part, this incentive works to your advantage.

Loans

If you've ever borrowed money, you certainly know the impact of time on cost. A fifteen-year mortgage will cost you more per month but less over the term of the loan than a thirty-year mortgage. If you are using a construction loan for your project, the clock starts ticking as soon as that loan is issued, and you incur a daily cost for the privilege of borrowing that money. If that loan will convert to a less expensive mortgage when the project is complete, you have

Pitfall

The clock starts ticking on your construction loan and doesn't stop until the last contractor payment is made. Not until then can you convert it to a mortgage at 2 to 3 percent less.

a financial incentive to get this job done in a timely manner. And if you're watching the fixed mortgage rates sneak up as you're trying to finish your project, getting the project done as soon as possible becomes even more crucial.

Insurance

A construction project has inherent risks, including theft of materials, fire, and the safety of the people, materials, and equipment on site. You will have insurance to cover these risks. With each passing day, your project evolves a little more from a higher-risk building site to a less risky finished space. Your insurance costs will reflect this (see chapter 10). The sooner you finish the project, the less you will pay out in insurance premiums.

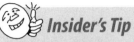
Expediting the Project

You can push people only so hard. Expediting things will cost you. There will be times during your project when a key deadline may be in jeopardy if you don't pay a little extra to have something unanticipated shipped right away. Try to keep these expenditures to a minimum—again, with good up-front planning.

More Than One Way to Tell Time: Types of Schedules

Like the project budget, the project schedule is a living document, not a finite thing. It's first used to set timeline goals and later becomes a tool by which you measure progress when deciding just about everything associated with the project. How long will it take to get those windows? How much work should be done by now if we are to pay this amount? Should we tell the in-laws Christmas will be at their place this year? Below are explanations and samples of the two schedules you'll need for tracking time on your project.

> *Time, like money, is measured by our needs.*
>
> —GEORGE ELIOT

 **Pitfall**

The toughest thing about a construction schedule could be getting your hands on one. But without one, how will you measure progress?

The Construction Schedule

A construction schedule is the last thing most contractors prepare or share because it's based on so many assumptions in the early going. However, it's essential to you for two reasons. It forces the contractor to break that project down and get his mind around it before he begins. You want him to have done this, since his surprises are your surprises. It's also the best tool you have as an owner for measuring progress. So even if you have to cajole and accept a schedule that's filled with disclaimers, don't start the project without one.

The construction schedule should include (a) tasks to be completed by trade in chronological order, (b) start date and end date of each task, and (c) start date and end date of the whole project.

DIV.	DESCRIPTION	COST	WEEK NUMBER												
			1	2	3	4	5	6	7	8	9	10	11	12	13
1	General conditions	$6,500	▓												▓
2	Site work	$5,073	▓	▓										▓	
2	Selective demolition	$4,556	▓												
3	Concrete	$5,414		▓											
4	Masonry	$7,664			▓								▓		
6	Rough carpentry	$9,414			▓	▓									
6	Interior finish carpentry	$8,808									▓				
6	Exterior finish carpentry	$7,730						▓							
6	Cabinets	$1,850											▓		
7	Insulation	$4,775						▓							
7	Roofing	$9,836					▓								
7	Siding	$6,800						▓							
8	Doors and hardware	$5,800													
8	Windows	$4,800						▓							
9	Gypsum	$6,016							▓	▓					
9	Flooring	$4,400										▓			
9	Ceramic tile	$2,800													
9	Painting	$3,700								▓	▓			▓	
10	Specialties	$795												▓	
15	Plumbing	$11,500						▓					▓		
15	Heating	$12,834						▓					▓		
16	Electrical	$10,000						▓	▓				▓	▓	▓
	Bare Cost Total	**$141,065**													
	Contractor's 15% Overhead & Profit	$21,160													
	CONTRACT AMOUNT	**$162,225**													

CONSTRUCTION SCHEDULE—DORSEY HOUSE ADDITION

Today's computers make it easy to create fancy schedules in several formats, but I like the bar chart best for easy understanding. In the construction schedule above, the concrete foundation work should be done by the end of the second week, the framing (rough carpentry) will take another three weeks, and as is normal, many trades will be working on the interior finishes at the same time between the eleventh and the thirteenth weeks.

The Draw Schedule

A "draw" is a payment, or "drawing down of your funds," made to the contractor upon receipt of a requisition, also called an invoice or bill. A draw schedule is a dated plan showing the disbursement of all the money you intend to pay the contractor through the end of the project. It relates directly to the construction schedule. In creating the draw schedule, you or the lender will establish how many payments will be made over the course of the project and the dollar amount of each anticipated payment based on the percentage of work scheduled to be completed, less retainage.

Retainage is money earned (for work completed) but held back from the contractor until the completion of the entire project. The standard approach is to hold 10 percent of the value of all completed work. This helps ensure that an owner is not paying out more than the work is worth, and over the course of a good-sized project, this retainage adds up to quite a good incentive for the contractor to finish. If you have a $50,000 project and you create a draw schedule showing five payments based on $10,000 worth of work for each draw, you will retain $1,000 (10 percent of $10,000) and pay the contractor $9,000. By the end of the project, the contractor will have received $45,000 and you will still be holding $5,000. You would release the retainage only when all the work was done satisfactorily (page 183).

Pitfall

When someone tells me, "I call and call, but I just can't get the contractor to come back," I know they've paid him too much.

A draw schedule is required by anyone lending you money for the project, and it's helpful to you in three ways. Both you and the contractor can plan ahead financially. You are much less likely to pay for work not yet completed. And you are less likely to have the contractor come to you, hat in hand, looking for money just because he needs some.

If you are not borrowing money, ask the contractor to present a draw schedule or work with him to create one in advance of project start-up. It's usually laid out on a monthly payment basis for large projects that last several months. However, you may lay it out on a biweekly or weekly basis for small, short term projects, such as a six week kitchen renovation. Anyone making or reviewing a draw schedule will need the project budget and the construction schedule to carry out the following five steps in tracking time passed and money spent.

Step 1: Use the construction schedule to estimate what materials will be purchased and what work will be complete by specified dates.

Step 2: Determine what percentage of the total work this represents in each of your budget line items. For example, the Dorseys' contractor estimates that one month after construction begins, the foundation will be complete, the first floor will be framed, and all the windows and exterior doors will be on site. This represents about 50 percent of the site work, 100 percent of the concrete work, 30 percent of the rough carpentry, and 65 percent of the cost of the windows and doors.

Step 3: Take your budget and look up the total cost of the work in each of these line items. Multiply each line item by the percentage you think will be complete for that first requisition as shown above.

REQUISITION #1—DORSEY HOUSE ADDITION			
LINE ITEM	**TOTAL COST**	**% COMPLETE**	**INCLUDED IN FIRST DRAW**
Site work	$5,073	50%	$2,536
Concrete	5,414	100%	5,414
Rough carpentry	9,414	30%	2,824
Windows and doors	10,600	65%	6,890
Total anticipated work and materials for first month			$17,664
General conditions	6,500	20%	1,300
Subtotal			$18,964
15% overhead and profit	21,060		2,844
Subtotal			$21,808
Less 10% retainage			(2,180)
TOTAL FIRST DRAW			**$19,628**

Step 4: Add those sums together, and deduct the percentage you are holding back for retainage. The total is the amount of the first anticipated draw. Repeat for subsequent scheduled draws through the last planned payment when the retainage will be paid to the contractor as well.

Step 5: Put these dates and draw amounts on paper, and you have a draw schedule (see below). Payment is made only if the materials are on site and the work is done in accordance with the anticipated milestones. You will have to adjust the amounts to be paid and/or the dates to pay them if work or delivery of materials is delayed.

DRAW SCHEDULE—DORSEY HOUSE ADDITION					
WORK COMPLETE	**DRAW 1**	**DRAW 2**	**DRAW 3**	**DRAW 4**	**DRAW 5**
Site work (1st half), concrete, rough carpentry, windows and doors	$19,628				
Rough carpentry, roofing, windows		$24,865			
Exterior finish carpentry, insulation, siding, doors and hardware, rough-in (1st half) for plumbing, heating, and electrical			$45,097		
Interior finish carpentry, gypsum				$16,689	
Site work and masonry (2nd half), cabinets, flooring, ceramic tile, painting, specialties, finish work (2nd half) for plumbing, heating, and electrical, retainage of $14,368					$55,946
CONTRACT AMOUNT					**$162,225**

Notes: Each draw amount includes 20% of the general conditions number, plus the cost of each described work item completed along with corresponding overhead and profit at 15%, less 10% for retainage. Retainage from the first four draws is added back into the final draw amount.

What Was That Other Thing?
Additional Things to Track

You will find everything easier to track if you get all your time-sensitive tasks, pending decisions, and other deadlines in one place. I recommend figuring out what they are and using different colored pens to note them in the appropriate date slots on your copy of the construction schedule. Hang it on the fridge or keep it in your day planner for easy reference during the course of the project. You may have some of the following time-sensitive issues.

Supplies

You may be providing some special materials to be included in the project: that great stained-glass piece you got at the flea market, the antique front door you scavenged on vacation, or the light fixture that triggered this whole dining room makeover in the first place. You may also be required to choose cabinets, carpet, wallpaper, tile, and other finishes for which allowances have been included in your project cost. Make sure those supplies and selections get to the contractor on time.

Inspections

Depending on your project, several people may be inspecting the work completed: you, an architect or project manager, the building and mechanical inspectors, and the bank appraiser. Track these appointments for inspections against the milestones in your construction schedule.

Insurance

Your insurance agent may ask to be notified at critical junctures in the project, including completion of the foundation, enclosure of the space, firing of the heating systems, and when the space is habitable.

Your Personal Deadlines

Life goes on, and the more of an involved owner you are, the more you have to ensure that the construction schedule creates as little stress as possible in the rest of your life. Things like when the kids get out of school, when the baby is due, care for ailing parents and even the annual Fourth of July barbecue may be time-sensitive issues worth noting.

It's hard to fully appreciate that time is money until you see deadlines unmet on a construction site. Apply your knowledge of schedules and pre-empt experiencing this firsthand.

CHAPTER 12

Mother, May I?
Getting Through the Permit Process

This chapter will list and assist with all the sign-offs and blessings to be obtained from the planning office staff as well as review boards, the building inspectors, and even the neighbors.

- Nothing to Fear: Knowing the Process and Its Players
- People Pleasing: The Steps for Permit Approval
- Good to Go: Once You've Got the Permit
- Step Lightly: Making Changes to the Neighborhood

Nothing to Fear:
Knowing the Process and Its Players

Your home must be built, expanded, or renovated in accordance with the ordinances of your state and town. How you go about getting your property permitted depends on where you live. If you're doing a build-to-suit home, the developer will probably handle all permitting. However, if you are building a new home or an addition, or making over your existing home, you or someone representing you will have to obtain a building permit. Requirements vary from state to state and also from town to town. Some towns are quite lax, and some are very stringent. In general, the more rural the location, the fewer steps there are to permitting, with the exception of areas prone to hurricanes, floods, erosion, or earthquakes. These areas have become more stringent by necessity.

> *Big fleas have little fleas upon their back to bite 'em. And little fleas have lesser fleas and so ad infinitum.*
>
> —OGDON NASH

Insider's Tip

Permitting is the only bureaucratic process in your construction project. The wheels turn slowly, and you don't always get the answers you want the first time through. Plan your time and other commitments accordingly.

The best way to get started in the process is to go to the town clerk's office, or the planning office if your town has one, and ask what hurdles your municipality makes you clear, what the timelines and fees are for each step, and what materials and information you must provide. Chances are good they will have a checklist of all you need to do, with the appropriate contact people included. Be aware of the oddly symbiotic yet bureaucratic relationship among all the entities involved in getting your approval to build, expand, or renovate. The departments and boards described below are interrelated, and you must meet the requirements of one before you can seek approval from the next. However, these disparate offices work independently too, with their own set of rules and ways of doing things. Don't assume they know what's going on before or after them in the process.

Staff Affection

If your town has a planning office, it will have a town planner and maybe other staff members. These people are a great resource for you. They have seen tons of plans and hundreds, even thousands, of owners with questions. They will assist you with the application process and review your initial submittal. The first things a staff person will look at are the location of your property, dimensional standards including lot coverage, building height, and your proposed setback from adjacent properties. This will require a site plan (a bird's-eye view), with all dimensions accurately noted, that at least addresses these factors. Some municipalities require stamped drawings produced by a licensed architect (see below).

Based on that initial review, the staff will let you know what approvals need to be obtained and how to go about applying, scheduling, and paying for those. You may be asked to present your project to one or more of the community boards described below. Typically, these boards meet every two to four weeks. Since these meetings are a forum for public comment, your application must be "notified". This means an overview of your application will likely be posted in the local newspaper fifteen days prior to your scheduled slot on the board agenda, and all abutting property owners will receive a notice in the mail. A staff person may visit your

Site Plan—Dorsey House Addition

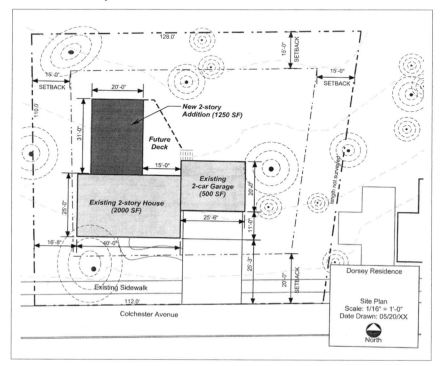

What Your Contractor Can't Tell You

site to verify the information submitted in your application and be prepared to give input to the board(s).

Don't be intimidated by the process. With the exception of those permits that must be pulled by licensed professionals, the process is made for laypeople. I have sat on boards that give approval for building or renovation in my town, and we love to see homeowners who are enthusiastic about their projects and looking to do things right. However, if you live in an area where the permitting process is really complicated and requires more time and education than you care to invest, you may want to hire a permit expeditor. The staff will probably mention this option and offer you some contact info on expeditors if using them is common practice where you live. If you're using an architect, they often help with this.

Go Early, Go Often

Most of us have heard the phrase "held up in the permit process." This problem usually comes about in one of two ways. One, the owner didn't allow enough time for the process and has work scheduled to begin before obtaining approvals and a building permit; or two, the owner missed a step or blew something off and is now asking for forgiveness from a skeptical town planner or building inspector. The key is to get into this process early. Then you will know what will be expected of you and your project won't be held up while you wait to bring required

> **Pitfall**
>
> If you're called to task because your construction project was not permitted properly, that's the contractor's responsibility, right? Wrong. The permit follows the property, and you are responsible for both the permit and the problem.

changes to the next meeting a month in the future. Remember, although the process is fairly straightforward, it is bureaucratic and the people within it represent the best interests of the municipality. Unlike most of the people involved in your project, they do not work for you. You need to satisfy them, and the best way to do that is to do as you're told, be ready to compromise, don't commit a lot of time or money to design before you have some sense that it will be approved, and always ask for permission, not forgiveness. It's even valuable to stop by the appropriate offices before you begin designing. Meet any pertinent staff and inspectors face-to-face. Share your ideas for your building, and make sure you understand what will be required later. Establishing good relations with the permit people is always time well spent.

When Ignorance Is Not Such Bliss

There's a common misconception when it comes to permits. Since contractors often obtain permits, owners think it's the contractor's responsibility. Wrong. The owner of the property, not the person contracted to build it, is ultimately responsible for ensuring that all work is permitted and inspected. If you agree to have the builder or a subcontractor get the necessary permits, first find out for yourself what is required, and be sure to have those permits in hand before work begins. If you intentionally or inadvertently dodge the permit process, you may get away with it only to find you have problems when you go to sell the property. For instance, if the footprint of your property has been altered, it may encroach on a setback, and it certainly won't match the description in the title to your property. Yup, it was a sad day when I attended a deck demolition party. It's much better to be a good doobie when it comes to permitting.

People Pleasing:
The Steps for Permit Approval

In your location, what you are having built may require any of the following types of approval. Each section below includes a definition of this step in the approval process, the people you will encounter, typical issues addressed, and advice from professionals in those respective departments.

Zoning

Your town has ordinances that apply to areas, or zones, on the town's map. Some areas are zoned residential (homes), some commercial (business), some industrial (manufacturing), etc. Not every eventuality is covered in the zoning ordinances, so the zoning board hears owners seeking clarification or exception to these ordinances. The board is typically made up of volunteer community members with interests in law, town planning, real estate, or architecture. For diverse representation, the board strives for a balance of its members in terms of these interests as well as where they live in the community. An owner may go before a zoning board for a variance granting relief from a particular zoning ordinance, or to appeal the denial of a permit based on an interpretation of a zoning ordinance at the staff level. The zoning process also gets you on the municipality's property tax roll.

Typical Issues: An owner wanting an in-home business may seek conditional use approval granting exception to the rules of property use in a residential area. Another owner may want a variance on the number of dwelling units allowed because she wants to add on a mother-in-law apartment.

Advice from Pros: Whatever the reason, if you need to go before a zoning board before you can move forward with your project, stop everything and wait for that approval. Bending the rules of zoning ordinances is not a slam dunk, and the board will need a compelling reason to make an exception for you without setting a bad precedent.

Planning

Planning focuses on the division of land and what sits on it. If your town requires planning approval but does not have staff that has authority to give that approval, your project will have to go before a planning board for any construction project that requires subdivision of land or the addition of built materials, including parking surfaces and other significant

Isn't the greatest rule of all the rules simply to please?

—MOLIÈRE

What Your Contractor Can't Tell You

changes to the site. The board is made up of a mix of community volunteers from different neighborhoods with some knowledge of planning, along with interests in site plans and architectural design. You should bring a large site plan or handouts of your site plan that can be easily viewed by all, showing all pertinent dimensions of the lot, the buildings, the driveway, trees, and boundaries.

Typical Issues: Relationship of the lot and proposed structures to the neighborhood, the street, and neighboring properties. Access for fire and emergency equipment, and visibility to and of oncoming motorists.

Advice from Pros: Your site plan can be homemade, but make it clear and well detailed with all dimensions indicated.

Design Review

Now they're really meddling, right? Design review has to do with the aesthetic qualities of your proposed project, and its context in the neighborhood in terms of scale, character, and massing. Usually, this review is triggered only by location in certain designated zones that are deemed to be sensitive to the impact of . . . well . . . aesthetic mistakes. The goal here is compatibility with the neighborhood, and the design review board's job is to ensure you achieve that. The board is usually made up of community volunteers with expertise in architecture and design. The members will review your designs regarding the exterior of the building(s) and any other site improvements. For this meeting, you will likely be asked to bring a site plan and all four elevations (side views) of the building(s).

Typical Issues: What's in keeping? Is what you are proposing an asset or a liability to the surrounding neighborhood in terms of size, style, and appearance?

Advice from Pros: Even if you are not planning to have an architect on your project, now would be a good time to consider having a professional prepare some simple schematic drawings. Your builder could also provide these, and so can you—but please at least use a ruler. Scribbles on a napkin from an owner shouting, "Trust me, it will look great!" tend to send up red flags at this juncture.

Depending on what you're asking for in terms of zoning, planning or design, your request may be posted in a local newspaper and sent to your abutting neighbors. Then those neighbors and the larger community have a chance to voice their concerns and/or support of your project. Guess which they voice.

Other Review Boards

Some locales have unique steps in the permitting process such as historic review, urban review, or environmental quality review relating to the wetlands, shoreline, or other natural resource being protected. In addition, residential developments often have associations that review in accordance with their own bylaws.

Advice on Boards

Nationwide, municipalities are trying to streamline the process and reduce the number of approval steps by combining zoning and planning review under one board. So in your area, the steps listed above may be handled by individual boards or may now fall under the purview of just one or two boards.

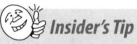

Insider's Tip

If you are going before a municipal board for approval, it would be a great idea to attend a couple of their meetings before you appear before them with your project. The meetings are open to the public. In some municipalities they're even televised locally. They are interesting, and you will learn a lot about what will be expected of you.

The boards usually accept staff recommendations, so satisfying those staffers is a wise first step. No one involved in the process is supposed to help you with design, except to review and make recommendations as needed, so come prepared. Homeowners are often accompanied and even represented by their builder or architect at board presentations. After presenting your project and answering questions, you will come out of any board meeting with one of four decisions:

- Approval of your application and plans as submitted

- Conditional approval of your application, meaning you are approved under certain specified conditions

- Denial of your application with suggestions as to what you need to change and submit for approval at the next meeting

- Denial of your application without suggestions, indicating your plans are too far out of the realm of feasibility for anyone to make suggestions. Back to the drawing board if you get this response.

Lastly, if you don't like the answers you get and disagree with a board's interpretation of the ordinances, politely ask them to show you the ordinance that gives them the authority to make this decision. That's where any negotiation begins and ends, with the ordinance. Sometimes even the board members forget that.

Building Permits

To obtain the actual building permit, you will need thorough plans. If you went before a board with minimal plans, this next and final step will require more. You need to have plans that show not only the fin-

> "There are two great rules in life, the one general and the other particular. The first is that every one can in the end get what he wants if he only tries. This is the general rule. The particular rule is that every individual is more or less of an exception to the general rule."
>
> —SAMUEL BUTLER

ished product but the materials that will go into it as well as detailed dimensions. It is the building inspector's job to do a plan review to ensure that what you're planning to build meets all pertinent building and safety codes. This will include review of the foundation, framing layout, and all proposed systems, including electrical, heating, and plumbing, you name it.

The mechanical systems, including electrical, plumbing, heating/air-conditioning, and gas, will require separate permits obtained by the trades specializing in those fields from inspectors specializing in those fields. For instance, your electrician will apply for and receive an electrical permit from the electrical inspector. Your building permit will be issued only after all the necessary mechanical permits have been issued. Your subcontractors are very familiar with their part of this process, leaving you to focus on the bigger picture, the building permit.

Although it's your job as the owner to ensure that your project is properly permitted, towns that require licensing of construction contractors usually require that they obtain the building permit. In places that do not require licensing of builders, owners are often allowed to obtain permits as well. Either way, it's a great idea for the contractor and owner to see the building inspector together. That way, you will hear everything the inspector says to the builder and learn what deficiencies there are in your plans that may cost you later. This review process is more subjective than you might imagine. Usually, some amount of horse trading goes on, and the contractor is given some specific instructions. Your contractor may try to dissuade you from joining in, but you want to be privy to this discussion between contractor and inspector if you possibly can be.

If your town gives you the option of who should pull the permit, who should it be? Some owners like to get it just to save a little money, since a contractor will charge a bit for his time to do it. Don't be cheap! I like to have the contractor get the permit. Though it's good for an owner to be part of the process, it's also good to have the contractor take responsibility directly for satisfying all requirements of the permit, following all instructions from the building inspector, and scheduling all inspections. Since he plans to continue working in this community, it is in the contractor's best interest to keep the respect of that building inspector. Let his self-interest work for you.

To summarize, you may want to approach this last leg of permitting like this. Set up an initial meeting with the building inspector to discuss your project in broad terms, maybe before you even have any plans or a contractor on board. When the time comes, have the contractor file the building permit application and schedule a meeting for both of you to review the plans with the building inspector. Get copies of all paperwork for your files, because no matter who does the legwork, the permit follows the property, not the people involved. The contractor will receive and post the permit on site, comply with what the inspector tells him to

An ounce of action is worth a ton of theory.

—FRIEDRICH ENGELS

do to address code concerns, and schedule all necessary inspections of the construction project in progress.

Typical Issues: Structural integrity, sufficient capacity of all systems, rise and run of stairs, egress from second-story windows—anything that might elicit concerns about soundness and safety of the proposed building.

Advice from Pros: Use the time while you're waiting for zoning or other approval to meet with the building inspector. He can get you ready for the next step so you don't lose time in the process.

Handling Building Inspectors

Is the building inspector in your area infamous? Do all the contractors fear him? Are there local legends about the terrible things he's made people do or structures he had demolished after they were built? In my opinion, if he's a good inspector in a busy building community, all the above are true, and here's why. He is responsible for making sure hundreds of things get built correctly each year. When someone successfully sues the owner of a new building after tripping on the steps, or the roofs of a development fly off in a tornado, whom do you think they turn to and blame? The building inspector. If he lets a place get built in violation of code, it's his fault. He can't be everywhere at once, and he can't let builders think they can just do as they wish when he's not looking. What I call the cold-war mentality is his best option. He needs people to think he's crazy enough to push the button if someone's caught doing things wrong, and occasionally he makes an example of just such a someone. Although he has a heavy burden and maybe a tough shell to bear it, this inspector is your ally. He may make your contractor's life hell at times, but don't let that relationship overshadow how he can benefit you. He has no financial stake in your project and so is the most objective and professional set of eyes reviewing your plans. Use him. Flesh out your plans in detail with him. Hide nothing, and ask how you might do things differently, better, or cheaper.

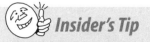 **Insider's Tip**

Don't let anyone scare you away from the building inspector. He's your secret ally.

 **Insider's Tip**

Permitting fees can really add up. Don't forget them when budgeting your project cost.

Oh Yes, the Pound of Flesh

Of course, there is no way to get through city hall without paying some fees. Fees differ widely from place to place in their amounts and how they are calculated, so check with your municipality and get a fee schedule so that this expense comes as no surprise. You might have to pay an application fee for starting the approval process at the zoning or planning level, another for the building permit itself, and another for your home's impact on the town's infrastructure and services.

Some towns use flat fees of under $100 to submit an application, and some charge based on the square footage or estimated construction cost of the total project for both the application submittal and the building permit. Say you want to build a 2,000-square-foot house for an estimated $200,000 in Niceville, USA:

Application Fee: In Niceville, you'll pay $6 per $1,000 of estimated construction cost, or 0.6 percent, for the zoning application. On a $200,000 construction project, this would cost you $1,200.

Impact Fee: Your new home has an impact on the town's expenses. The town can expect to incur more costs for roads, traffic lights, water, sewer, police, fire, schools, and even the library. The existing property tax payers are not expected to pick up all the expenses generated by other peoples' desire to build in their town. So you, the homeowner, may be required to pay an impact fee to help Niceville keep up with the increased demands on its infrastructure and services. This is a onetime fee, usually based on the square footage of your proposed home or addition. Two dollars per square foot is common. If you are building a 2,000-square-foot home, you would pay a $4,000 impact fee levied by the town through the Niceville planning office.

Building Permit Application Fee: The Niceville Department of Public Works will liberate you of another 0.6 percent of your total estimated construction cost for the building permit—another $1,200.

So to build that estimated 2,000-square-foot, $200,000 house in Niceville, the total fees would be:

BUILDING PERMIT FEES	
Application to the planning office	$1,200
Impact fee	$4,000
Building permit fee	$1,200
TOTAL FEES	**$6,400**

Good to Go:
Once You've Got the Permit

When your plans have been approved and permitted, a large yellow card will be issued. It is to be posted in an obvious place on the work site. This permit gives you permission to build in accordance with the plans you submitted. You or your contractor will need to schedule required inspections along the way. Typically, the building and mechanical inspectors need to do some or all of the following inspections:

• Foundation inspection is conducted by the building inspector and should take place before the foundation has been backfilled so that he can inspect waterproofing, foundation insulation, footing drains, and water and sewer pipe penetrations as well as the foundation itself.

- Rough-in inspections are conducted by electrical, plumbing, and other mechanical inspectors after all wiring, piping, ductwork, etc., have been installed, but before the framing is enclosed with wall surfaces.

- Rough-framing inspection is conducted by the building inspector to ensure the building is framed to be structurally sound and in accordance with the plans submitted. The rough-in work by the subcontractors should be completed before the rough-framing inspection is conducted, since the penetrations through the framing for wiring, pipes, and ductwork may have an impact on the structural integrity of that framing.

- Final inspections are conducted by each of the inspectors to assure total compliance with the plans and code, and to ensure that this dwelling is safe for habitation. Your final approval comes in the form of a certificate of occupancy which gives you permission to occupy this space.

These inspections mark significant milestones in your project, and they can delay work from progressing in a timely fashion while you wait for the inspector to give you approval to go on. Be sure you or your contractor is on top of scheduling these inspections. If you make a significant change in the scope of work, such as increase the building size, change a roof pitch, or add air-conditioning, be sure to inform the building inspector before the work begins. You don't want him to think you're trying to pull a fast one, sneaking in work you didn't get permitted in advance.

Step Lightly:
Making Changes to the Neighborhood

With all the decisions you have to make and coordination you have to manage for your construction project, it's easy to forget those around you. When it comes to the neighbors, remember, they will be there long after the contractors are gone. Think of how fascinated you've been watching a project unfurl where you now live and how inconvenienced you've been by the mess and noise. If the first thing a new neighborhood sees of you is a messy, noisy construction site, you may have some fences to mend when the process is over. Neighbors can even stall or stop you from getting a permit if they contest it with sufficient grounds. However, it's hard to be a nasty neighbor to people who you know have made an effort to take your needs into consideration. If you're building new you have no home yet, so the neighbors can't bring over muffins and welcome you to the neighborhood. You must go to them. Do so before the project begins, introduce yourself, and tell them the timeline and daily work hours of the project. Give them your phone number and ask them to feel free to call you with any problems regarding the construction. This way you will find them a lot more accepting of your project and better neighbors in the long run. When the project is complete, be sure to invite them to the housewarming party and thank them for their patience and support.

A building permit in hand means your plans satisfy code requirements and meet the standards of your community. Once your neighbors give their blessings, you're done explaining your project to anyone but friends and family.

CHAPTER 13

Ready to Build?...
Not So Fast
Pulling It All Together

Everyone gains comfort from a clear definition of success before a project begins. In this chapter, we'll review what you need to ensure before the workers come.

- Just Like Santa: Make a List and Check It Twice
- Long Time No See: The Preconstruction Meeting
- Ensurance: Make Sure These Things Are Done
- When Are They Leaving?! Renovation Tips

Just Like Santa:
Make a List and Check It Twice

You have come to understand a lot about what makes a good project. You have made many choices about what information to apply and what information to forgo. Look at the questions below and make sure that you've addressed any tasks that you've chosen to include in the preparation of your project.

- Do you love your designs?

- Do you have a well-defined scope of work to convey your designs to all players?

- Do you have a contractor who is the right choice for you and your project?

- Do you have a fixed price for the work or a solid approach laid out for another method of holding your costs in line?

- Do you have a signed contract?

- Do you have a construction schedule?

- Do you have money in place with a draw schedule and healthy contingency?

- Do you have your insurance in place?

- Do you have certificates of insurance from the contractor?

- Do you have permits and a rough schedule for inspection?

- Do you have needed surveys, perk test, and confirmed utility connections set up?

- Do the neighbors know who you are and what's happening?

- Do you have a good division of duties planned with any significant other?

- Do you have in place anyone you may have chosen to help monitor (page 6)?

- Do you have a list of any materials you will have to select and when?

Long Time No See: The Preconstruction Meeting

After you've settled on the right contractor, there's often a lengthy period during which everyone is running in different directions to pull the permits, get through the contract, satisfy the lender with budgets and necessary paperwork, and wring hands over lots of little details. It's a busy time, and yet all the players who will be on the job site may not see each other and focus on the scope of work for several weeks—months even. When the dust settles you're ready to begin. Have a "preconstruction" meeting to get everyone together face-to-face. Confirm that you all understand what's about to take place and are ready to start.

The Owner's Briefcase

Now would be a good time to set up your equivalent of a toolbox. For this and all future meetings, I recommend you bring the following:

- Date book. You'll be scheduling lots of things.

- Calculator. You'll be surprised how much math work takes place.

- Camera for visual documentation of the project

- Notebook and pen to take meeting minutes

- Copies of the budget, the plans, the specifications, and the contract. Together these make up the project guidelines, and you may need to refer to them during discussions.

- Change order forms. Having these at meetings may help you turn around decisions quickly (page 177).

- Lien waiver forms (page 130). If you're asking for them for each payment period, you'll have one handy each time the contractor hands you a requisition.

- Copies of minutes from previous meetings

- Tape measure—good for verifying reality

- Mud boots

Insider's Tip

You may want to use a three-ring binder for the growing stack of paperwork that you'll be collecting. For taking notes, I like to use those little black-and-white composition notebooks with bound pages. Since pages cannot be inserted or removed, these notebooks are accepted by legal typess as an accurate chronological account of a project in the event of a dispute.

The Who's Who of Your Team

In attendance should be:

- You, the owner(s)

- The general contractor

- The architect, designer, owner's representative, or other consultant who may be helping you with project management

- The first big subcontractor on the job, probably the excavator. (Having a subcontractor at these meetings is not common practice, but if you can get him to take a few minutes to join the meeting, I think it's worth it. He sees you're watching the store, and you can confirm that he knows his mission.)

This project is about to shift gears dramatically. Now is your chance to set the tone, to let everyone understand how you plan to participate and what your expectations are.

Speak Now or Forever Hold Your Peace, Folks

You should do the following at the meeting:

- Have all parties give updates on their completed tasks and verify their readiness and availability. Take the pulse of the group, and flesh out any last-minute concerns or apprehensions. Cover the scope of work, costs, and schedules.

- Review any ground rules specific to your project: parking facilities, work hours, phone use, cleanup, safety procedures, etc.

- Talk about the paper trail all parties will generate: revised drawings, requisitions, change orders, warranties, and manuals. Share and review the forms to be used. Talk about turnaround time, and determine who processes what and who gets copies. You, the owner, get copies of everything.

- Mention that no changes to the scope of work will be paid for unless they have been approved by you in advance.

- Outline monitoring that can be expected: job meetings, site visits, photography, bank inspections, requisition review, etc. It's only fair, and it helps to spell this out before work begins so the contractor doesn't feel as though he's being accused of bad behavior when you watch your project like a hawk.

- Set the weekly job meeting schedule that's most convenient to all parties. Contractors usually prefer to meet after 3:00 p.m. when they are still on site but the crews are headed

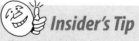 **Insider's Tip**

Try to schedule the job meetings for midweek. That way enough work has been done in the week to generate questions yet there's time left in the week to achieve solutions and get any necessary materials on site for the coming week.

home. It's still light out and generally a good time if you can get away from work or the kids.

- Discuss how and when each person likes to be contacted. Create a list of phone numbers, cell phone numbers, pager numbers, fax numbers, addresses, and email addresses, and distribute to all. The more available you are, the better. If you're an early riser and willing to take calls early, let the contractor know that. They are often standing at a sales counter at 6:30 a.m. wishing they could call you about something.

- Discuss who may give directives. From the contractor's point of view, there may be three or more people at the table. Whom does he listen to? Who has authority? If your spouse or partner comes on site and says the opposite of what you said the day before, what would the contractor do? Can the architect give directives on the site without checking with you first? Talk this out. Neither playing Telephone nor backdoor communication is good for the project.

- Close the meeting with the pep talk of your choice.

Ensurance:
Make Sure These Things Are Done

- Ensure that you have systems in place for anything that happens regularly, like paying the bills and making changes to the scope.

- Ensure that the contractor perceives you as an asset, not a hindrance. Go ahead of the general contractor to clear the path between him and anything that impedes his work and is your responsibility. There are many things an owner can do. If you're doing a renovation in your occupied home, move and cover the furniture yourself, remove valuables that may tempt, tend to pets, kids, utilities, keys, parking, and storage. Let the contractor know you're ready to convert your home to a work site that's low-risk and efficient.

- Ensure that any down payment is accounted for in your budget and that you have protection of that investment built into your contract.

- Ensure that up-to-date plans and specifications have been distributed to everyone who needs them. All subcontractors should have full sets. Though their work may be shown on only one page, conflicts can arise when they can't see where and how other people's work is planned to overlap with theirs. You'd hate to have to pay to move ductwork because the HVAC guy couldn't see you planned to have plumbing pipe in that location. Have a set that stays at the site at all times for anyone to refer to.

- Ensure that you have an accurate list of all subcontractors. Get a list of all the major suppliers too, even if surreptitiously. If things get rough, you may want to call them and see if they have received payment for the materials and supplies on site.

- Ensure that any personnel you wanted on the job are coming and will stay with the job to the end. No baiting and switching.

- Ensure that no one has the wrong idea about you and your money. If you haven't done it already by necessity, it's time to change the tone of the money talk. Don't let the discourse stay on broad numbers. Put on your Scrooge hat. Scrutinize any new pricing from this point on (page 73).

- Ensure that the natural assets on your property are protected. Tag any trees to be saved, and guard their root systems from truck traffic. Get protection over any shrubs you don't want harmed. If your project involves land clearing, have an approach in place for all the felled trees and the topsoil (page 47).

- If you've got all this "ensurance" in place, you're doing as well as most professionals, and this bodes well for a successful project. On to the site!

When Are They Leaving?!
Renovation Tips

A renovation in occupied space presents unique challenges for those doing the work as well as those living in the space. For the duration of the project, your home is the contractor's workplace. Try to foresee what level of invasion you'll be comfortable with, and define it up front. If you do it right, you will miss the contractors once they leave. Here are some tips for your happy coexistence.

In planning the project, think about ways you can streamline the scope of work to have the least impact on your lifestyle as possible. Do all exploratory work before construction work begins. Peek in those walls, pull back that floor covering. Also get unit prices for the things you cannot see (page 28). This will prevent the waste of time that goes with the other approach, which is to get the whole crew on site, open wallls, dicker over prices, order materials, wait and reschedule the work crew.

If your renovation project includes both functional and aesthetic items, alternate them. Insulate the attic, then paint the kitchen. Upgrade the wiring, then strip the mantel. This will give you ongoing rewards on both fronts and usually goes a long way to keep the peace in a marriage.

Get anything preassembled that can be. Once you think about this, you may be surprised by just how much can be built elsewhere and brought in for installation: the kitchen cabinets, the wall of built-ins, the window seat, lots of stuff. Materials are offered for purchase in varying degrees of completion. You can get prehung doors and windows, prefinished flooring, preprimed lumber, prepainted shelves. There are also many quick-drying products these days, including urethanes, Sheetrock compound, and adhesives. Explore your options with your contractor.

If you plan to move into a place and then renovate, do two steps of the project before you unpack the truck. Paint the inside of the closets and cupboards so you don't have to handle stored things more than once. And refinish the floors because you can do a lot of work around your possessions, but you cannot make them levitate.

If an addition is part of your project, talk through the "tie-in" with the contractor. If you all plan well, most of the work can take place outside your living space, with the connection to the existing space being the last thing done. Not having full access to everything at once is slightly more complicated for the contractor, but he can likely do it.

Once workers are on site, it will be hard to resist asking them to do any little thing you see in your home that needs doing. Do not ask for additional work in a casual manner. This could jeopardize the larger schedule and be thrown in your face later as the reason the project is running late or over budget. You can get the extra work done. Just try to structure it. Even if you're working off a little laundry list of tasks, amend your scope, contract, and schedule as you go. This will help keep the contractor from grinding his teeth.

Close Quarters

Due to the sheer proximity of the workers, you cannot help but have a more intimate relationship with them. Be mindful of this dynamic, and set some boundaries. Be sure your primary relationship with them is professional. Spell out the terms for the following:

- When utilities, kitchen, and bathrooms might be out of service
- What's their space and what's off-limits to them
- Where they can park
- Where they can store materials
- Their use of your power, water, bathroom, and phone
- Address heat loss from open doors
- How to handle turning lights off, locking up, and setting alarm systems
- Relations with your kids and pets
- What you prohibit hearing from a radio
- Language you will not accept

To my parents' embarrassment, my eldest brother's first word was "bashard." We had a construction project going on at that formative time in his life. He grew up and went into construction, so it all worked out fine.

Controlling the Mess

This part can really be maddening. Dust gets everywhere, the floors are unrecognizable, handprints cover the walls you didn't need worked on. Only about half of the contractors I know are good about controlling this, so be specific about your requirements up front, or you'll find yourself shouting, "Was he raised in a barn?!" Here are the housekeeping procedures that will help:

Inside

- Wrap it good. Apply and tape rosin paper on any uncarpeted floors. It's cheap and will hold up through a lot, leaving your floors nearly pristine.

- Use painter's tape and thin sheets of plastic from a paint store to seal off any openings that will not remain operable. For those that will remain operable, you need a little more. On the days when the big dust flies, as when Sheetrock is sanded, I add a damp sheet hung over the plastic and a damp towel on the floor. This really catches the mess that bounces off the plastic and sneaks through in traffic.

- Even if you think they're out of the line of fire, cover the plants with light fabric. They choke and die easily from construction dust. And you have better things to do than wiping individual leaves for the next few months.

- Designate a cutting and sanding area. Your first choice is outside, second is the garage, and third is inside in a place you can enclose.

- The contractor should agree to pick up, sweep up, and store everything at the end of each workday.

- For cleaning up Sheetrock dust, avoid the temptation to use a damp sponge. Vacuum, wipe up with micro-fiber, but no moisture. Trust me.

Outside

- Park your car out of harm's way.

- Insist on daily nail pickup. For a big outdoor project, the contractor can rent a rolling magnet for this before he leaves the site for good. This may prevent you from getting a punctured tire a year later.

- If work is taking place around exterior plants or landscape beds, the contractor should never cover the plants with plastic, but rather use light-colored fabric to reflect the hot sun. If there's a paint project going on, he should collect all paint chips and drips on drop cloths laid around the base of the house. Otherwise, you'll be cleaning paint out of your mulch or grass forever. And if the old paint contained lead, it will contaminate your soil.

Keeping It Safe

Neighborhood kids love construction sites. What could be more fun—or dangerous? Good daily cleanup goes a long way in keeping a work site safe. Also specify the following:

What Your Contractor Can't Tell You

- No power equipment should be left plugged in overnight.

- No electrical wires should be left exposed.

- If a painter wants to use a heat gun for the removal of old paint on siding, consider how combustible the materials are behind that siding, and think about it hard.

- Schedule the use of any toxic materials, and insist they be stored out of reach.

- Ladders must be put away at night.

- No excavation equipment should be left idling when vacant, or turned off with the key left in it.

- Any exterior hazards like large holes or scaffolding must be wrapped with protective fencing.

Security

The contractor cannot vouch for the conduct of everyone he's bringing into your home. Subcontractors will bring in people he's never met, and he himself may be hiring day laborers he doesn't really know. Remove temptation. If you will have workers in your home when you're not there, remove your valuables, such as jewelry, guns, and cash. It has been my experience that other types of items that go missing are seasonal items not in use at the time. Six months after the workers have gone, you can't find your skis, or you head off to the concert in the park saying, "Honey, I'm sure we had binoculars." So keep an eye on the stuff in the back of your closets and the basement too. If your home is filled with valuables, you may want an insurance rider during the construction phase as well as requiring of the contractor that no one with a criminal record of theft be permitted on any of the crews.

Insider's Tip

If something goes missing from your home during a renovation, it won't likely be something you use every day. Watch the rarely watched stuff.

Controlling the Noise

Lots of people in construction have hearing damage. That ought to tell you something. It can get pretty loud, and most of the noise is unavoidable, although it can be managed. Set work hours that will keep you and your neighbors sane. Contractors like to start very early. If early access is okay with you, but not the noise, find a middle ground. For instance, you could permit them to show up at 7:00 a.m., but no hammering, heavy equipment, or power tools until 8:00. Radios will be coming with the workers. Set the volume standards. Also ask that unnecessary shouting be kept to a minimum . . . until the housewarming party.

Once you've reassembled your team and ensured that everyone's ready and everything's in place, it's time to execute those plans. On to the site.

CHAPTER 14

Let the Games Begin
Managing the Construction Phase

If you didn't believe it before, you probably do now: The plan is the thing. This book has thirteen chapters on setting your project up, and only this one on managing it while it's under construction. If you've done the things in the other chapters that are applicable to you and your project, this is all you'll need to make your dreams a reality.

- Who's on First: Establishing the Roles and Rules for All
- Watching the Store: Monitoring the Project
- For Richer or Poorer: Budget Management
- The Homestretch: Project Closeout

Who's on First: Establishing the Roles and Rules for All

At long last, it's time to get down to making something tangible. Five things will take place during the construction phase of your project:

- Construction work will be carried out.

- There will be ongoing interpretation of the plans and specifications.

- Revisions will be made to the scope of work addressing decisions previously left pending.

- Interested parties will monitor the construction work.

- Payment will be made for the work completed.

Here's what sometimes baffles people—if you have a good contractor, solid plans, permits, and you've all agreed on a price for the project, what more is there to do but watch them work? Somehow, plenty. Think of it like making a movie. If you have actors, costumes, and a good script, you still need a director to pull it all together. For a big project, if you haven't done so already, you may want to consider hiring someone expert in construction management to help oversee the project on your behalf. This is almost essential if you're building or renovating a distant second home and cannot have a regular presence on site.

The Main Players

You, the owner, will monitor the construction work, pay for the work, and make decisions when asked. From the point of view of the other parties,

> 6 6 *Ah, to build, to build! This is the noblest art of all the arts...* 9 9
>
> —HENRY WADSWORTH LONGFELLOW

"the owner" is everything else associated with you too. If you're part of a couple, there's the dynamic of your relationship and how that contributes to or detracts from the project. There's the best friend who tags along at site visits and flirts with the electrician. There's the banker, the kids, the pets, and your vacations. Sure it will be your finished space, but until that time, respect the fact that it is a work site. Do everything you can to make it an efficient one for the contractor.

If there is an architect, designer, or owner's representative on the project, that person can help monitor the project for progress and quality control, and interpret the plans for the contractor. To a great extent, he can also act as liaison between you and the contractor, ensuring that you understand the issues at hand and helping you make necessary decisions.

The contractor, his crew, and subcontractors are responsible for obtaining materials and carrying out the construction work as planned and agreed to in the contract. The contractor is also responsible for alerting you to problems he may have in interpreting the information conveyed on the plans, as well as participating in creating their solutions. Lastly, he will submit requisitions for payment.

If you have an architect on your project, the triangular relationship of owner-architect-contractor can be fascinating and challenging. Just be mindful of the many dynamics at play. You, the owner, now have a well established relationship with the architect, and the contractor is the last to join the team. Since you have completed the design phase, unless the plans do not

 **Pitfall**

You, the architect, and the contractor can become a hate triangle if you don't understand the role each plays in the construction phase.

hold up in the field, you are done with most debate with the architect. The two of you are now of a shared mind as you get the contractor to build as planned. This can feel a bit like two-on-one to the contractor unless you bring him into the fold quickly.

Like an employer, you are paying both the architect and the contractor, but you do not have their knowledge base. This creates a reliance on them and maybe a personal struggle to trust what they each say at times. When they give you conflicting input, who do you trust? Well, one of the features of the triangle is that the architect has no incentive to underbuild, due to his liability. The contractor has no incentive to overbuild due to the cost of labor and materials. So from your point in the triangle it's often the midrange option that's right. For instance, when I hear an architect suggest 2" x 8"s and the contractor's saying 2" x 4"s, I can't help but suspect that 2" x 6"s will likely suit the need best.

From the contractor's point of view, he must wait and see who really has authority over what. He may be bound by a contract that favors the other two parties. He may have a good or bad past with this architect. At any rate, it's the architect and contractor who work in the same construction community and will likely cross paths or swords again. By the way, the contractor knows your architect's strengths and weaknesseses from the plans. Some contractors are very leery of architects and see them as being empowered by their contracts, and qualified more in the theoretical than the practical nature of building. Contractors with this opinion might say something like, "This guy couldn't actually build a thing in the real world."

There may also be class, socioeconomic, and gender issues at play among the parties. Try to level the playing field and be a model of mutual respect.

Communication and Conduct

You can always lighten up, but it's hard to tighten up. Be sure to start things out as professionally and pleasantly as possible. Set a tone of equity, high standards, and mutual respect. You have plenty of time to become good buddies as all goes well due to your good planning. There are no stupid questions. Get everything you need explained to you until you understand it. You should never have to feel like a stranger on your own site, with mystery work going on around you.

You will likely be tested early in the project. The contractor will make a change and tell you about it later. If you have chosen a high level of owner participation for yourself, now is the time to be a bit of a jerk—just this once. Hold off on paying any up-charge that comes out of this, or make them do the work as planned. Do what you must to make them understand that you need to be in the loop, and restate that you stand ready to make lightning fast decisions when given all the information. When it comes to other people making final decisions about your project, nip it in the bud.

The most destructive and expensive pitfall of residential projects may be the namby-pamby owner. When I hear, "I jokingly said I thought he was overcharging me, but he didn't say anything," or "I said I thought the window might look better up higher, but he just went and put it in low anyway," I know this project is doomed. You cannot hint, cajole, or whine your way to a successful project. Be as decisive, clear, and direct as you can. Now is the time to get used to looking someone right in the eye and telling him what you want. If this is impossible for you, use your partner, architect, or a hired owner's representative to convey your wishes.

Don't gossip. Don't bad-mouth your partner's decisions. Don't let the contractor take you out for coffee and insult the architect. Once you have hired the team members, be loyal to each and every one of them. Be aware that you are at the center of several three-way relationships, there is big money at stake, and everyone there has more experience than you in manipulat-

> *Whenever one has anything unpleasant to say, one should always be quite candid.*
>
> —OSCAR WILDE

ing these circumstances to their advantage. So stay out of the mud, stay focused, and do your best to bring out the best in everyone on the job.

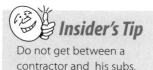 **Insider's Tip**

Do not get between a contractor and his subs.

You will spend some phone time dealing with the contractor's administrative person, typically a woman. Don't get uppity. The power base may actually be the woman behind the man. Introduce yourself and enlist her support, but respect her allegiance to the contractor. She holds a lot of sway, processes your paperwork, and frequently is the contractor's wife.

Pecking Order

Respect the chain of command. If you have hired a general contractor to execute your project, remember that the subcontractors are working for him, not you. He is responsible to you for their work, and this is a good thing. It's the other side of the team speaking with one voice. If you give subcontractors directives on site, you will start a bad game of Telephone and weaken the strength of your contract. If you see something that concerns you, go directly to the contractor to sort it out. Your relationship with subcontractors should be almost purely social unless you are addressing issues at a job meeting or the contractor invites you into a three-way discussion. Failure to respect this chain of command can cause confusion, bruised egos, and cost increases.

The Couple On Site

You, the owner, may in fact be a plural. If so, try to think of yourselves as a professional team. You and your colleagues from work don't go to meetings with outsiders and bicker or air the company's dirty laundry, so don't do it with your spouse or partner on a job site. Do your wrangling off site. Speak with one voice on site. Divide your duties clearly, and let the other members of the team know your respective job descriptions on the project. For instance, maybe you can swing by the site a couple days a week on your way home from work, but only your spouse can attend the weekly job meetings. Maybe you will be the one coordinating and relaying all decisions regarding finishes and fixtures, while your spouse will go through the permit process.

The Clammed Up Contractor

This is the guy who has trouble expressing himself, is very embarrassed to reveal he has made a mistake, and fears your reaction. This situation is like parents hoping their teen will come to them with big problems. Why? Because they share that kid's best interests and think they could contribute to a solution. The cover-up solution the kid comes up with could be awful. Same here. Don't just say you're open to hearing all. Make it happen by being an obvious supporter from day one. Let the contractor know you know there will be mistakes. They are inevitable, and you'll all work through them together.

> *Not only is there no God, but try finding a plumber on Sunday.*
>
> —WOODY ALLEN

The Guarded Architect

If you are using an architect and his plans, watch how he interprets the plans to the contractor when little conflicts arise. Out of the twenty-five architects I've worked with, only one actually admitted to a design error and offered to pay for the mistake. Architects don't want to admit to inferior design and ask clients to pay extra for a solution. You'll recall that the AIA contract documents give them power to be pretty tough on the contractor. To keep the peace and be ethical, you may have to set a staunch contract clause aside, step in, and mediate a solution that seems fair to all. Here's an example.

Fair Play

I was once working with a great team to renovate a community center. The architect designed an exterior landing with no rails around it. I asked if it needed rails. The architect said it did not because it was twenty-five inches off the ground and code did not require rails on landings under thirty inches off the ground. I knew he had the letter of the law right, but given how the land dropped away and this building held crowds, it was a long shot. Though he had approved the plans, when the building inspector saw it, he said, "No way. Put rails on that thing." Who pays for them? The contractor wanted to charge for the rails, and the architect wanted him to do it for free because the contractor was the one who had met with the inspector to pull the permit. The contract said that the builder was required to build according to code regardless of what was drawn. And what's code? What the book says or what the inspector says? I had pointed out the problem early on, so I certainly didn't want to pay an expensive change order for it. If the architect and I had made the contractor do it for free, he would have hated us, and rightly so. We came to a better solution. Since I was getting extra value in the rails to be added, I was willing to pay what they would have cost as part of the initial bid, but not the increased change order price being offered by the contractor. I asked nicely, and the architect agreed to pay that difference. The contractor was so pleased not to bear the brunt of this that his price dropped too. Win, win, win.

Shhhhhhh

There are times on a site when everyone can suddenly go mute. There's a concern with something major like the dimensions of a big beam that carries the weight of the floor above. Everyone knows the solution. It's easy, but they're not talking. It could be fear of liability. You have two choices. You can offer to pay for an engineer who's licensed and insured to render an opinion and give a directive, or you can say to the builder or architect, "I won't hold you responsible for this, but what's your solution?" Hear them out and then decide what to do based on your comfort level.

Trust in Allah, but Tie Your Camel

Even with a project well set up, and even if you have a fixed price for it, there is opportunity for the contractor to be an opportunist who takes unfair financial advantage of the situation. He's controlling the budget to a large extent now. He is ordering materials and crew, submitting requisitions for payment, proposing prices for change orders, and most important, he is supposed to be executing the work as specified while applying a high level of quality control. However, he can do a shoddy job on things that may be covered up before you arrive on site. He can propose outlandish change order prices on items that if not approved could stop the works. There are a hundred ways for a contractor to get more and give less than you all agreed upon in your contract. They know that in time you will come to appreciate this vulnerability. It comes down to a fine balance between trust, circumspection, and readiness to act on your part.

What I Hear You Saying Is . . .

There are several ways for people to take in information. In your family and at your workplace, you may have all come to share common styles, but you're in a new setting now and don't want to waste time forcing that style if it doesn't work. Be cognizant of what works best with the different members of the team and adjust accordingly. If you start to hear "I don't remember you saying that" once too often, stop hitting your head against the wall and try another way. Your options include oral and written communication, direct or through a third party, formal or informal, in meetings or out on site, face-to-face or by phone, email, or snail mail.

Finish the Finishes

As you start the construction phase, your specifications probably include the materials to be used but not necessarily the colors for paints, stains, cabinet finish, hardware finishes, countertops, vinyl flooring, carpet, bathroom fixtures, tile, etc. Just after the job gets under way, go and get samples of every one of these things, or ask the contractor to provide samples (page 59). Either way, get started on these decisions long before the contractor asks. It can take you months to get comfortable with all your finish selections, but your contractor doesn't care what colors you want. He just wants your decisions the minute he asks for them, and it may not occur to him to ask for them until the day he needs to order the necessary materials.

Give 'Em Their Propers

If you are doing a good job as a leader, the workers will look to you for approval. So compliment freely. You can also create so much goodwill with the occasional small, kind gesture. On a freezing day, show up just before break time with hot coffee and doughnuts for everyone. On a scorcher, show up with cold beer at the day's end. Make the workers copies of photos that include them. Leave a silly note in the portable toilet. Such efforts go a long way to letting the crew know that you appreciate them for doing a good job for you. The gesture will be returned tenfold by a crew that takes pride in its work.

Watching the Store: Monitoring the Project

When construction work is under way, your site will evolve daily. There's a lot to respond to and keep track of. Keep your construction documents (plans and specifications) close at hand and do the following.

Job Meetings

I usually leave for work shouting, "I'm off to Santa's workshop!" because the job sites can be such fun, bustling, crowded places. But this also means whoever is running the job can have a lot of other things on his mind. So no matter how many times you see and speak to a contractor on site during a given week, it's nice to sit down together, review the status of the project, and make sure everyone knows what's coming up. In fact, when I survey owners who have had successful projects of more than two months in duration, they usually refer to the benefits of having attended weekly job meetings. Chaos is the enemy, and this is a great way to settle things down and stay informed. Here's how job meetings work.

You set a weekly meeting time with the significant players. This may just include you and the contractor, or it may include your spouse or partner, an architect, an architect's assistant, and the contractor's superintendent on the job. Contractors are understandably reluctant to dedicate a lot of time to this, as some owners tend to turn them into unproductive coffee klatches. Don't. Come

Pitfall

If you don't have meetings and take notes, you'll get very tired of hearing, "That's not what I thought you said," and "I just thought . . ."

prepared, be succinct, and try to keep the meeting under an hour. Guest visitors such as subcontractors, engineers, suppliers, and other designers might be included if their attendance is requested. Someone is designated to take and distribute meeting minutes (page 167). Doing this is a bit of a hassle, but the one taking the minutes is keeping the most formal record of the job and so holds some power as to how this project is conveyed to others in the event of trouble.

The following is covered at each job meeting:

Approval of Last Week's Minutes: If someone disagrees with the content of the minutes from the prior week, this is their chance to ask for an amendment or let the record stand. Example: "I think Ellen said she did *not* want the white grout."

Old Business: Revisit last week's issues. Put to rest those that are complete and talk about further action needed on the others. Example: "Regarding site work, all the drainage pipe is laid, but there's no conduit in for the electrician to run his power line underground, so we can't backfill yet."

New Business: Everyone should come prepared to talk about upcoming issues. Example: "They're predicting a lot of rain this coming week. I want to adjust the schedule a bit to get the building wrapped. That would mean a delay of the interior framing shown on the schedule. We'll make up the time later on that. Everyone okay with that?"

The Schedule: Revisit the schedule focusing on the immediate future and anything that might impede the work. Example: "Are we still on track for the floor installation? Will they be here on Friday? If not, we need to stop the plumbers. They're scheduled to install the toilets on Monday, and they can't with no floors in." Note which subcontractors are coming on site for the first time. Discuss their work, and if you like, ask the contractor to invite them to the next job meeting. It could be for a brief hello or to talk about substantive matters and coordination.

Change Orders: These are often generated and discussed at job meetings. Sometimes the need for one is brought to the owner's attention one week, and the change order proposal outlining a proposed change is brought by the contractor for review at the next meeting, if time permits. Example: the contractor says "I got that picture window all framed up like it was drawn, but you better check this out and see if you want it moved."

Paperwork: In the boxes of supplies and equipment delivered, you will receive manufacturer's instructions for installation and application. These will help you in monitoring the project. You will also get owner's manuals and warranties which you should take off site to file (page 125).

Although it is not a standard meeting topic, a "wish list" is something very handy for you to keep updated and bring to the meetings. Most people do not have unlimited funds and so end up cutting some items from their initial scope of work. Be sure to keep a list of these items that you would like incorporated into the project if the entire contingency is not spent on the contracted scope of work. Use this list to prioritize your expenditures, and look at it together with the construction schedule from time to time, because each decision regarding a wish list item has a deadline. For instance, the decision on whether or not to upgrade the windows from vinyl to wood must be made early in the construction schedule. The decision on whether or not to upgrade from vinyl flooring to ceramic tile can wait until near the end of the project. Be sure to let the contractor know about possible changes well in advance, or you may face a restocking charge for materials already on site. If these options have been given alternate prices in the initial pricing of your project, you will already have fair prices to consider.

Documentation

Keeping good records of all communication has two benefits. It helps all parties to focus their tracking of the project. It also provides a record of conversations, decisions, and actions that will be helpful if there is conflict

Job Meeting Minutes #5 — Dorsey House Addition

Date: May 21, XXXX
Location: Job site
Weather: Sunny, 72 degrees
Minutes written by: Bob Mansfield

Attending: Ken and Marcia Dorsey (owners), Bob Mansfield (general contractor), Tom Houle (project super), Larry Cobb (electrician)

OLD BUSINESS

Insulation: Bob got the price for blown-in, dense-pack insulation requested last week. The Dorseys rejected the proposed change. We'll stick with the batting insulation as specified.

Still no window delivery yet.

The framing lumber that Ken didn't like has been removed and replaced.

The painter is still waiting for exterior paint colors so he can tint the primer. The Dorseys will provide the color selections by the end of the week.

The Dorseys approved the change order proposed last week to go from "three-tab" roof shingles to an "architectural" style. All parties signed the change order. The shingles are in stock and the sheathing and felt paper are up, so this change shouldn't alter the schedule if the weather holds.

NEW BUSINESS

Marcia would like to add some framing in the walls for hanging pictures throughout the house. Bob says he'll use scrap lumber and charge for about three hours of labor. He'll bring the change order next week. Marcia will mark the height she wants on the studs in the family room.

Bob asked for a more detailed drawing showing how the arched entry from the family room to the existing building ties in at the existing framing. Tom will ask Rebecca, the architect, for a detail showing that, and for her to stop by the site and walk Bob through that if necessary.

Door hardware: The hinges are back-ordered in the brushed nickel finish that's specified. We could put in something else but it wouldn't match the knobs and locksets. The Dorseys changed the finish selection to antique brass throughout. Bob will check for availability.

Per Marcia's request, Larry Cobb joined the meeting. He and Marcia toured the site and confirmed the locations of all fixtures, outlets, switches, thermostats, and phone jacks.

Ken noted that the chimney looks great but the mortar is too dark for the old look they're trying to achieve for the face of the fireplace. Bob will work with the mason to get the mortar lightened up for the interior finish work.

on the job that must be sorted out by a third party. As with contracts, the very act of recording helps immeasurably in preventing trouble.

The job meeting minutes should include the date of the meeting, names of attendees, and notes on items listed above, including attribution of the statements noted. Direct quotes are great. There should also be a follow-up section for notes on things that happened after the meeting but before the notes were written. For instance, "The flooring guys showed up, so we're still on schedule for the plumber to put in the toilets." The pros also note the weather conditions ("65 degrees and rainy"), since some materials have restrictions regarding their installation in certain weather. Whoever keeps the notes should be encouraged to write and distribute them no later than three days after each meeting. Showing up with them in hand at the next meeting is close to worthless, since no one will have time to review them. If the architect or contractor is taking the job meeting minutes, be sure you take your own notes, compare them to the meeting minutes for accuracy, and insist on changes, when important, to accurately reflect what went on.

Pitfall

Even on a very pleasant project, there will come a day when the contractor rattles off each and every little thing he's done for you. This is usually in response to what you thought was a reasonable request after all you've done for him.

Create and maintain what I call the Give-and-Take List. This is not a standard part of project record keeping but a little secret tool that will serve you well. A lot of give-and-take will take place on the typical construction project. Some small changes don't seem worth a change order. Sometimes acts of kindness are done for one another as a matter of common courtesy. Some mistakes will be made and overlooked. Keep a little running list of these items in the back of your notebook. I guarantee you, sooner or later, the contractor will list all the favors done for you. You will be amazed at his steel trap mind. Without this list, there you'd be, flat-footed, knowing that you'd given as much as you'd taken, but not able to join in the game since you didn't know you were supposed to keep score. Share the items on this list only if and when you have to in a negotiation.

If your team is communicating by email, set up an archive folder to save all correspondence, and use the "read receipt" option to verify that the intended recipient has opened your email. Save the read receipts too. Contractors tell me that email has added a whole new element to their communication. They say some owners come home and write rambling, angry letters with half-directives and misinformation all through them. Most contractors are used to taking the written word very seriously on a job site. In order to ensure they still can, be very careful how you use this medium, and try to rely on the notes from face-to-face meetings instead. Also take notes of phone conversations.

> "I have been bully-ragged all day by the builder, by his foreman, by the architect, by the tapestry devil who is upholstering the furniture, by the idiot who is putting down the carpets, by the scoundrel who is setting up the billiard table and has left the balls in New York, by a book agent whose body is in the backyard, and the coroner notified. Just think of this going on the whole day long and I am a man who loathes details with all my heart! But I haven't lost my temper."
>
> —MARK TWAIN ON HIS HARTFORD, CONNECTICUT, HOUSE PROJECT 1873

If you haven't yet bought a digital camera, this would be a great time to get one. Take lots of pictures with the date and time feature, and not just for the scrapbook. Get shots of delivered materials, including mechanical equipment, boxes with model numbers, and lumber that's stored on site. Photograph the progress of construction, and try to focus on those items that will get covered up later. Get shots of the foundation before it's back-filled, the framing before it's sheetrocked, the subfloor before the finish floor's laid on, and so on. These pictures will be the best record you'll have of the materials that came on site and how they were stored and installed.

Site Visits

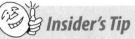

Insider's Tip

Whether you are living in a building being renovated or living three hundred miles away from a custom home being built, you must have a presence on site. There are four reasons to show up throughout the course of the project: for general monitoring, for an inspection of the rough framing (page 148), for requisition approval, and for project wrap-up, including creation of a punch list (page 182) and final inspection (page 148).

If you happen to be well-heeled, don't flaunt your wealth on site. It's tough to keep the change order prices down if you're dressed in Armani and pulling up in the Range Rover.

General Monitoring

Site visits shouldn't last for long if the crew is there. They can be more leisurely on weekends and after hours. Mix it up if you can. It's nice to have the contractor tour you around briefly to show you the most recent accomplishments, and it's also nice to be there on your own, to compare what you see on site to the plans and take it all in. When coming to the site, bring a notebook, pen, and camera. Keep the contractor's liability in mind. He will appreciate it if you don't wear open-toed sandals or let the baby crawl around the open stairwell.

If you're very ambitious about monitoring, there are plenty of books out there with which you can educate yourself on the technical aspects of construction. Go to the site during off-hours, and bring the tools you need to check things out. Take your set of plans and a tape measure for verifying dimensions, especially the depth of anything out of a dump truck, like gravel, sand, or topsoil. Take a flashlight for looking in attic spaces and wall cavities. Take a five-foot level to check that the framing for the door headers is level and the jambs are plumb. If you're really into this aspect of things, you can take a moisture meter to test the moisture content of lumber arriving on site. You want under 19 percent moisture for dimensional lumber and under 15 percent for finish lumber. Take a polarity tester that tells you if outlets have been wired correctly. Again, the greatest benefit of monitoring is the fact that you do it and the contractor and subcontractors know you're watching. Call the contractor with any concerns that arise from such monitoring. If you do this early in the project, you will be raising the bar for quality control throughout. On the other hand, try to exercise some discretion about this. Have you seen those price charts at the auto mechanic's? They say, "$70 an hour or $90 an hour if you watch."

If your project is on a time-and-materials basis, things are a little different. This approach is most appropriate for small projects and those with a lot of unknowns, so they typically take place in the home you're living in. Good. You can monitor the time easily. Hang that piece of paper on the inside of a kitchen cabinet. When you hear the contractor's wheels hit your driveway, write down the time and date, and do the same when he leaves. When you get a bill, compare it to your time tracking and review the cost of materials submitted to you. The first time I did this, it was with great trepidation that I told the contractor he billed me for 30% more time than I recorded. I handed him my sheet and with a little shrug and the swipe of his pen he cut 30% from his labor number. I remember thinking "well, that went well".

Rough Framing

When a new space is framed, you are looking at the skeleton of your home. You can have your first 3-D look at what your 2-D plans have conveyed. It's a great time to take stock of your designs. Your architect or contractor can help you with this, but you are the one who will live in and use the space, so this task is more about your impressions. Before anything goes in or on those framed walls, go to the site and confirm that this space will really meet your needs. It's relatively inexpensive to adjust your plans now, but it would be prohibitively expensive later. Bring your copy of the plans, a tape measure, chalk, and the dimensions of your major pieces of furniture and appliances if need be. With plans in hand, use the chalk right on the floors to map out any interior walls not yet up. Also draw the furniture and the appliances. Does it still work? Are the door and window openings made as drawn, and more important, do you like them? Do the headers for the doors and windows line up the way you anticipated? Do they let light in as you hoped? Will the kitchen layout suit you? Will door swings be in conflict with your layout? Do the traffic areas feel comfortable? Kneel to the height you'll be at when seated. Do the window locations still work to capture the view? Note any changes you would like to consider. Pencil them onto your set of plans, and bring them to the attention of your team immediately.

> 66 *We shape our buildings: thereafter they shape us.* 99
>
> —WINSTON CHURCHILL

Insider's Tip

Don't believe your eyes when it comes to the appearance of the size of your new space under construction.

Don't panic if newly built space looks smaller than you thought it would. It seems to shrink and expand in appearance. The foundation hole looks so big. The backfilled foundation looks so small. The framed space can feel insufficient, but once sheetrocked, it seems to expand again. And if you have a very open floor plan it will look larger once furniture goes in. Rely on dimensions, and if you're concerned, compare those dimensions to finished space elsewhere.

Don't fret over inactivity or hyperactivity on a new home site as long as the schedule is being met. The crew sizes and number of subcontractors will ebb and flow throughout the project, and the faces will change. There's a lot of activity when you begin, with excavators, utility people, concrete delivery, etc. Then a smaller crew settles in for the framing, and subcontractors come and go for their rough-in work. The end of the project may seem like mayhem as all the subcontractors are on site at once doing their finish work. Just follow your schedule, and you'll see who's coming and why.

For Richer or Poorer: Budget Management

In terms of math skills, managing a construction budget is relatively easy. There's no highbrow accounting involved, so even if you're not a numbers person and couldn't figure out a tax form if your life depended on it, you should still be able to do this. You will use two tools; the draw schedule, reflecting anticipated payment of lump sums, and the budget, which shows both the sum total of the project and the individual line items that make up that total. You have five things to focus on:

- The down payment

- Change orders

- The contingency

- Processing requisitions for payment

- Maintaining the overall budget by reflecting expenditures

The Down Payment

You may have agreed to pay the contractor a down payment for project start-up. This is designed to cover any of his out-of-pocket expenses, including the purchase of materials, mobilizing his crew and subcontractors, and renting equipment such as scaffolding (page 13). The only difference between a down payment and a requisition should be that the down payment is for work to be completed and a requisition is for work that has been completed. The down payment, though a lump sum, should be applied against the draw schedule and the budget just like a requisition. For instance, if you are paying the contractor $10,000 as a down payment on a $150,000 project, you would reflect this as the first payment on your draw schedule, then show $140,000 remaining to be paid on this project.

Now break down what the down payment is for, and apply those costs to the various line items in your budget. Maybe $2,200 goes to general conditions for the job trailer, phone hookup, and renting a lift; $6,400 goes to materials: $3,000 for masonry block, which would apply to the masonry budget, and $3,400 for dimensional lumber, which would apply to the rough carpentry line item. The remaining $1,800 of the $10,400 is for getting electrical power in from the nearest pole and would be applied to the electrical line item. Now calculate the percentage of the work that these costs represent in each line item (page 11). Everyone on the project now knows that these items have been paid for, and what percentage of each line item they represent.

The Dreaded Change Orders

Again a change order is the mechanism for amending the contract. It can reflect a change of no financial consequence. It can reflect a downgrade in materials or a decrease in the scope of work, resulting in a decrease in the contract amount. However, most often it reflects an upgrade in materials or an increase in the scope of work, resulting in an increase in the contract amount.

Typically, the owner or contractor brings the need for a change to the other party's attention. The contractor then proposes a cost for the change and states how it will affect the schedule. If the owner approves the cost and amendment to the schedule, a change order form is filled out and signed by all parties.

The change order process is also a great mechanism for helping everyone fight the tendency to just deal with all the accounting later. It's the good guy contractor who is focused on the construction work and may have priced your project overoptimistically who will likely be remiss in keeping up with the books. Without using the change order process throughout the project, as described below, he may well do his bookkeeping halfway through the project and realize he's losing his shirt. Then what?

All change orders should be discussed and approved before the related change in the scope of work is executed. If you receive a bill for work you didn't ask for or approve, something is wrong. Assure the contractor that you will be an attentive and available owner who will respond to change order proposals as soon as possible. Every project I do seems to start out with one of these test cases, a bill for work I didn't know about. I like to set those aside for consideration of payment at the end of the project. If you can do that, it stops that little approach, but fast.

Why People Hate Them

Just the words "change order" strike fear in the hearts of owners and architects. Change orders reveal the gaps in the construction documents. They are usually brought to your attention by the contractor, who seemingly could have made you aware of deficiencies in the scope of work before you signed a contract for a fixed sum that did not include this work. The less thorough your plans are, the more the cost will rise during the construction phase because change orders cost you money, usually more than you think they're worth. Plan on being charged at least 50 percent more for the work than you would have paid if it had been included in a base bid before a contract was signed. Don't even bother asking why.

You suffer a certain degree of powerlessness now that the project is under way. Say you get a price from the contractor to switch the way a door swings by taking it out, flipping it around, and reinstalling it. He gives you a price of $1,200. Well, the door, which is already paid for, cost only $350, so how could this little bit of labor cost so much? How can this cost be justified? It can't, but what can you do? Pick a fight? Get another contractor in to do the work? Again, most of the solutions to problems are built in back at the planning stage. This is why you need those good construction documents and a formula in your contract for calculating change orders that will get you a bit closer to fair change order numbers. It works in reverse the same way. You may be dumbstruck by how little money you're offered to deduct something.

From the contractor's point of view, change orders are a powerful tool for recouping losses and making a bigger profit. If a project has incomplete or flawed plans, how he chooses to use this tool is up to him. It can get really ugly. Some large construction firms even give their staff members a percentage of the change orders they generate as an incentive to keep the costs going up. Appalling! One of the smartest contractors I know told me he likes to start a project by submitting lots of tiny change orders, even those that have no cost change at all. That way, he says, he gets the owners comfortable with the form and signing their names to it before he hits them for the big money. He knows that especially early on, an owner wants to keep the peace and is reluctant to fight over change orders. Owners tend to bend and bend until they snap on this issue. Try another tack. Set a precedent of extreme scrutiny for those early change orders, even if they're minor. Your reaction is being judged. You are teaching people how to treat you on this issue. Think of it as performance art if you have to, but don't be an easy mark and just blithely accept any proposal put before you.

The Four Reasons for Change Orders

Unforeseeable Conditions: No one could have anticipated the need for this work. Example: Until the contractor stripped off the old shingles, no one knew or could have known that the roof sheathing you were hoping to reuse was rotten and covered in mold.

Design Errors and Omissions: Some portion of the scope of work is not included in or properly conveyed in your plans and specifications. Example: The plans for the conversion of a barn to a home show a new wall going in right where an old wall is, but they don't show removal of that old wall.

Owner Generated Change: Example: You decide you can afford granite kitchen counters after all.

Design Improvement: There's a better way of doing something than you all thought when you designed it. Example: The contractor says he could chamfer the edges on all the exposed timbers to give your timber frame addition an older look.

In these examples, the reasons for change orders are correct, but if you think that they were all unpreventable, you have another think coming. Welcome to the world of change orders. Now let's talk scrutiny and preventive measures.

When a contractor proposes a change order, here's how to go about considering whether it should be paid, who should pay for it, and how much. If in doubt, check to make sure this work isn't covered in the documents. If it's not, which of the four reasons above apply?

Unforeseeable Conditions: Once something is discovered, yes, you have to pay to get it addressed. This type of change order is usually a missed opportunity for foresight. In the case of the preceeding example about roof sheathing, stop and think if the issue at hand was really unforeseeable or just unforeseen. You could have done a little exploratory work, letting someone peek under the shingles to be removed. If you didn't want to or couldn't disturb the shingles, you could have gotten a unit price for sheathing replacement in advance (page 28). But now the shingles are off, the roof must be completed right away before it rains, and so you must pay for sheathing. Given these circumstances, you're now not in much of a position to haggle about the sheathing price.

Also think about whether someone else could have been reasonably expected to foresee this. In the event that the architect should have known, then that's more an issue of error or omission masquerading as an unforeseeable condition. You may want to ask him to contribute to the cost of this, but his doing so is a long shot. If it's the contractor you believe could and should have known about the unforeseen condition, then take it up with him.

If there is value added to the project, regardless of who you think is at fault, you should pay for that value. Then the question becomes how much. I say you should pay the amount the work would have cost you if it had been included in the base bid in the first place, as it should have been, not an inflated change order rate. This is a reasonable counterproposal to a high cost change order that you think was born of the contractor's omission through no fault of yours or your plans.

Design Errors and Omissions: If you provided your own designs, then your position regarding an error or omission in those designs is much like that of an owner generated change. However, if your plans and specifications were produced by a licensed architect, he has errors and omissions insurance. Typically, a claim is made only for a significant problem like a major structural design error, and this usually happens after the fact, like a roof collapse. For the small stuff, like changing a door or kitchen cabinet to resolve a dimensional error, it's not very common for an architect to pony up and pay for his mistake. I have never understood or really accepted this myself. I am always willing to pay whatever amount is reasonable for the value added to the project for such a correction. However, I will try to hold the architect accountable for the rest, especially if someone's yanking my chain and trying to say the change order is necessitated by one of the other three reasons when it's not. For what it's worth, the policy on big projects with state or federal money is that the owner will pay up to one percent of the total construction cost toward change orders brought about by design error. Sounds fair to me.

Owner Generated Change: To my mind, if the change order is purely owner generated or triggered by any other out-of-the-blue reason, you should be ready to pay the full freight and just negotiate the fairest price you can. In the example above, the change order for the upgrade to a granite counter-top could have been better addressed by an alternate price when the contractor was first pricing the project (page 29).

Design Improvement: Provided you already have a decent fallback plan in the original scope of work, this is the least onerous of change orders. It may even be generated just by the contractor's sense of pride in his work. So typically, the circumstances are more in your favor, and you can all come to agreement on a fair price. In the fourth example above, you can take or leave the suggestion to chamfer the timbers.

The Combo Platter: If it's a change necessitated solely by the oversight of one or another of the parties you've hired, and there's no value added to the project, you could try to leave the table and say, "This just isn't my expense." Most change orders fall in a gray area, however. On the one hand, someone should have seen it coming, but on the other, the change will add value to the project, so you must pay something. You could ask for some shared responsibility to be reflected in the price. Again, you don't want to pay the inflated change order price, but rather something closer to the price that would have been included in the base bid had the item not been overlooked in the first place. You may be the lame duck in these negotiations, with little going for you other than a winning smile and an appeal to the contractor's sense of fair play. So try to keep the focus on fair pricing, with the assumption being that the contractor is a fair and reasonable person. Don't whine or throw a fit, or the game's over and he wins.

The Change Order Proposal

Once you've determined that the change order is legitimate in concept and you accept the reason for it, you must analyze the proposal itself. You will review the proposed revision to the scope of work, the cost, and the impact on the schedule, and apply some of the strategies mentioned above.

The Scope of Work: Does the proposal thoroughly describe the solution or change you've agreed on, with all materials and labor included?

Cost: Is the price fair? First just check the math proposed to see if it adds up right. If you find a math error in your favor, point it out to the contractor. Doing so is worth a lot of goodwill in these negotiations.

Now check the calculations for double dipping. Say you have decided to increase the depth of a wall of bookshelves from ten inches to fourteen. You may get a change order proposal that shows all the materials and labor for the ten-inch shelves deducted from the project at a woefully low price, and all the labor and materials for the fourteen-inch shelves added at an astronomical price. This is double dipping and not right. You should pay only for the difference between the price of the original project and the price of the amended project. In this case you could argue that the new shelves would be about 50 percent bigger than the old ones, so you want to pay 50 percent more in materials only.

Use suppliers to confirm the cost of materials if need be. Try not to use the supplier the contractor is buying from. He may not want to help you.

Regarding labor, just apply some common sense. If the change order reflects six man-hours of labor to change a piece of door hardware, this just doesn't pass the giggle test. You may suggest the work be done on a time-and-materials basis to call this bluff. Then be there to watch the work. It won't happen many more times if you do.

If you are revising the scope of work downward, the same cost issues apply in reverse, and so when planning a project, deducts should never be seen as a way of recouping funds. In other words, don't say, "We'll just put the flagstone patio in the plans, and if we run out of money near the end, we'll pull it out of the project." You'll lose your shirt, and that's why alternate pricing was invented (page 29). To my mind, the low deduct change order is actually often more legitimate than the high add. After all, the contractor was counting on that work for income and has already coordinated it into the plan, schedule, crew needs, and shopping list. He may even have materials for it that have to be returned.

What if you're offered savings? Your contractor comes to you and says he can get windows just like the ones in your plans but much less expensive. He proposes a savings to you of $500. Sounds great, huh? It may be, but don't just say yes. First you have to confirm that those windows are in fact comparable to the ones you already have him committed to buying. Then call a supplier, preferably not the one he's using, and find out the cost. He may be a saint and be giving you all the savings, or the real savings may be $1,500. I

Insider's Tip

If the contractor comes to you with an offer of big savings for switching a material in the project to one that's cheaper, consider his motivation. Is he the best Boy Scout ever, or are you not seeing all the savings?

think it's only fair that the contractor pocket something for finding you the bargain, but I think 25 percent or so would be an ample finder's fee.

Impact on the Schedule: People neglect to address this issue because a single change order may have little or no impact on the schedule. Beware of the incremental increases. They add up, and one day late in the game, you

Change Order
(Instructions on reverse side)

PROJECT:
(Name and address)
DORSEY HOUSE ADDITION
59307 COLCHESTER AVE
BURLINGTON, VA

TO CONTRACTOR:
(Name and address)
MANSFIELD CONSTRUCTION, INC.
2612 MAPLE ST
BURLINGTON, VA

CHANGE ORDER NUMBER: 1

DATE:

ARCHITECT'S PROJECT NUMBER: —

CONTRACT DATE:

CONTRACT FOR:

OWNER ☒
ARCHITECT ☐
CONTRACTOR ☒
FIELD ☐
OTHER ☐

THE CONTRACT IS CHANGED AS FOLLOWS:
(Include, where applicable, any undisputed amount attributable to previously executed Construction Change Directives.)
UPGRADE ROOF SHINGLES FROM THREE-TAB TO ARCHITECTURAL STYLE.

The original (Contract Sum) (Guaranteed Maximum Price) was $ 162,225

The net change by previously authorized Change Orders $ 0

The (Contract Sum) (Guaranteed Maximum Price) prior to this Change Order was $ 162,225

The (Contract Sum) (Guaranteed Maximum Price) will be (increased) (decreased)

(unchanged) by this Change Order in the amount of $ 760

The new (Contract Sum) (Guaranteed Maximum Price) including this Change Order will be $ 162,985

The Contract Time will be (increased) (decreased) (unchanged) by _____ (—) days.

The date of Substantial Completion as of the date of this Change Order therefore is _____

NOTE: This Change Order does not include changes in the Contract Sum, Contract Time or Guaranteed Maximum Price which have been authorized by Construction Change Directive for which the cost or time are in dispute as described in Subparagraph 7.3.8 of AIA Document A201.

Not valid until signed by the Architect, Contractor and Owner.

REBECCA GREENFIELD
ARCHITECT *(Typed name)*
(Signature)
REBECCA GREENFIELD
BY

MANSFIELD CONSTRUCTION
CONTRACTOR *(Typed name)*
(Signature)
BOB MANSFIELD
BY

MARCIA DORSEY
OWNER *(Typed name)*
(Signature)
MARCIA DORSEY
BY

©2000 AIA®
AIA DOCUMENT G701-2000
CHANGE ORDER

DATE   DATE   DATE

may hear that the schedule can't be met because of "all those change orders." Always enter something, even "zero" in the line for "Contract Time".

The Change Order Form

When you've come to agreement on the terms of a change order, it should be reflected in writing. AIA has a handy change order form you can use to process your change orders (above). Remember, these are little changes made to the original contract agreement, so you should execute them as they arise, and reflect the costs in the budget and the time impact in the construction schedule. Using this change order process is precisely how you keep a budget from slipping out of control.

It's fine for several work items to be grouped together under one change order. If you want to make your own change order form or review one submitted to you by the contractor, just be sure it covers the following and that you have filled in all the blanks.

Homemade Change Order Form

Date _____

Names of parties and location of project _____

Change order number_____

Description of proposed change _____

A calculation section:

    Original contract amount _____

    + Change to contract from previous change orders_____

    + Cost of change order being proposed_____

    = New contract amount with proposed change order included _____

Schedule: increase or decrease in length of project in days _____

Signatures of contract parties _____

The Contingency

The well planned contingency fund is a pot of money you set aside to pay for unanticipated work or work whose final cost cannot be established at the beginning of a project. In other words, it's what you use to pay for those change orders. On new construction projects such as custom homes and additions, if you have good construction documents and you aren't likely to ask for many changes along the way, your contingency is fairly safe in terms of the building itself. Most of your unknowns are underground. Just what will you find when they excavate? How far will you have to drill for water? This site work happens right up front. If you are looking at a nine-month building schedule and see half your contingency disappear in the first two weeks, it can be terrifying. Don't panic.

Renovations are a different matter. I carry 10 percent even on well planned renovation projects because they tend to involve existing space that's often imperfect and has hidden problems like rot or bad wiring.

Most contractors will ask what the contingency amount is. Don't tell, or deny you have one. There's just no upside to anyone knowing you have a pot of money that he can tap into. In fact, if he thinks you don't

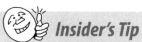 **Insider's Tip**

I usually carry 5 percent of the total construction budget as a contingency on new construction projects. If we make it through the site work and I still have at least half of that left, I feel I'm in good shape.

APPLICATION AND CERTIFICATE FOR PAYMENT AIA DOCUMENT G702 (Instructions on reverse side) PAGE ONE OF ___ PAGES

TO OWNER: KEN & MARCIA DORSEY

PROJECT: DORSEY HOUSE ADDITION

APPLICATION NO.: 2
PERIOD TO: 4/21 - 5/21
PROJECT NOS.:

Distribution to:
☑ OWNER
☐ ARCHITECT
☑ CONTRACTOR

FROM CONTRACTOR: BOB MANSFIELD

VIA ARCHITECT:

CONTRACT DATE: 3/1/XX

CONTRACT FOR:

CONTRACTOR'S APPLICATION FOR PAYMENT

Application is made for payment, as shown below, in connection with the Contract.
Continuation Sheet, AIA Document G703, is attached.

1. ORIGINAL CONTRACT SUM .... $ 102,225
2. Net change by Change Orders .... $ 760
3. CONTRACT SUM TO DATE (Line 1 ± 2) .... $ 102,985
4. TOTAL COMPLETED & STORED TO DATE .... $ 49,437
   (Column G on G703)
5. RETAINAGE:
   a. ___ % of Completed Work $ 4,943
      (Columns D + E on G703)
   b. ___ % of Stored Material $ —
      (Column F on G703)
   Total Retainage (Line 5a + 5b or
   Total in Column 1 of G703) .... $ 4,943
6. TOTAL EARNED LESS RETAINAGE .... $ 44,494
   (Line 4 less Line 5 Total)
7. LESS PREVIOUS CERTIFICATES FOR PAYMENT 18,257
   (Line 6 from prior Certificate)
8. CURRENT PAYMENT DUE .... $ 26,237
9. BALANCE TO FINISH, INCLUDING RETAINAGE 18,491
   (Line 3 less Line 6)

CHANGE ORDER SUMMARY	ADDITIONS	DEDUCTIONS
Total changes approved in previous months by Owner		
Total approved this Month	760	
TOTALS	760	
NET CHANGES by Change Order	760	

The undersigned Contractor certifies that to the best of the Contractor's knowledge, information and belief the Work covered by this Application for Payment has been completed in accordance with the Contract Documents, that all amounts have been paid by the Contractor for Work for which previous Certificates for Payment were issued and payments received from the Owner, and that current payment shown herein is now due.

CONTRACTOR: MANSFIELD CONSTRUCTION, INC.

By: Bob Mansfield   Date: X/5/XX

State of: VIRGINIA
County of: FAIRFAX
Subscribed and sworn to before
me this FIRST day of JUNE, XXXX

Notary Public: [signature]
My Commission expires: X/X/XX

ARCHITECT'S CERTIFICATE FOR PAYMENT

In accordance with the Contract Documents, based on on-site observations and the data comprising this application, the Architect certifies to the Owner that to the best of the Architect's knowledge, information and belief the Work has progressed as indicated, the quality of the Work is in accordance with the Contract Documents, and the Contractor is entitled to payment of the AMOUNT CERTIFIED.

AMOUNT CERTIFIED .... $ ___
(Attach explanation if amount certified differs from the amount applied for. Initial all figures on this Application and on the Continuation Sheet that are changed to conform to the amount certified.)

ARCHITECT:

By: ___   Date: ___

This Certificate is not negotiable. The AMOUNT CERTIFIED is payable only to the Contractor named herein. Issuance, payment and acceptance of payment are without prejudice to any rights of the Owner or Contractor under this Contract.

AIA DOCUMENT G702 • APPLICATION AND CERTIFICATE FOR PAYMENT • 1992 EDITION • AIA® • ©1992 • THE AMERICAN INSTITUTE OF ARCHITECTS, 1735 NEW YORK AVENUE, N.W., WASHINGTON, D.C. 20006-5292 • WARNING: Unlicensed photocopying violates U.S. copyright laws and will subject the violator to legal prosecution.

CAUTION: You should use an original AIA document which has this caution printed in red. An original assures that changes will not be obscured as may occur when documents are reproduced.

G702-1992

---

have a contingency, he may ask to investigate existing space more fully and be more likely to reveal deficiencies he sees in your plans up front.

Requisitions for Payment

A requisition is a request for payment, usually submitted monthly or even biweekly by smaller contractors. When the contractor hands you a bill, should you pay it? Should you pay all of it? The goal is never to pay out for more than the value of the accomplished work. If you pay this requisition in full and, God forbid, the contractor died tomorrow, could you get your project finished for the money you have remaining? All parties will be looking closely at the budget to answer this question.

The requisition amount should be for 90 percent of the value of the work completed, with a breakdown of the percentage complete for each budget line item. Ten percent of the value of that work will be held as retainage until the end of the project to ensure that the contractor finishes the job.

If you have a draw schedule, it will show an estimated or fixed amount to be drawn from the budget at each requisition period. You just need to feel assured that the contractor has met the milestones set for that time frame that correspond to those anticipated payments. The contractor may request release of half the retainage prior to final completion. A ten percent retainage represents the bulk of his profit on the job and may be more than the value of the remaining work toward the end of the project. So it's not an unreasonable request on his part. Use your discretion on this. Always ask yourself, "Can I get the rest of the work done for the amount of retainage I am holding at this time?"

If you have a construction loan, the bank will send an appraiser to verify that the work completed and the amount being charged for it correspond to the draw schedule. Again, this does not speak to quality. The bank appraiser is not necessarily an expert in construction and is not responsible for instructing the contractor. You need to ensure that you are happy with the work for which the bank is about to pay. After all, it's your money they're handing over. This would be the very best time to get outside help. An independent property inspector with great expertise in construction can come to your site for an hourly fee, find deficiencies, recommend solutions, and approve the work done for each payment. For as little as $1,000 for a custom home construction project, you could know that any problems have been caught and remedied, allowing peace of mind as you move from milestone to milestone.

The Requisition Form

For small renovations, it's fine to accept a handwritten invoice, but try to apply some of the concepts from the more formal requisition process. Make sure the math works. Make sure the bill notes what work has been done. Have the contractor write "paid in full" and sign it when you pay him.

For full-blown projects, you'll want a more formal record of the cash released. You should use a requisition form. Unlike the change order form, the submission of the requisition represents the beginning of a process. The contractor is proposing you pay him a certain amount of money for a certain amount of work and materials he's purchased for the project. The AIA has a handy form for this too. It's called *Application and Certificate for Payment* (page 178). Whether you use this or one from either you or your contractor, for a large-scale project for which you're making more than a couple payments, it should include spaces for the following:

Processing the Requisition

Be sure the contractor is aware of the time it will take you to process the requisition. If you're paying out of your own bank account, maybe you need a couple days to check that the work is done, or let a professional

Homemade Requisition Form

Date _____

Names of parties and location of project _____

Requisition number _____

A calculation section:

   Original contract amount _____

   + Change to contract from change orders to date _____

   = Current contract sum _____

   Total value of work completed and materials stored to date _____

   − Retainage held to date _____

   = Total earned less retainage to date _____

Current contract sum (above) _____

   − Previous payments to contractor _____

   − Current payment due _____

   = Balance to finish including retainage _____

Signatures of contract parties _____

verify that for you. If the bank or other lender will be making the payments, they can tell you the turnaround time for processing.

If you are requesting lien waivers, you should expect to receive one in exchange for your approval of a requisition (page 129).

What you need to watch out for from the first bill to the last is front loading. That's charging for work not yet completed and materials not paid for and on site. Determining the percentage of work completed is not a hard science. If you look at your kitchen addition under construction and it has the windows on site but not installed, maybe the requisition proposing a draw of 90 percent of the money in the windows line item of the budget is excessive. Just say, "I'd be more comfortable if we called this 50 percent complete," and start the conversation. I know it sounds tough to challenge a contractor on this, but contractors are used to little modifications in the bill, and you should try to think of yourself as helping him keep the project on track. Whatever scrutiny you bring to the first requisitions will be contagious, and you'll be more impressed with the accuracy of the following ones. The first requisitions may be proportionately high in relation to your overall budget. This is because the contractor is buying out the project: getting all his materials purchased and on site. It's okay to pay these requisitions as long as he's shopping only a couple weeks in advance, the materials are stored properly, and you have insurance to guard against any loss to you or the contractor.

If things aren't going well on the project, scrutinize the requisitions even harder for overcharging. Any contractor in his right mind would try to get all the money off a sinking ship, but then what would you have left to pay for a solution?

Usually, subcontractors will grumble to you at the job site if they have not received payment. Heed these grumbles, talk with your contractor immediately, and whip out a lien waiver for the general contractor to have the subcontractor sign as soon as he receives that delayed payment. Then monitor more closely.

If things really start to derail and you are considering not paying a requisition, call a lawyer for advice or consider enacting the dispute resolution clause in your contract. Withholding payment from a contractor is an act of war you may regret. This is not like a store with an inventory and you decide to freeze payment on a credit card purchase when you find a hole in the shirt you bought. The contractor is laying out up to 1,000 percent of what he hopes to get from the job in profit. It's a high risk endeavor for any builder. He lives on very tight margins and his worst fear is that you might hold back payment. So don't abuse the power of the checkbook. Whenever possible, negotiate a solution instead.

Once you've approved the requisition, update your budget with the information on the requisition.

Maintaining the Budget

Let the contractor's requisition be the trigger for managing your budget. Once you have approved a requisition, update your budget for work complete in the various line items, including change orders.

The Homestretch:
Project Closeout

By the end of a big project, you have met with people and monitored work, paid requisitions, and made design decisions for months. At this point, even if the project has gone smashingly well due to all your diligence and the great work of those you hired, it may be getting old. Try to stay focused just a bit longer so you can all part happy with the finished product and each other.

Before you make the final payment, there are a few things you want in hand:

- If it's required, you need to have the building inspector hand over a certificate of occupancy permitting you to live in the finished space.

- A lender will walk you through what you and your contractor may have to do to satisfy that person. Likely, you will be asked to sign a "sworn construction statement" verifying you built with the money what you said you would. The lender's appraiser will come to the site to verify the payment sought on the final requisition. If you are closing out the construction loan and converting it to a mortgage, they will do a title search and probably require a signed lien waiver from the contractor, each of the subcontractors, and the big suppliers to ensure that no one intends to make a claim against your property for outstanding bills. Even if you don't have a lender involved, it would be a good idea to get those lien waivers before making the last payment.

- Depending on what kind of insurance you've used, your insurance agent will need to be satisfied that the site is safe and free of further building related risk. Give that person a call to say you're done, and see if there are any other requirements of you or the contractor.

- Do you have copies of all warranties and owner's manuals? Have you scheduled a warranty walk-thru with the contractor for a year after the project is complete (page 126)?

- Do you have plans that reflect not just what you originally planned to do, but what you actually did? These are called as-builts, and they may come in very handy in the future when you're looking for the septic tank or wondering if there's a wire in that wall. Your contractor can create pretty accurate as-builts just by marking up your original plans. They don't have to be beautiful, just accurate.

The Punch List

At the end of the project, the contractor will be looking for final payment and release of the retainage. You will be looking for the completion of any annoying little tasks, like touching up the paint where the carpet layers dinged it or getting a replacement glass shade for the light fixture the plumber hit. This list of little things a contractor has to do is called the punch list. The contractor should prepare the punch list (page 126) with proposed dollar values for each task to be done. You should look at the list and add to it as needed, but don't you create the first draft of the list. You might miss something and end up alleviating him of having to do that item. An architect can help you with this, but at this point it's really your opinion that matters. The standard approach is to then multiply the total value of the punch work by 2 and hold this money against completion of the project while releasing the final requisition payment and retainage (page 126).

For example, you are near the end of a $100,000 project. The last requisition is for $25,000—$15,000 for the last month's work and $10,000 for release of the retainage you've held through the project. There is an estimated $750 worth of punch work to be done. You multiply that by the industry norm of 2 and hold the resulting $1,500. So you will pay $23,500 of the last requisition. You will pay the $1,500 when the punch work has been completed.

Be careful not to treat seasonal work too casually, though. If the bulk of your project finishes in a season that doesn't permit exterior painting, landscaping, or other seasonal work, be sure you hold plenty. For significant tasks like this, get a price from a third party and hold twice that amount.

The money you are holding against the completion of the punch list should definitely be held to the bitter end. It's little enough, and at this point you have nothing more than this money and the goodwill between you and your contractor to get those annoying little loose ends tied up. When the last brushstroke of paint is on and the last seed of grass is sown, you can release the last bit of money to the contractor.

A Job Well Done

It's a sign of great planning and supervision on your part if you are delighted to invite the key people who worked on your project to your housewarming party. Tell them to bring their business cards, and raise a glass to them with a sterling toast. Also let them know of a good time to show the place off to their customers and spouses if they'd like to do that.

Provide letters of thanks and recommendation, and tell them they can put you on their list of satisfied customers who will give a great reference.

Conclusion

This book was written with the following thought in mind: If owners knew 10 percent of what professionals know, they could avoid 90 percent of their problems when building. But who can stop at 10 percent? There's a lot of information in this book, from creating your vision to setting your standards and enforcing them with the team of people you assemble. Much of it will not apply to your project. Much of it you will not choose to focus on specifically. Much of it is unknown to professionals you may deal with, as it's written from the perspective of an informed and participatory owner—something they don't see every day. However, the principles behind each bit of information remain the same. They are always in play and are always pertinent, and they are these: You have the right to protect your interests and are obligated to respect the interests of others. Don't worry if you can't execute each task exactly as spelled out in these pages. No two projects or sets of players are alike. You will have many opportunities to do just as instructed in this book step by step. Other times, you will be able to apply only the spirit of the information, making your own way through to your own method of doing things. The point is to gain the perspective of a competent owner with an approach to your project that will make you your own best asset. I hope this book helps you to do that.

By now you probably know how much work is ahead of you, and it may seem a little daunting. But what could be more satisfying than to actually live in a job well done? You and the people you form bonds with will come together to make your vision a reality. You will likely never forget this time in your life. You will cherish the scrapbooks of it and remember it as an adventure like no other. And if you're like most owners who build, you will start thinking of the next project before the paint dries on this one. I wish you the best of good fortune. May your dream house come true.

> "'Mid pleasures and palaces though we may roam, be it ever so humble, there's no place like home."
>
> —JOHN HOWARD PAYNE

Talk the Talk
A Glossary of Terms

ABS acrylonitrile-butadiene-styrene

abutting property owner neighbor who shares your lot line

add an increase in the scope of work and/or cost

additional insured covered by another party's insurance policy

aggregate gravel or crushed stone added to concrete

AIA American Institute of Architects

air exchange the exchange of interior air for exterior or fresh air

allowance an amount of money allotted for the purchase of yet-to-be-specified materials

alternate price the prearranged price for altering a task or material in the scope of work

as-builts plans reflecting the work executed to construct a building and all its systems

awning window a single-sash window hinged at the top, typically seen in basements

backfill to place and compress soil around a foundation; to fill in an open excavation hole

back order delay in supply of a product from the manufacturer to the distributor

balusters vertical supports under a handrail to make a banister system

bar graph a diagram including two sets of information and horizontal lines representing a logical sequence of relationship between them

base bid a cost proposed scope of work that is fully determined

bearing wall a wall or partition that supports the weight of a portion of the building above in addition to its own weight

berm raised edge, ledge, or shoulder

bid price submitted for consideration

bidding	soliciting proposed prices from more than one contractor
bid package	the information necessary for a contractor to produce a bid, including plans, specifications, and contract
biscuit	elliptical sliver of wood inserted and glued into notches of two pieces of wood to be butted together
board foot	unit of measure equal to one square foot of lumber one inch thick
BOCA	Building Officials and Code Administrators International, which publishes the BOCA National Building Code and establishes minimum requirements for materials and methods of construction
bow	a window system that protrudes from the plane of the wall in which it is installed
box valance	window treatment, a three-sided, fabric-covered armature spanning the top of a window
building inspector	municipal employee who reviews, amends, and approves plans and construction work for compliance with building codes
building permit	a written consent for the execution of construction work in accordance with approved plans
built materials	materials installed, applied, or assembled in or on a structure
bulkhead	exterior, enclosed stairway to basement
butt joint	a connection made from square end to square end
buy out	to purchase the bulk of materials needed for a portion of a project
carbon footprint	impact on the environment
carry	to include or account for
casement	a crank-out window assembly
certificate of completion	a letter from the bank appraiser to the lending bank, certifying that the project was completed in accordance with the plans and specifications
certificate of insurance	a document certifying that a contractor is insured
certificate of occupancy	written approval of completed construction work and permission for space to be occupied

chamfer	a 45-degree bevel cut into a 90-degree outward corner
change order	an alteration to the terms of a construction contract, usually an addition, deletion, or amendment to the scope of work, with cost and scheduling implications resulting
change order proposal	a written proposition of the terms of a change order
clean-out	an opening in drainage pipe
clear	without imperfections
conditional use	permission to use land or building space under certain stated conditions, in a way other than ordinarily permitted by regulation
conduit	a hollow tube or vessel used to contain and protect lengths of electrical wire or plumbing pipe
construction documents	plans, specifications, and building contract
construction management	the management of a construction project, or a specific method of providing contracted construction work
construction schedule	a timed plan for building tasks
contingency	funds allotted to cover the cost of unpredictable expenses
contract	written, legally enforceable agreement between two or more parties
contractor	one of the parties to a contract
contract structures	various approaches to construction work and related duties and liabilities, reflected in owner-contractor agreements
cost estimate	an approximation of expense associated with a task and/or materials
crew	group of workers
cross-member	brace between lengths of lumber
culvert	a pipelike construction of concrete that passes underground to direct and drain water
cut sheet	written, diagrammatic, and photographic information regarding a product
deduct	a deletion of, or amendment to, a task or material that results in a lessening of cost
designer	one who designs
dimensional lumber	wood used for creating structural support of a building

dimensional standards	rules about measurements
double dipping	a form of overcharging by unfair and inaccurate miscalculation
double-hung	a window that has two operable sashes installed one over the other
drainage tile	pipe used to collect and transfer water underground
draw schedule	a timed plan for payment
drip line	the line on the ground under the eave of a building at which water lands from the roof above, or the line on the ground under the outer edge of the tree's canopy
drywall	also called Sheetrock, plasterboard, and gypsum board, sheets of plaster encased between two layers of paper and used as an applied surface to walls
egress	location at which one can exit a building or space
elevation	drawing of a building on a vertical plane showing a view of the front, rear, or sides of a building
faux finish	material such as paint or concrete applied to surfaces so as to look like a different material or finish
fill	gravel, soil, or similar material used to reshape or backfill land
finger-jointed	a means of creating lengths of moldings by joining short pieces of wood
finish	material applied to surfaces to enhance beauty, function, and comfort
finish lumber	wood used for aesthetic, not structural purposes
finish weld	the bonding of two pieces of metal by heating and cleaning the joint to create an aesthetically pleasing product
fixed	predetermined and committed to
fixed fee	a cost that is fixed
footing	a concrete or stone base beneath a wall or column
footing drain	drainpipe at a footing
footprint	the perimeter outline of a building
form	a mold to receive poured concrete

front-loading	assigning more costs at the beginning of a series of requests for payment
general conditions	expenses incurred to run a construction project, or rules for contract parties
general contractor	a builder who works under contract and hires and supervises subcontractors
GMAX	guaranteed maximum price, or fixed fee
header	horizontal structural support over a door or window
HVAC	heating, ventilating, and air-conditioning
I-beam	a metal joist shaped like an "I"
impact fee	a charge levied against an owner of a property to offset a municipality's expenses associated with that property and its use by the owner
jamb	a vertical side post used in the framing of a doorway or window
job meeting	an assembly of the parties associated with a construction project for the purpose of monitoring progress and facilitating administration of the construction contract
kept in house	not sold to a secondary mortgage institution
lead time	the time between the ordering and receipt of a material
LEED	Leadership in Energy and Environmental Design
lien	a process by which an aggrieved party may make a financial claim against another
lien waiver	a document signed by the recipient of a payment, waiving the right to place a lien on a property
lift	also called cherry picker or lull, a piece of equipment used to elevate workers to perform work some height off the ground
lintel	a short beam spanning a door or window opening and supporting the wall above it
liquidated damages	a predetermined fee levied (usually daily) against a contractor for tardiness in completion of work by an agreed upon date
loss leader	item sold for less than its value to encourage the purchase of higher-priced related products
lot coverage	the amount of land area covered by a building or other site improvements

low-e	reflective insulation
lumen	unit of measurement for the flow of light, equal to that of one candle
mark-up	a charge for services associated with handling a material or coordinating a service
massing	proportions, presence, occupation of space
mechanical	pertaining to HVAC, or more broadly, pertaining to machinery or operable house systems
millwork	wooden objects made in a mill
module	a portion of a structure assembled individually for incorporation into a larger unit
mortise and tenon	a method of connecting timbers, a piece of wood with a notch, hole, or cut on the end to receive a corresponding projecting part on the end of another piece of wood
mud	drywall compound
muntin	molding dividing or applied to the glass of windows or doors
non-permeable	cannot be penetrated by water, non-porous
notify	the public posting of information
open-book	full disclosure of all actual costs
outgas	to emit gas
panel	a wall section
paper contractor	a contractor who assembles a crew by hiring carpenters and laborers for each individual construction project
paver	stone or ceramic block installed in ground for a road, driveway, or path
penetration	a hole made to permit pipes, wires, conduits, or ductwork to pass through
percentage complete	a tool for assessing value, measurement of work done
performance specification	an instruction to a contractor or subcontractor to design and price a system to meet certain standards of performance
perk test	a test used to determine the rate at which soil drains water
permit expeditor	a person hired to assist an owner in obtaining a building permit
permitting	the process of granting a building permit
plan review	to read and critique blueprints

What Your Contractor Can't Tell You

plans	also called blueprints or drawings, pictorial representation of finished work and materials
plumb	vertically straight
point load	weight borne by a post
point of refusal	the point at which no more is produced or released
polarity tester	instrument for determining proper wiring
popcorn	blown-on synthetic finish material
positive grade	land sloping away from building
pulled	obtained
punch list	list of work items remaining
PVC	polyvinyl chloride
rabbeted	cut with a groove running along an edge of wood
rebar	reinforcing bar, used to provide structural support and stability in concrete
reface	to apply new material on the exterior or facade of something
reflective value	a measure of light that bounces off a surface, depending on color and texture
reimbursables	expenses for which one seeks payment
release the retainage	discharge funds held until completion of a project
requisition	also called request for payment, bill, or invoice
resilient channel	a V-shaped metal strip applied between wall framing and Sheetrock to provide sound insulation
restocking charge	fee charged by suppliers to accept and handle returned purchases of materials
retainage	money earned but held from payment until the completion of a construction project
rise and run	the height and depth of a step
rosin paper	soft, absorbent paper used to protect surfaces
rough carpentry	structural building, framing, working with dimensional lumber
rough-in	installing plumbing or electrical materials in a framed space
R value	measurement of a material's ability to insulate
sash	a frame holding the glass of a window or door

scarf joint	a connection between two boards on the same plane joined by overlapping 45-degree tapered ends
schematic design	initial conceptual drawing
scope of services	the summary of work to be performed by an architect, contractor, subcontractor, or other service provider
scope of work	the work that is done to execute a plan
setback	distance from property line at which a building or site improvement can be located
shopping the project	revealing one contractor's cost estimate to obtain lower pricing from another
sight line	line of vision
site plan	drawing or blueprint of property and site improvements
sixteen divisions	means of categorizing construction work and materials
slab	a horizontal concrete surface such as a basement floor
soffit	roof overhang
solid surfacing	synthetic stone (e.g., Corian)
span	a distance
specifications	detailed instructions regarding methods and materials of a construction project
square-stock	finish lumber with 90-degree edges
staggered framing	a partition wall made of two rows of studs with alternating studs supporting opposite faces of the partition for sound insulation
stamped drawings	blueprints created and marked with the seal of a licensed architect or engineer
statutory employer	legally, you as the boss
stress skin panels	wall system applied to outside of framing
structural	supporting
structural welding	functional welding without regard to aesthetics
subcontractor	member of the trades who works under contract for a general contractor
subfloor	supporting floor system between floor framing and finish floor surface material
submittal	a detailed description of material to be installed or applied given upon request by contractor to owner or architect

What Your Contractor Can't Tell You

substrate	any component that lies beneath or within what it supports
super	job superintendent or foreman
supplementary conditions	additional contract clauses beyond the standard bundle, specific to owner and/or project
swale	a low area or depression in land
take occupancy	gain control of and access to a built space
take-off	calculation of labor and materials needs based on information in plans and specifications
tank port	opening at the top of an underground tank
tint	colored powder added to concrete or mortar
title	legal document detailing right of ownership
to code	in compliance with all pertinent building codes
toe kick	the vertical face of the recessed space under lower kitchen cabinets
to scale	proportionately accurate
trade price	the discounted price contractors and subcontractors pay for materials
trades	workers and companies of specified fields in construction including excavation, framing, electrical, plumbing, painting, etc.
true divided lights	individual panes of glass separated by muntins, as opposed to simulated divided lights
turning radius	measurement of length necessary to rotate an object within a space
two-party check	a check that cannot be cashed without the signatures of both parties shown in the "Pay to" section
unit price	price to do a designated task on a per-unit basis
up-charge	increase in cost
upset limit	a cap on spending
value added	enhanced worth
value engineering	cost containment, cost saving, sometimes resulting from creative redesign
variance	exception to a rule, regulation, or ordinance
vernacular	indigenous to a specific style or era
walk-thru	touring of the site
whole-house fan	a large fan installed in the attic floor operated from the story below, it can exchange the air in a whole house in minutes

wick	to draw in or transfer moisture
work triangle	the three-sided traffic area between sink, refrigerator, and stove
zone	division of controls of a heating system by area
zoning	restriction of the types of construction and use of property by designated areas within a municipality

Inspirations
Other Resources

There's a wealth of information at your disposal. Below are some recommended books, Web sites, videos, television programs, periodicals, computer-design software, and workshops that you may find inspirational.

Architecture and Residential Home Design

200 Budget-Smart Plans, by Paulette Mulvin

The House Plans Bible, by Creative Homeowner

Architectural Graphics, by Francis D. K. Ching

Architecture: Form, Space & Order, by Francis D. K. Ching

Adobe Houses for Today, by Laura Sanchez

Creating the Not So Big House: Insights and Ideas for the New American Home, by Sarah Susanka and Grey Crawford

The Distinctive Home: A Vision of Timeless Design, by Jeremiah Eck

A Field Guide to American Houses, by Virginia McAlester and Lee McAlester

Homing Instinct: Using Your Lifestyle to Design and Build Your Home, by John Connel

Luxury Dream Homes, by Home Planners Inc.

New House Book, by Terence Conran

The Not So Big House: A Blueprint for the Way We Really Live, by Sarah Susanka

A Pattern Language: Towns, Buildings, Construction, by Christopher Alexander, Sara Ishikawa, and Murray Silverstein

Patterns of Homes: The Ten Essentials of Enduring Design, by Max Jacobson

Feng Shui: A Practical Guide for Architects and Designers, by Vincent Smith and Barbara Lyons Stewart

Timber Frame Construction: All About Post-and-Beam Building, by Jack Sobon, Murray Silverstein, and Barbara Winslow

American Institute of Architects, www.aia.org

Home Planners, www.eplans.com

Punch Pro Home Design, www.punchsoftware.com

Quickspecs by Guidelines, 800-634-7779

Yestermorrow Design/Build School, www.yestermorrow.org

Fine Homebuilding magazine

Home and Garden Television, www.hgtv.com

> *"Do thou, then, breathe those thoughts into my mind."*
> —MICHELANGELO

Renovation and Historic Buildings

Additions: Design Ideas for Great American Houses, by Fine Homebuilding

Big House, Little House, Back House, Barn, by Thomas Hubka

A Building History of Northern New England, by James Garvin

Home Renovation, by Francis D. K. Ching

How Buildings Learn: What Happens After They're Built, by Stewart Brand

Old House Journal magazine

The Old Way of Seeing, by Jonathan Hale

Renovation: A Complete Guide, by Michael Litchfield

The Resourceful Renovator: A Gallery of Ideas for Reusing Building Materials, by Jennifer Corson

This Old House magazine

Green Design

Natural Remodeling for the Not-So-Green House, by Carol Venolia and Kelly Lerner

The Healthy House, by John Bower

Green Studio Handbook, by Alison Kwok and Walter Grondzik

Natural House: A Complete Guide to Healthy, Energy-Efficient, Environmental Homes, The, by Daniel D. Chiras

New Independent Home: People and Houses that Harvest the Sun, by Michael Potts

The Solar House: Passive Heating and Cooling, by Daniel D. Chiras

Green Building Products, by Alex Wilson

Center for Resourceful Building Technology, www.crbt.org

4-Star, 5-Star Energy Rating, www.energystar.gov

LEED, www.nrdc.org/buildinggreen/leed.asp

Project Management

Building Construction Illustrated, by Francis D. K. Ching and Cassandra Adams

Building Your Own House, by Robert Roskind

Independent Builder: Designing and Building a House Your Own Way, by Sam Clark

Project Management in Construction, by Sidney M. Levy

American Institute of Architects, www.aia.org/documents, 800-365-2724

Dreamhouse Institute: Construction Management Workshops for Homeowners, www.dreamhouseinstitute.com

How Contractors Find Change Orders and Extras by Guidelines, 800-634-7779

Managing Home Construction: Hometime Video, Two Tape Series, www.hometime.com, 1-800-992-4888

National Association of Home Builders, www.nahb.org

R.S. Means, www.constructionbook.com

Materials and Methods

Journal of Light Construction magazine, www.jlconline.com

Home and Garden Shows: www.southernshows.com, www.macevents.com, www.showevent.com, www.hgtv.com

Shelter Supply: Providing Energy Efficient Supplies, www.sheltersupply.com

Sweets Catalog: Building Products, www.sweets.com

Interior Design

Seven Layers of Design, by Christopher Lowell

The Home Decorator's Bible, by Anoop Parikh

The Complete Idiot's Guide to Decorating Your Home, by Mary Ann Young and David Nussbaum

Decorating Idea Book, by Heather Paper

Choosing Color, by Kevin McCloud

Landscape Design

Education of a Gardener, by Russell Page

Residential Landscape Architecture, by Norman K. Booth and James E. Hiss

Right Plant Right Place, by Nicola Ferguson and Fred McGourty

Fine Gardening magazine

Garden Design magazine

Clearwater Landscape Design online, www.clearwaterlandscapes.com

Master Landscape Pro software; www.punchsoftware.com

Stories and Perspective

Home, by Witold Rybczynski

House, by Tracy Kidder

Mr. Blandings Builds His Dream House, by Eric Hodgins and William Steig

The Perfect House, by Witold Rybczynski

Legal

American Institute of Architects, www.aia.org/documents, 800-365-2724

Nolo: Law for All, www.nolo.com

Quicken Family Lawyer, www.broderbund.com

Index

Abbreviated Standard Form, 119
Affordability, of project, 72. *See also* Budget
AIA. See American Institute of Architects
Air barriers, 55-57
Air-conditioning, 65-66, 69
Air exchange, 7, 65-66, 69
Allowances, 28, 66, 70, 89, 108
Alternate prices (pricing), 28, 108
American Arbitration Association, 128
American Institute of Architects (AIA), 196
    architects and, 30, 33, 161
    change order forms, 175-76, 177
    contract forms, 117-18
    requisition forms, 178, 180
Appliances, 62-63
Application and Certification for Payment, 180-81
Application fees, 146, 147
Appraisers, 4, 9-13, 182
Approaching design, 15, 16-20
Approaching projects, 1-4
Arbiters, 8, 128
Arbitration, 128
Architects, 4, 30-44
    conflicts with, 22-23, 162
    guarded, 161
    hiring, 36, 38-42
    interviewing, 38-40
    job description, 30-32, 36-37
    payment structures, 33-35, 38-40
    references, 92-93
    schematic design and, 31, 33, 43-44
    types of, 36-38
    working with, 37-38, 40-41, 42-44, 159-60
As-builts, 182
Associates, 4
Association of General Contractors (AGC), contracts, 117

Automobile insurance, 123
Awning windows, 58
Bankers (banks), 4, 9-13, 74. *See also* Appraisers; Loan officers
Base bids, 28-29, 107, 114
Bathtubs, 65
Better Business Bureaus, xiii, 90, 98
Bid analysis, 114-15
Bid dates, 113
Bid day, 114
Bidders, 108-15
    considerations of, 111-13
    instructions to, 105, 106-07
Bid forms, 105, 107-08
Bid packages, 105-08
Bid period, 111-13
Bids (bidding)
    architects and, 32
    base, 28-29, 107, 114-15
    competitive. *See* Competitive bids
    ethics and, 109-10
    schedules, 108-15
Bills (invoices), 135, 179. *See also* Requisitions for payment
    sample, 178
Block walls, 51
Blueprints. *See* Plans
Board review, 4, 141, 142-44
Boilers, 65
Bookstores, as design resource, 16
Brickwork, 51-52
Broom finish, 50
Budget, 78-82, 170-81. *See also* Cost estimates
    for architects, 33-35
    change orders and, 108, 122, 171-75
    closeout of project and, 181-83
    as commitment tool, 82
    construction loan and, 9
    contingency, 48, 80, 150, 177
    design considerations and, 20-21
    down payments, 13, 122, 153, 170

five things to focus on, 170-81
flexibility in, 28-29
as goal setting tool, 79-80
as monitoring tool, 72, 82
as negotiating tool, 81-82
as refining tool, 80-81
requisitions for payment, 137, 178-81
as sales tool, 81
time and, 132-34
Buildable lots, 8-9
Builder's risk insurance, 124
Building inspection schedule, 9, 147-48
Building inspectors, 144, 145, 146-48
Building permits, 47, 144-46
application fees, 146
construction loan and, 9
process and players, 139-42
steps for approval, 142-47
Build-to-suit contracts, 89
AIA contract form, 118
Business automobile insurance, 123
Cabinetry, 53-55, 63-64
Calendar, tracking, 15, 108, 137
Camera documentation, 168
Carpenters, 6
Carpentry, 43, 63-64
Carpeting, 61
Casement windows, 58
Case work (shelving), 53-54, 63-64
Ceiling coverings, 59-61
Certificate of completion, 10
Certificate of insurance, 9, 123
Certificate of occupancy, 87, 148
Chain of command, on project, 161
Change order proposals, 174-75
Change orders, 171-77
architects and, 32
bid forms and, 108
contract and, 122-23
distaste for, 171-72
forms, 176-77
job meetings and, 165
reasons for, 172-74
Checklists, 14-15, 150-51
Give-and-Take, 168
punch, 126-27, 182-83
wish, 16, 165
Civil engineers, 5, 48
Clammed up contractors, 161
Cleared sites, 47-49
Clerk of the works, 6

Closeout of project, 181-82
Commercial general liability insurance, 123
Commissions, for loan officers, 10, 12
Communication, 160-163
email, 167
Community boards, 4, 140, 142-44
Competitive bids (bidding), 83-84, 104-08
AIA contracts, 118-19
four elements of, 105-08
four stages of, 108-15
Completion dates, 122, 131
Concrete, 49, 50
Conditional use approval, 162
Conduct, communication and, 160-63
Conflicts, 22-23, 161-62
Construction budget. See Budget
Construction documents, 24-28. See also
   Contracts; Plans; Specifications
record keeping and, 14-15, 138, 165-68
Construction loans (loan officers), 4, 9-13
closeout of project and, 181
contractors and, 98
draw schedules and, 9, 136, 137
insurance and, 123
time and costs, 133
Construction management (CM), 86-87
AIA contract forms, 118
resources, 198
Construction managers, 6, 86-87
Construction phase, 158-183
architects and, 32-33
budget management, 170-81
closeout of project, 181-83
monitoring project, 164-70
roles and rules for, 158-63
Construction plans, 14-23. See also Plans
approaching design and, 15-20
design decisions and, 21, 24-28
do's and don'ts, 18-20
money and design, 20-21
to-do list, 14-15
working together as a couple, 22-23
Construction schedules, 134-35
bid forms and, 106-07
contracts and, 122
plans and, 45-46
sample bar chart, 135
tracking, 14-15, 138

Contact numbers, 153
Contingency, 78-80, 177
Contract administration services, 33, 36
Contractors, 90-101. *See also* General
    contractors; Subcontractors
    change orders and, 171-72, 174-75
    clammed up, 161
    conflicts with, 22-23, 161-62
    construction phase and, 159-60,
      161-63
    cost estimates and, 72-77
    ethics and, 109-10
    guarantees, 126
    hiring, 90-96
    insurance for, 95, 123
    interviewing, 91-92, 95
    money and reputation of, 96-98
    optional contract protections,
      129-31
    owners and, 98-99, 111-12, 159-60
    protecting your project and, 98-99,
      102
    qualifications, 95-96
    references, 92-93
    working with, 96-103, 159-63
Contract parties, 121
Contracts, 83-98, 116-31. *See also*
    specific types of contracts
    awarding, 114-15
    benefit of, 119-20
    common problems with, 116-17
    must-haves to include, 120-26
    optional protections, 129-31
    standardized, 118, 126
    types (structures), 83-98
Conveying systems, 64
Copper plumbing, 65
Corrective work, 39, 116, 172, 174
Cost estimates (estimating), 72-77,
    84-85
    assessing, 76-77
    methods of, 73-77
    order of magnitude, 74, 76-77
    plans and, 45-46
    square foot cost, 74
    systems estimating, 75
    unit price, 75-76
Cost estimators, 5, 43, 73, 75
Cost plus contracts, 88-89
Costs and time, 132-34
    expediting the project, 134
    general conditions and, 133

insurance and, 134
labor and, 132
loans and, 133
Couple conflicts, 22-23, 161
Covenants, 9
Customized clauses, 126-27
Deadlines, tracking, 138
Deduct changes, 175
Defective workmanship, 39, 116
Design/building contracts, 84-85
    AIA contract form, 118
Design errors and omissions, 39, 162,
    172, 173
Designers, 5
    architects versus, 30
    contractors and, 69
Design improvements, 172, 173, 174
Design phase, 14-71. *See also* Architects
    approaching plan, 15-18
    architects and, 31-32
    construction documents and, 24
    decisions and, 24-28
    do's and don'ts, 19-20
    flexibility in, 28-29
    materials and scope of work and,
      68-71
    money and, 20-21, 28-29, 80-81
    needs versus wants, 16-18
    permits and review, 142-43
    resources, 197
    sixteen divisions and, 45-71
    working together as a couple,
      22-23
Digital camera documentation, 168
Dimensional lumber, 53-55
Dispute resolution, 127-28, 181
Divisions of materials, 45-69, 73
Documentation, 165-168. *See also*
    Construction documents;
    Contracts; Record keeping
    preconstruction meeting and,
      151-53
Domestic conflicts, 22-23, 161
Doors and windows, 57-59
Double dipping, 174
Down payments, 13, 122, 153, 170
Draftspeople, 4
Drainage, 5, 49, 51, 66
Drawings. *See* Plans
Draw schedules, 135-36, 137, 179
    bid packages and, 107
    construction loans and, 9

sample, 137
steps for, 135-37
Dream house, 15, 16, 18, 20
Drywalling, 59-60, 125
Durability, design decisions and, 21
Electrical engineers, 5
Electrical systems, 67-68
Electricians, 7
Elevations, 24
Email communication, 167
Employers' liability insurance, 95, 123
Energy efficiency, 55-56, 58, 65-66, 68
Engineers, 5
Ensurance, 153-54
Environmental quality review, 144
Equipment, 62-63
Ethics, bidding and, 109-10
Excavation, 47-49
contingency, 48, 176
unit pricing for, 29
Excavators, 7
Exterior carpentry, 53-55
Exterior painting, 53, 59-61
Family Lawyer, 117, 199
Fees
for architects, 33-35, 39
for permits, 146-47
File Index, 15
Filing system, 14, 15. *See also* Record
keeping
Final payments, 181
Finish carpentry, 53-55
Finishes, 59-61
construction phase and, 163
design decisions and, 19-20
metals, 52-53
Fire suppression systems (sprinklers), 66
Fixed fees, for architects, 33-34, 39
Fixed-price contracts, 121-22
Float finish, 50
Flooring, 8, 61
Footing drains, 49
"Foresight good, hindsight bad," 2, 17
Form, design decisions and, 20
Forms, AIA
change order, 176-77
contract, 118-19
requisition, 178-80
Foundation inspections, 147-48
Framers, 7
Framing, 53-55
Front-loading, 180

Function, design decisions and, 21
Furnaces, 5, 66, 69
Furnishings, 63-64
General conditions, 46-47, 106, 133
General contractors, 6, 46
change orders and, 71-72, 74-75
conflicts with, 22-23, 161-62
construction phase and, 159-60,
161-63
cost estimates and, 72-77
ethics and, 109-10
hiring, 90-93
insurance for, 95, 123
interviewing, 91-92
money and reputation of, 96-97
optional contract protections for,
129-31
qualifications, 95-96
references, 92-93
working with, 96-103, 159-63
General liability insurance, 123
Give-and-Take List, 167
Glossary of terms, 187-95
GMAX (guaranteed maximum price),
87
Goal setting, budget and, 79-80
Goodwill gestures, 163
Gossip, 160
Gravel base, 49
Green design, 68
resources, 198
Ground rules, for projects, 152
Grout, 59
Guarantees, 126
Guarded architects, 162
Guidelines' Quickspecs, 27, 197
Hiring
architects, 36, 38-42
contractors, 90-96
Historic preservation, 71, 198
Historic review, 144
Homeowner's insurance, 124
Home shows, 16
Hot markets, 76, 95, 113
Hourly rates, for architect fees, 34
HVAC, 7, 65-66
Impact fees, 147
Incentive clauses, 131
Inspections, 10, 147-48
construction loan, 10, 11
Installer conflicts, warranties and, 125
Insulation, 55-57

Insurance, 47, 123-25
    bid packages and, 106
    closeout of project and, 182
    for contractors, 95, 123
    for owners, 124
    schedules and, 138
    time and costs, 134
Interior decorating, 5, 19-20, 63-64
    resources, 199
Interior decorators, 5
Interviews
    architects, 38-40
    contractors, 91-92
Investment, return on, 20-21, 45
Invoices, 135-36, 178, 180-81. *See also*
    Requisitions for payment
    sample, 178
JAMS/End Dispute, 128
Job meetings, 42, 152, 164-65
    minutes, 165-67
Job site visits, 102-03, 161, 168-70
Kitchen appliances, 62-63
Kitchen cabinetry, 16, 53-55
Laborers, 6
Laminate shelving, 63-64
Landscape architects, 5
Landscapers, 7
Landscaping, 47-49, 154
    resources, 198
Laundry facilities, 51, 62-63
Lawyers, 8, 119
Lead paint, 60
Lead time, 69-70
Legal resources, 197
Lenders. *See* Loan officers
Liability insurance, 123-24, 162
Libraries, as design resource, 16
Liens, 96, 129-31
Lien waivers, 129-31
    construction loans and, 9, 182
    preconstruction meetings and, 151
    requisitions and, 180
Lighting, 67
Line items, 46, 80, 136-37, 170, 177-79
Liquidated damages, 122, 131
Lists, 14-15, 150-51
    Give-and-Take, 167
    punch, 126-27, 182-83
    wish, 16, 165
Litigation, 127-28
Loan officers, 4, 9-13
    closeout of project and, 182

contractors and, 95
    draw schedules and, 9, 135-37
    insurance and, 178-81
    time and costs, 133
Log cabin kits, 87
Loss leaders, 69
Low-flow plumbing fixtures, 66
Lumber, 53-55, 71
Maintenance, design decisions and, 21
Manufacturer's instructions, 125, 127,
    165
Masonry, 51-52
Masons, 7
Materials
    divisions of, 45-69
    synthetic, 54-55, 56-57, 71
    warranties, 125
Mechanical engineers, 5
Mechanical inspectors, 148
Mechanical permits, 145
Mechanical subcontractors, 7
Mechanical systems, 65-66, 145
Mediation, 128
Mediators, 8, 128
Meetings. *See also* Job meetings
    preconstruction, 115, 151-53
Metals, 52-53
Mildew, 61, 66
Mind-set, 1-4, 100-01
Modular construction, 87
    AIA contract, 118
    renovation and, 154
Moisture content, 54, 168
Moisture protection, 55-57
Money. *See also* Budget; Cost estimates
    design phase and, 20-21, 28-29,
      80-81
    time and, 132-34
Monitoring, 161, 164-70
    budget as tool for, 80-81
    contractors and, 102
    documentation, 165-68
    job meetings, 42, 152, 164-65
    site visits, 102, 161, 168-70
Mortgage companies, 10, 12, 81, 133,
    183
Municipal boards, 4, 140, 142-49
Namby-pamby owners, 160
Negotiated contracts, 85, 181
Negotiations
    architects and, 32
    budget and, 81-82

Neighborhood, making changes to, 143, 148-49

Networking, for contractors, 90

Note taking, 151, 165-67

Off-hours site visits, 168

Office personnel, 4, 6

On-site monitoring, 102, 161, 168-70

Open houses, 16

Order of magnitude, 74, 76-77

Overcharges, 160, 180

Overhead costs, 47, 76, 97

Owners, 4
    architects and, 37-38, 40-41, 42-44, 159-60
    change orders and, 172-74
    construction phase and, 159-61
    contractors and, 97, 98, 159-61
    insurance and, 124
    meetings and, 151
    namby-pamby, 160
    permits and, 141-42, 145-46

Painters, 7, 60

Painting, 59-61, 125

Paper trail, 14, 15, 137-38, 165-68.
    See also Construction documents; Contracts; Record keeping
    preconstruction meeting and, 151-53

Paving subcontractors, 7

Payments. *See also* Down payments; Requisitions for payment
    for architects, 32-33, 39
    final, 182
    withholding, 181

Pecking order, on projects, 161

Performance specifications, 27-28, 40

Permits, 139-49. *See also* Building permits
    process and players, 139-42
    steps for approval, 142-47

Personal deadlines, 138

Pilfering, 100, 157

Planning approval, permits and, 139-40, 141, 142-43, 144

Plans, 24-26, 153
    bid packages and, 105-06
    contractors and, 44
    permits and, 140, 141, 142-43
    ready-made, 2-3, 26, 33
    record keeping and, 14
    sample, bird's-eye view, 25, 140

scope of work and, 121

Players, 4-8
    construction phase and, 158-59
    permits and, 139-42
    preconstruction meeting and, 151

Plumbers, 7

Plumbing, 65-66

Polarity testers, 168

Popcorn ceilings, 60-61

Positive reinforcement, 163

Preconstruction meetings, 151

Principals, 4, 96

Proactive owners, xiii

Professional manner, 160

Profits, 79, 98-99, 103

Progress meetings, 42, 152, 164-65
    minutes, 165-67

Project approach, 1-4

Project budget. *See* Budget

Project closeout, 181-83

Project managers. *See* Construction managers

Project monitoring. *See* Monitoring

Project schedules. *See* Construction schedules

Project tracking, 15, 138

Property taxes, 142

Punch lists, 126-27, 182-83

Punch Pro, 45

Qualifications, of contractors, 95-96

Quality standards, 27, 120

Quicken Family Lawyer, 117, 199

Railings, 52, 53

Ready-made plans, 2-3, 26, 33

Real estate open houses, 16

Record keeping, 14-15, 138, 165-68.
    See also Construction documents; Contracts
    preconstruction meeting and, 151

Recycled materials, 69

References
    architects, 40-41
    contractors, 92-93

Reimbursables, 34

Renovations, 154-57
    architects and, 42
    in close quarters, 155
    conflicts on, 22-23
    contingency plans, 177
    controlling the mess, 156
    controlling the noise, 157

resources, 198
safety and, 156-57
security and, 157
Requisitions for payment, 135-36,
179-80
down payments versus, 170
form for, 178, 180
processing, 179-81
Research, 2-3
Resources, 197-98
Restocking charges, 165
Retainage, 182-83
contracts and, 117
draw schedules and, 135-36, 179
Return on investment, 20-21, 45
Review boards, 142-44
Roofers, 7
Roofing, 56, 173
Rough framing, 53
inspections, 148
monitoring, 169
Rules for change orders, 122-23. *See also*
Change orders
Salability, and return on investment,
20-21, 45
Sample forms, AIA
change order, 176-77
contract, 117-19
requisition, 178, 180
Schedule of values, 32, 107, 114
Schedules, 134-37. *See also* specific
types of schedules
in bid forms, 107
change orders and, 171-72, 175-76
in contracts, 122
of inspections, 147-48
monitoring project, 159, 164-70
plans and, 45-46
time on costs, 132-34
tracking, 137-38
types of, 134-37
Schematic designs, 31, 33, 43-44
Scope of work, 80-81, 121
change orders and, 171-77
job meetings and, 152
Sealing and caulking, 55-57
Seasonal work, 183
Security, during renovations, 157
Security systems, 57, 68
Septic systems, 7, 47, 49
Setbacks, 141
Sewer systems, 9, 47

Sheetrockers, 7
Sheetrocking, 60, 125
Shelving, 53, 63
Siding, 55, 56-57
Sight lines, 18
Signatures, 9, 108, 117, 128
Site plans. *See* Plans
Site visits, 102-03, 161, 168-70
Site work, 47-49
contingency, 177
unit pricing for, 28-29
Sixteen divisions, 45-69, 73
Sketches, 31
Small projects, contracts for, 119
Soundproofing, 59-60
Special construction, 64
Specialties, 61-62
Specialty items, 64-65
Specifications, 24-25, 26-28, 121, 153
bid packages and, 105-06
record keeping and, 14-15
Sprinklers (fire suppression systems), 66
Square foot costs, 74
Staff affection, permits and, 140-41
Standardized contracts, 117-20, 126-27
Start dates, 134
Stealing, 100, 157
Steel trowel finish, 50
Stone work, 47-49
Structural engineers, 5
Subcontractors (subs), 7, 152
bid forms and, 107-08
construction phase and, 161
Submissive behavior, 71
Submittals, 71
Superintendents (supers), 6
Suppliers, 8
change orders and, 175
conflicts and warranties, 125-26
costs and, 125
as design resource, 16, 70-71
Supplies, 19, 62-63, 138
Surveyors, 5
Sworn construction statement, 182
Synthetic materials, 54, 57, 71
Systems estimates, 75
Technical designs, 36
Television, as design resource, 16
Testing services, 5
Thermal and moisture protection,
55-57, 168
Thermostats, 69

3D Home Design, 44

Tiling, 61

Timber framing, 54

Time and costs, 132-34
    expediting the project, 134
    general conditions and, 133
    insurance and, 134
    labor and, 132-33
    loans and, 133

Time-and-materials contracts, 34-35
    AIA contract, 118-19
    and cost plus, 88-89
    monitoring projects and, 169

Titles, 129, 130, 142, 182

To-do lists, 14-15, 150-51

Toe kicks, 63

Topsoil, 48

Town clerk's office, 4, 129, 141-42

Townspeople, 4, 16. *See also*
        Community boards; Zoning

Trade discounts, 70, 77

Traffic space, excessive, 19

Trends, in design, 18, 21

Trim, 54

Trusses, 53-55

Underground conditions, 47-49, 177

Unforeseeable conditions, 173

Unit prices (pricing), 28-29, 75-76, 108

Upset limits, 35

Urban review, 144

Utility connection fees, 47

Vacuum systems, 62

Vapor barriers, 50, 55-57

Ventilation, 55-57, 65-66, 69

Vinyl siding, 56-57, 71

Walk-thrus, 109-11
    warranty, 126, 182

Wall accouterments, 61-63

Wall finishes, 59-61

Warranties (warranty terms), 125-26,
    182

Waterproofing, 55-57

Web sites, 118, 197-99

Weekly job meetings. *See* Job meetings

Windows and doors, 57-59

Wiring, 67-68

Wish lists, 16, 165

Withholding payments, 181

Wood and plastic, 53-55

Workers' compensation, 95, 123

Writs of attachment. *See* Liens

Zoning, 4, 8-9, 142, 144

Zoning boards, 142-44

About the Author

Amy Johnston is a construction manager and owner's representative based in Burlington, Vermont. She grew up renovating homes with her family and went on to renovate several of her own. She has spent the past twenty years managing the design and construction of homes, affordable housing projects, historic downtown restorations, and commercial spaces, totaling more than two hundred buildings. As liaison between the parties on so many projects, Amy enjoys a unique perspective on the dynamics of successful design and construction. She also participates in writing building code and sits on her city's Design Advisory and Historic Preservation Boards. Amy speaks publicly on related topics, and appears frequently on CNN.